The Social Context
of Health Care

ASPECTS OF SOCIAL POLICY

General Editor: J. P. Martin

Professor of Sociology and Social Administration
University of Southampton

The Social Context
of Health Care

Paul Brearley
Jane Gibbons
Agnes Miles
Eda Topliss
Graham Woods

Department of Social and Administrative Studies,
Barnett House,
Wellington Square,
Oxford.

MARTIN ROBERTSON · London
BASIL BLACKWELL · Oxford

First published in 1978 by Basil Blackwell & Mott Ltd.
and Martin Robertson & Co. Ltd., Oxford.

ISBN 0 631 18120 2 (paperback)
ISBN 0 631 18110 5 (boards)

Photosetting by Vantage Photosetting Co. Ltd.,
Southampton and London
Printed in Great Britain by
Richard Clay (The Chaucer Press), Ltd.,
Bungay, Suffolk

Contents

Introduction

Good doctors have always been aware of the importance of the social circumstances of their patients. Often this has been a matter of common-sense observation by the intelligent family doctor, but on a more scientific level there has been a long and honourable tradition of medical interest in the environmental factors which aid the spread of disease, and so often nullify the effects of therapy.

This is not the place to rehearse yet again the achievement of the Victorian pioneers, such as John Simon, whose pressure and example induced our forefathers to pave, drain and clean their streets, to provide pure water and to remove safely the multitude of effluents produced by an industrialized society. The task of their modern successors is no less important even though the objects of their vigilance, the modern forms of pollution, may be somewhat different.

This book is not concerned with public health in that traditional sense, but with what might, perhaps, be regarded as a development which blends that approach with that of the socially conscious physician. Increasingly two things are becoming clear, as several contributors to this volume point out. First, the greatest scope for the diminution of ill-health lies in prevention at a personal level by the adoption of healthier ways of life; obvious examples are to reduce or give up smoking, with its influence on lung cancer and respiratory conditions, and to cultivate the complex of habits thought to reduce the risk of diseases of the heart and circulation – avoiding excess weight, taking exercise, limiting the consumption of animal fats and, once again, giving up smoking. Second, the very successes of medical science in reducing the toll of diseases, conditions and accidents that used to be lethal for younger age groups, has left a population of survivors likely to be beset by longer-term and less soluble problems. As Eda Topliss puts it in her chapter on Health Care Policies, 'the health services will need to develop an overwhelming emphasis on care rather than cure'.

1

These fundamental changes in the nature of the problems posed by ill-health have had, and will continue to have, a major influence on the organization not only of medical care, but of social work. It is, therefore, vital for professionals in health care and in social work to appreciate the magnitude of what has been occurring, and to consider the long-term implications for all the services concerned. This book has arisen out of such an awareness by a group of colleagues, all at one time working in the Department of Sociology and Social Administration in the University of Southampton, involved in teaching medical students, health visitors and social workers. It brings together material of three main types – a discussion of the nature of health and ill-health, accounts of policies and the machinery for providing health care, and lastly discussions of the problems of caring for three major groups whose social and medical problems are particularly closely intertwined.

Each chapter is self-contained, but all have a common concern to consider social influences on health and the implications these have for the organization of health services.

In the first chapter Agnes Miles begins by demonstrating how the very concepts of health and ill-health are strongly affected by social standards, so that the patients whom a doctor sees have only come to him after they have interpreted their symptoms as being serious enough to justify consulting him. This is not necessarily a direct reaction to the presence of symptoms, but depends on the impact those symptoms have on the patient's daily life. Indeed conditions that do not have direct effects, even though significant to the clinician, may well be ignored. It seems very clear, for example, that people's tendencies to view themselves as needing medical care are related to factors such as their social class, ethnic group and, above all, the extent to which they are socially isolated.

Agnes Miles' discussion goes on to consider another change of far reaching significance. This is what has inelegantly been termed the 'medicalization' of health. Partly because to be sick is to adopt a role which may confer a degree of acceptability on previously deplored behaviour, and partly because of the undoubted achievements of medical science, medicine is increasingly seen as providing solutions to problems not previously within its scope. Hence, as Illich dramatically expresses it, 'people have become patients without being sick'. In consequence doctors are more and more likely to face patients whose needs go beyond the traditional requirements for medication.

Eda Topliss provides an historical and analytical account of some major issues of policy confronting those responsible for the National Health Service. Present-day questions are given a better understanding through a concise description of their history, and changing patterns of need for medical care are brought out so as to indicate their policy implications. Such a discussion may be somewhat repugnant to those trained to care for individuals, but with a Health Service employing nearly a million people and accounting for about 12 per cent of public expenditure it is unrealistic to think that professionals can simply practise without reference to all manner of limitations and, indeed, exhortations, relating to their daily tasks. Perhaps the most significant illustration of these pressures was the creation and recommendations of the Resource Allocation Working Party which, for the first time, attempted in a systematic way to examine the distribution of resources to the N.H.S. Regions in relation to numerous indices of health and the provision of health care services. The implications of this attempt are an important issue in Eda Topliss' chapter.

In a sense the very existence of Graham Woods' chapter is evidence of the changes that have taken place. One of the most fundamental changes in the years since the creation of the National Health Service has been the trend for family doctors to work in groups, sometimes in health centres, and usually with substantial collaboration from nurses, health visitors and sometimes social workers. It represents the implementation of ideas about primary health care long discussed in the medical profession, but only slowly put into effect. Linked with policies favouring community care, the reorganization of the health service since 1974 has probably meant that primary health care is getting more real consideration (as opposed to paying lip-service to the concept of the family doctor) than ever before. Where there is a genuine synthesis of medical treatment, sustained care, prevention and social support it can be argued that this concentration of effort can be regarded as a specialism in itself, thus relieving general practice of its status as a poor relation of the established specialties.

The mentally ill constitute the first of the major groups of patients discussed in the second half of the book. They are numerous and until recently their care has tended to be ineffective and to have commanded low priority in comparison with the more dramatic treatment of acute physical conditions. Nevertheless, as Jane Gibbons shows, emotional distress is one of the most universal human conditions, experienced by almost all at one time or another, and the development of new forms of treatment has transformed clinical medicine and created new demands for the provision of services in the community. Mental illness provides one of the clearest examples of the importance of the social context of health care. There are strong relationships between illness and status, with social mobility and isolation, and with stressful experiences; the regimes of some mental hospitals themselves have undesirable features, being either too restrictive or too stimulating environments. Most important is the milieu of the home: difficult personal relationships may have helped to generate the illness or hamper recovery, while the existence of a mentally ill member may be a great strain on others in the house.

Having considered the substantial research literature Jane Gibbons goes on to examine developments in the care of the mentally ill. In particular she discusses the fashionable concept of 'community care' and concludes both that a clearcut division between hospital and community is undesirable, and that community care sometimes causes real hardship for families.

The last two groups discussed, the disabled and the elderly, share important features brought out by both authors, Eda Topliss and Paul Brearley. They are almost by definition dependent in some degree, and those who care for them have to exercise fine judgment in balancing their medical and social needs. The disabled may be handicapped in a variety of ways but are not necessarily ill, and they are under medical supervision as the aftermath of an accident or episode of illness; they need care which helps and enables them to live fuller lives. This care need not, and indeed should not, encompass the whole of the patient's life. The aim is to maximize the patient's autonomy, and there are clear dangers that forms of direct supervision, appropriate in the care of the acutely ill, may be applied without thinking to people who, in all respects apart from their disability, are free individuals entitled to live as they please. As Eda Topliss puts it:

> A disabled person may choose to take [a risk], in order to guarantee the privacy he values more. Some relationships formed between disabled people in residential care may be extra-marital, promiscuous or homosexual. That is true of some relationships outside residential care too. The disabled person who enters residential care does not thereby expect to surrender moral choice, nor is there any reason for him to do so, whether in the matter of sexual morality, or in other spheres.

In short, it must never be forgotten that one of the concerns of those providing any form of care should be to establish the proper limits to their activities; to do what is necessary but no more, and always to remember the aim of working for the restoration or enhancement of the patient's autonomy.

Almost all the points made about the disabled apply also to the elderly, with the added complication, as Paul Brearley shows, that they may actually suffer from multiple illnesses in addition to the effects of age as such. It is, however, far too easy for the elderly, lacking a clear social role, to be assumed to be 'sick'. Far from this being the case it is vital for medical care to prevent the loss of functions, and an important part of the task of the caring team is to identify people at risk and to take preventive action before it is too late.

Each contribution should be read for its own subject matter, but various common themes are brought out in a concluding chapter by Eda Topliss. This is not the place to anticipate her assessment, but at this point it might be worth suggesting that readers could find it worthwhile to make serious efforts to imagine themselves in the roles of doctor, patient, administrator, social worker and so on as appropriate, when reading the various chapters. What is important is to understand what faces each person involved in the health service, particularly the patients for whom it exists. What is it like to receive attention, or to give it, to be free to go home or to think of home as a place one has had to forsake for an institution with rules and restrictions? How far are these relevant to the patient's condition?

All health care has a social context. If care is to be truly beneficial, then that context must be understood by all concerned. This book shows how changing patterns of ill-health and developments in medical science have transformed the problems facing all those involved in health care. In response the framework of the health service has itself been changed, and within it new techniques and working arrangements have evolved to an extent which has not, perhaps, been fully appreciated.

If understanding of what is happening can be increased, then health care is likely to be more effective in the true sense of combining technology with humanity. In the last resort technical efficiency that does not give due weight to its social context may well be less effective because it is inhumane.

CHAPTER 1

The Social Content of Health

Health, like happiness, is an elusive concept. Several definitions exist, but none is entirely satisfactory, and it is curiously difficult, for professionals and laymen alike, to answer the seemingly simple question: 'who is healthy?'

The World Health Organization, at its inception in 1946, defined health as 'a state of complete physical, mental and social well-being, and not merely the absence of disease and infirmity'. This definition, viewing health positively as something more than the absence of disease and emphasizing the relationship of physical health to mental and social well-being, has despite the criticism retained its appeal, especially by comparison with narrower, more negative definitions of health.

To describe health as so complete a state of well-being is to postulate an ideal rather than to provide a realistic working definition which differentiates between those who are healthy and those who are not. Many people would regard themselves as healthy without experiencing a state of complete physical, mental and social well-being.

For an individual, there is a difference between 'being healthy', i.e. free from disease, and 'feeling healthy'. Many problems of life – physical, mental and social – can contribute to a feeling of being unwell despite the absence of any discernible pathological condition. Conversely, someone may feel quite well and healthy and yet be suffering from a disease unawares. For the individual both aspects of health are of importance: certainly, the absence of disease is not enough for well-being, but the presence of disease may be a threat to life.

Good health can be experienced positively or negatively, as something tangible or as an absence of health-related problems. One respondent, in a research on attitudes to health and illness (Herzlich, 1973, p. 53), said of health that 'it is to feel in good form, happy, content, with a good appetite, sleeping well, wanting to be up and doing; it is to feel well and strong, that's what good health is'. However, another remarked: 'when you are in good health, you don't think about it, you think of other things'.

A different definition, given from a sociological perspective, comes from Talcott Parsons (1964) who describes health as a state of optimum capacity for the effective performance of valued tasks. Parsons focuses attention on the social importance of health: healthy individuals are able to function well, to perform social roles; ill-health reduces their ability to do so.

In this chapter lay conceptions of health in contemporary Western societies will be discussed, then social patterns of health behaviour and, finally, some current problems associated with trends to 'medicalize' society.

LAY CONCEPTIONS OF HEALTH

Health norms in society

In spite of the problem of defining health, most people are able to say whether they are healthy or not. This is the experience of various social researches: when asked to rate their health as good or not, people find little difficulty in doing so. The reason for this is that in every society there are accepted standards of 'normal' health and fitness, and ill-health is regarded as a deviation from these standards. As is often the case with accepted standards of normalcy, what constitutes normal health in society is not spelt out, not written down in black and white; it is something that is transmitted to children in socialization processes, something 'understood' by everyone, that 'goes without saying'. It is a sociological commonplace that what constitutes deviation from the norm is easier to define than is the norm itself.

Although unstated, norms govern thinking about health. For example, in a community where the entire membership is 'unhealthy' by Western standards because of endemic infestation by parasites which diminishes energy, this condition will be regarded as normal health; only outsiders will say that the people concerned are not healthy. For the population concerned there is no frame of reference according to which the condition could be considered a deviation (Sedgwick, 1973). Indeed, health norms are often based on frequency of condition. Similar to statistical criteria of normalcy, that which is frequent and widespread is accepted as normal. A commission on hookworm in 1911 found that this was regarded as part of normal health in parts of North Africa (Sedgwick, 1973); in a South American Indian tribe a condition marked by spots on the skin was so common that those who did not have the spots were considered 'abnormal' (Dubos, 1965).

In our own society it is accepted that hair will fall out and teeth decay; baldness and bad teeth are part of normal health.

Clearly, conditions such as hair loss, toothlessness, parasitic infestation and spots on the skin are perceived as normal health or otherwise according to the socio-cultural norms of the particular society in which they occur.

This appears true even when pain and discomfort are involved. Of course, pain is an essentially individual experience, not governed by social norms; after all, culture has nothing to do with the feeling I have when I drop a brick on my foot. But culture influences the evaluation of pain and discomfort as part of normal health or not; as something to 'put up with' or to feel disturbed about. In our society, a woman may experience a great deal of pain during childbirth and yet be regarded as quite healthy while she herself would accept it as normal. In the same way, discomfort and pain during menstrual periods tend to be regarded as normal.

Or consider the example, given by Peter Sedgwick (1973, p.33), of the following imaginary conversation between physician and client:

> *Client:* (telephoning Doctor) Doctor, I haven't consulted you before but things are getting desperate. I am feeling so weak, I cannot lift anything heavy.
> *Doctor:* Goodness, when does this come on you?
> *Client:* Every time I try to lift something or make an effort. I have to walk quite slowly up the stairs and last night when I was packing the big suitcase I found I couldn't lift it off the bed.
> *Doctor:* Well, let's have some details about you before you come in. Name?
> *Client:* John Smith.
> *Doctor:* Age?
> *Client:* Ninety-two last February.

In our culture we expect a man of ninety-two to experience weakness and infirmity. The experience of pain, discomfort or infirmity constitutes ill-health only in particular contexts which are culturally determined.

Social norms govern not only what is accepted as normal health but also the extent of the acceptable level of ill-health. A cold in the head is recognized as a deviation from health but it is a common experience, most likely to be self-limiting and not threatening. It is not considered as 'good', but it is regarded as inevitable, something to put up with. A person may consider himself as very healthy in spite of repeated colds. In countries where malaria or trachoma are widespread these diseases, although recognized as illness, are accepted as part of life, something most people have to tolerate (R. and E. Blum, 1965). Thus, expectations of health also have a bearing on the way that lay people regard their health.

How healthy do people consider themselves to be in Britain today? The most straightforward way to try to answer this question is by asking them. In a social survey, conducted by Dunnell and Cartwright (1972) in the 1960s, over 1,400 adults were asked to describe their health during the fortnight before the interview as excellent, good, fair or poor.

Self-rating of health by adults

Excellent	28%
Good	39%
Fair	24%
Poor	9%

It would seem that a large proportion of the population – 67 per cent according to this sample – regard their health as excellent or good. A similar result was obtained in another survey, by Wadsworth and his colleagues (1971), carried out in two London boroughs. Then, over 2,000 people were asked to rate their health as perfect, good, fair or poor, and 69 per cent of them answered 'perfect' or 'good'.

Rating one's health as excellent or good does not mean a total lack of health-related problems or symptoms. Many of those interviewed by Dunnell and Cartwright, when presented with a checklist of symptoms, said they had experienced several during the previous fortnight. Indeed, only 9 per cent of the total sample claimed to be free of any symptoms. (The corresponding figure in Wadsworth's study was only 4.9 per cent.) Understandably, those who rated their health as fair or poor reported more symptoms than did the others; but even those who regarded their health as excellent reported an average of 2.5 symptoms. This is a confirmation of the argument that some aches and pains are not considered deviations from health, and that certain other conditions are accepted as minor deviations which do not affect overall health status. In this research, symptoms reported by respondents who assessed their health as excellent or good during the two weeks prior to the interviews included headaches, skin disorders, accidents and troubles with feet and teeth. These rather common complaints, then, are seen as compatible with good health: most people experience at least some of them from time to time, they are part of normally accepted 'health'. Furthermore, as Dunnell and Cartwright suggest, these relatively peripheral or external symptoms are not seen as threatening.

Standards of normal health and the public's expectation in this regard are not static but change a great deal over time. In Western industrial societies, where standards of living in general have much improved during this century, there is little doubt that health expectations have heightened. No longer is it considered normal that women should die in childbirth, that illnesses such as diphtheria and scarlet fever should be accepted as inevitable and that infant mortality be looked upon as the will of the God. Just as the population in these societies expect better housing and better working conditions than they did in the early part of the century, they also expect better health. Concepts of health are changing, and the level thereof that is accepted as normal is rising.

The notion that health expectations in Britain are continuing to rise has found wide acceptance, but some of the evidence quoted in support is not straightforward. The pattern of certified sickness absences has shown that minor illness is increasingly regarded as justification for absence from work (Office of Health Economics, 1971) and it is argued that this is a possible consequence of rising health expectation, that people are more likely than before to regard, say, a headache or indigestion as something wrong and needing treatment if only by way of rest and self-prescribed medication. According to this view there has been a lowering of the threshold of the perception of ill-health, symptoms formerly 'shrugged off' are now thought to merit attention. However, sickness absences are bound up with many other changes in society: they may be due, amongst other things, to changing attitudes to work, to welfare provisions which render absence less of a hardship than in earlier times; they may be due to changing attitudes on the part of doctors who have shown themselves willing to certify sickness absences on the grounds of minor ailments and thus have created more demand for such certificates. Sickness absence may, in fact, be affected by a multiplicity of factors, not easy to separate.

Similarly, it is argued that owing to rising health expectations, there is an increasing tendency for people to consult their general practitioners regarding minor, trivial ailments. Certainly, general practitioners speak of too many such complaints (Cartwright, 1967), but the pattern of consultations is influenced by the free availability of health services, the increasing need for sickness certificates signed by doctors, and other factors which, again, are hard to separate from the influence of rising expectations.

Normal health in a society, then, is not equated by people with being completely symptom-free. However, it is a common experience of health workers that certain symptoms, 'aches and pains' are regarded as acceptable by some people, who continue their daily activities in spite of them, while the same symptoms are considered unacceptable by others, who will take action by asking advice, buying medication and taking time off from work. This indicates that although there are commonly accepted general standards of health, variations exist, as between individuals, in what is considered as acceptable health for them. Researchers, studying the way that lay people distinguish between health and illness, and the point at which they decide that their symptoms are not part of normal health but indicate possible illness, have found that two of the determining factors are the novelty and suddenness of the complaint and the extent to which it interferes with normal activities (Apple, 1960; Baumann, 1961).

Certain symptoms appear suddenly and with great force and within a short time the subject passes from a state of feeling healthy to one of feeling ill. Most infectious diseases produce symptoms of this sort and in such cases there is no question of regarding them as part of normal health, they very obviously indicate illness. By contrast, many symptoms tend to be looked upon by the individual as being no more than minor deviations from normal health and sometimes not even that. A sudden pain may send one man hurrying to the doctor while to another a similar but familiar pain is just 'that damned rheumatism again!'. The persistent cough, worsening slowly over the years, may yet be regarded by the sufferer as normal health, but for someone else the rapid onset of a coughing attack threatens danger. Yet one cough may be no worse than the other; it is the suddenness, the unusualness, which is likely to cause the symptom to be taken seriously.

The second determinant of the compatibility of symptoms with normal health is the extent to which they disrupt normal activities. Obviously, identical symptoms may affect one person's activities more than they would another's. For example, an attack of laryngitis would seriously interfere with the work of a lecturer, an opera singer or a politician about to make an important speech; it would affect the work of a clerk or engineer to a considerably lesser extent. These latter may accept a sore throat as something trivial while those in the former group may take alarm at once. The more important the activity being disrupted, the more seriously is the symptom apt to be regarded. Nevertheless, interference with purely leisure activities may also focus attention on symptoms otherwise regarded as trivial. The schoolboy would not fuss over a twinge in his knee until he realized that he could not keep up with the others at football; blocked ears might be tolerated, even by a music lover, until his enjoyment of a concert was spoilt. As Parsons pointed out, normal health is necessary for the performance of social roles.

Thus, research findings show that an individual may regard his health as normal, in spite of symptoms, provided that these are not novel, do not arise suddenly, do not disrupt activities and can be considered as minor deviations from health. Conversely, symptoms which come suddenly, interrupt activities and which, if only for these reasons, seem major deviations from an accepted state of health, are regarded as illness.

Not only minor ailments tend frequently to be accepted as part of normal health, some forms of chronic illness may be similarly regarded in certain circumstances. Chronic conditions are those which are lingering and long-lasting and not susceptible to easy cure. They may start in a small way and only very slowly worsen over time; the symptoms may come and go and the illness come to be regarded as part of normal health and tolerated accordingly as the onset is not sudden and the symptoms not novel.

Other conditions may require a somewhat adjusted life-style involving the avoidance of certain types of work, the observance of a dietary regime and so on, but provided such rules are observed and any necessary medication received, the individual may engage in many of his customary social roles. People with chronic conditions often accept their particular illness as 'normal' to them, that is, they redefine normal health to include the illness condition which is always with them. David Robinson (1971, p. 102), in a study of South Wales families, illustrates this:

Mrs B. had for the past four years been waiting to go into hospital for an operation for a heart condition. This condition made her short of breath, and she was permanently taking drugs. However, when asked to give a general description of the health of members of her family, she described herself as 'very healthy'. Similarly, Mrs I., who had a chronic, but controlled, kidney complaint which, in the six months prior to my first visit to see her, had necessitated two weeks in hospital, eight out-patient sessions, two visits to the doctor and eight home visits from the doctor, classified her own position as 'healthy most of the time'.

In Claudine Herzlich's study people described states which 'combined health with illness; where a status quo is reached'; one of her respondents said: 'I've had a stomach ulcer for ten years, but as long as I watch my diet it doesn't prevent me from enjoying good health' (Herzlich, 1973, p. 54).

It is perhaps more surprising to find that a progressive, disabling disease may be regarded by the subject as normal. In a recent study of patients suffering from multiple sclerosis, several respondents remarked that their overall health was good. One middle-aged man said that it was lucky his health was so good, as otherwise he would not be able to cope with his multiple sclerosis! (Miles, forthcoming).

If one has had, say, a heart condition or kidney complaint for many years, one's daily activities have probably been adjusted accordingly, and a routine of adjusted activities has been established. The chronic condition would not, then, be thought of as illness because it was not interfering with the established routine of normal activities.

So far in this chapter self-assessments of health have been considered. However, an individual's health is defined as good or bad, not only by himself but also by his family, friends and workmates, i.e. members of his immediate social group. These may regard a person's symptoms as compatible with health and advise him that there is nothing to be disturbed about, but on the other hand they might take a contrary view. Similar to self-assessment, definitions of health by others are influenced by the novelty and suddenness of symptoms and by the degree of interference with work. A persistent cough would be accepted by those long familiar with the person concerned as his normal health; the singer with laryngitis will be regarded as ill by himself and by others. Visibility and recognizability of symptoms are also relevant to health assessment by others, who can apply these criteria to a hoarse voice, spots or a swelling, whereas pain or depression can be described only by those experiencing them.

Definitions of health by self and by others may differ. Parsons (1951) pointed out that a person's claim to be ill has to be accepted by his social group as valid, otherwise he will be considered as a malingerer. A man regarded by others as 'legitimately ill' will be allowed to discontinue his normal social obligations. Likewise a claim to be healthy needs acceptance by others or else the individual will be regarded as ill and be required to give up his normal functions in the world of the healthy. A sufferer from an infectious disease would not be allowed to function normally at the risk of spreading the infection, no matter how eager he was to carry on; someone behaving in a socially unacceptable manner due to mental disturbance would almost certainly be prevented from carrying out social roles in spite of his claims to be healthy; a man may be eager to fight for his country but will not be able to do so if his claim to health is not accepted.

Variations in lay conceptions

Lay definitions of normal health, then, are made in social contexts and are governed by the broad cultural norms of a particular society. Not only do conceptions of health differ from one society to another, variations may also exist within a society, especially in large countries where population groups reflect a diversity of ethnic origins, religious beliefs and socio-economic positions. Studies in the United States and in Britain have shown that a number of differences exist in conceptions of health and normalcy between sections of the population and that at least some of these differences are associated with underlying cultural variations.

Several authors argue that differences exist between middle- and working-class people in their conceptions of health and in their orientations to health. Eliot Freidson (1973, p. 288) suggests that 'the working class person has a very concrete and literal approach to his health, which is based on how he feels. . . . The definition of symptoms and of possible illness tends to arise directly from sensations of pain, discomfort or incapacity.' By contrast, Freidson argues that the middle-class person has a different approach: '. . . detached, abstract objectivity . . . more often defines significant symptoms independently of discomfort or even incapacity; he is inclined to use intellectual criteria of "danger signals" that involve at best the anticipation of discomfort.'

Gerald Gordon (1966) noted that working-class Americans emphasized more than did middle-class ones the importance of symptoms which interfered with their usual activities. Especially for poor manual workers, someone was sick when he could not work.

Other researchers have suggested that the level of health accepted as normal by working-class people is lower than that so accepted by the middle class. In a survey conducted by the Health Information Foundation in the United States, a working-class respondent said that a 'working man has to get used to aches and pains' (Rosenblatt and Suchmann, 1964). Koos (1954) noted that lower-class women commonly experienced lower-back pain, but regarded this as part of everyday existence. The results of a research carried out in South Wales showed that 'tiredness' was never seen as a sign of illness by men in the working class, although it was so regarded by those in the middle class. The inference was that tiredness is a fact of everyday life in working-class families and accepted as such (Robinson, 1971).

Dunnell and Cartwright (1972) reported that 43 per cent of Social Class V (unskilled manual) respondents rated their health as poor or fair but only 17 per cent of Class I (professional) respondents did so. However, the average number of symptoms reported by working-class people was higher than that reported by middle-class ones, indicating the possibility that a difference exists between levels of health accepted as 'normal' by people in different social classes.

Nevertheless, one has to view these suggestions with caution: far too little evidence is available at present concerning lay definitions of normal health, no matter to which social class they are attributed. Especially is there a paucity of British data, and it is quite possible that when such data is collected explanations of variations in lay conceptions will not be found in simple social-class positions. According to the Wadsworth (1971) study in London, people who assessed their health as poor or fair were significantly more likely to have been widowed, separated or divorced. Such variables as marital status and living or not living alone may prove to have considerable bearing on the way that people view their health.

The possibility of differences in conceptions of health and illness being associated with ethnic group membership has also stimulated many studies, mainly in the United States. In a well-known research Zola (1966) found a considerable difference, as between patients of Irish and Italian origin, in their evaluation of symptoms as indicating illness or not. In another study, now regarded as a classic, Zborowski (1958) examined responses to pain by American patients of Italian, Jewish and Anglo-Saxon origin. He found that patients of Italian and Jewish origin responded to the experience of pain in an emotional fashion, and paid a great deal of attention to it (although these similar responses related to different underlying attitudes), while the Anglo-Saxons tended to pay less attention to the pain experience and to be more stoical. The Italian and Jewish patients later revealed that their mothers had tended to show what some might regard as over-concerned, over-protective attitudes to their children's health and had paid great attention to childhood colds, bruises, etc. Such patterns of childhood socialization might well influence adult attitudes and definitions of normal health and be reflected in immigrant groups in a country like the United States.

In contemporary Western societies an important characteristic of the subculture of various social groups is the extent of their compatibility with modern medicine. Different sections of the population vary in the degree to which their conceptions of health and normalcy resemble prevailing medical conceptions.

There is bound to be some discrepancy between lay and medical definitions of health. Indeed, we know that this is the case from the repeated complaints of the medical profession that patients consult them unnecessarily about trivial conditions while others neglect symptoms which doctors would assess as serious. Of course, many factors may influence a person's decision on whether or not to seek medical advice, but among them would certainly be his concept of health and his evaluation of symptoms as part of customary health or otherwise.

Lay cultures of Western industrial societies are more likely to include notions of health and illness similar to those of modern medicine than are the lay cultures of simpler, non-industrial societies elsewhere. Within contemporary Western societies, those sections of the population which are closest to members of the medical profession in their cultural norms and values are most likely to be closest also in their conceptions of health.

Empirical studies, in which the health knowledge of lay people was investigated, have shown that the best indicators of the layman's compatibility with modern medical conceptions are his socio-economic position and educational attainments. The term 'health knowledge' usually means the extent to which lay people define their health, describe the working of the body, and recognize and evaluate the importance of symptoms in accordance with modern medical knowledge.

Dunnell and Cartwright (1972) asked people whether or not they thought five illnesses, diabetes, polio, bronchitis, tuberculosis and anaemia, were catching. Working-class people were less knowledgeable than the middle class: 82 per cent of Social Class I respondents answered correctly regarding four or five of the illnesses, the proportion falling to 53 per cent of Social Class V. Also, a higher proportion of middle-class than working-class people thought, in accordance with current medical thinking, that a 'daily bowel movement' is not necessary for keeping healthy. In the United States a health survey showed that respondents with lower educational background were able to name fewer of the symptoms of diseases such as diabetes, polio and cancer than were those with higher educational attainments (Koos, 1954). Other studies inquiring into patients' knowledge of medical words, specific diseases, usefulness of vaccination, etc., confirm these results (Koos, 1954; Samora *et al.*, 1962; Feldman, 1966).

HEALTH BEHAVIOUR IN SOCIETY

In our society health is an important social value; there is a consensus of opinion concerning the desirability of health. To most people it would seem incomprehensible that health could be a matter of complete indifference to anyone.

According to Talcott Parsons (1964) health is a specially emphasized . value in American society, and much of his argument applies to Western societies generally. He pointed out that the emphasis given to health in American society is linked with other cultural values, such as an orientation to mastering the environment, rather than adjusting to it, to practical, secular pursuits and to indefinite progress. Health is emphasized because it is an essential condition for the attainments of these values. Illness is seen as a failure to master the environment and as an obstacle to progress.

It is inherent in the concept of social values that they are hierarchically arranged: certain things are valued more than others. No matter how important, health is only one valued thing amongst many and has to compete with them. In contemporary Western societies the preservation of life and health are important ideals to which great homage is paid; people often say that one's life and health come first. But it is one thing to put a general value on health, as something desirable, and quite another to behave in accordance with this valuation, especially when health comes into conflict with other priorities. Health considerations do not always dominate the behaviour of individuals, who frequently take risks detrimental to health. For example, a good case has been made out and been much publicized showing that cigarette smoking is associated with lung cancer, bronchitis, and increased death rates generally, but people carry on smoking.

Health-related decisions are taken in social contexts, in the light of competing priorities. David Robinson (1971, p. 14), in his study of South Wales families, found that respondents often had quite clear ideas of priorities and evaluated the importance of health risks accordingly. For example, one respondent damaged his knee while playing football, and according to his wife: 'It was stiff on Sunday and I said he'd have to go to the surgery on the Monday . . . but he wouldn't. He started his job with X's and you can't go sick on the first day. . . .' In the classic study of Koos (1954, p. 37), a respondent very neatly expressed his view that health considerations have to compete with other priorities of life:

I wish I could get it fixed up, but we've just got some other things that are more important first. Our car's a wreck, and we are going to get another one. We need a radio too. . . . But it's got to wait for now – there's always something more important.

Indeed, it is a common experience that possible risks to health are evaluated in the light of the requirements of the job, or the importance of not missing the annual holiday.

. Of course, lay people do make positive efforts to preserve and safeguard their health, and such behaviour has been studied by many researchers. Kasl and Cobb (1966) defined health behaviour as 'any activity undertaken by a person believing himself to be healthy, for the purpose of preventing disease or detecting it in an asymptomatic stage'.

Behaviour for the preservation of health finds expression in attempts to lead a healthy life (exercise, dietary measures and adjustments to life-style are in this category) and in the use of health care services for the prevention and detection of disease (in which category come regular check-ups, vaccination and the use of screening and ante-natal services). Both of these aspects of health behaviour will now be considered.

Attempts to lead a healthy life and to avoid risks to health embrace a whole range of measures such as watching one's diet, taking a daily 'constitutional', giving up or moderating smoking or drinking habits, ensuring sufficient sleep and so on.

Claudine Herzlich (1973, p. 97) found that one of the most frequently mentioned concerns was eating: respondents in her study were found to pay considerable attention to the quantity and type of food they consumed as well as to the balance of their diets. Adequate sleep and rest were held nearly as important as eating habits, and many health practices were founded on the idea of 'relaxation'. Indeed, leisure activities like games, walking, going away on holiday and gardening, can all be viewed as health measures. Once notions of stress and relaxation are introduced, increasingly more aspects of daily life can be viewed as relevant to health.

People adopt health measures selectively; ignore or reject some and accept others, according to individual needs. As one respondent said: 'I've got a good digestion and I don't bother about what I eat but I can't work if I haven't slept well, if I don't get my regular sleep.'

Another popular measure for ensuring health is the consumption of vitamins and tonics. Dunnell and Cartwright (1972) found that nearly a fifth of the adults in their sample had taken a tonic, a vitamin preparation or a medicinal food or drink during the previous two weeks.

In modern Western societies several types of preventive services, varying in popularity, are available. Ann Cartwright (1967) asked a sample of nearly 1,400 people whether they had had any sort of check-up or general examination in the previous two years. A quarter of this sample said that they had received what the author describes as a preventive or screening check during that time. Over half of these checks were arranged through workplaces or done when a mobile X-ray unit was at the factory or office. When the people in the sample were asked whether they would like a doctor to give them a regular check-up every two years, nearly two-thirds said that they would.

Preventive health measures are not equally popular with all sections of society. Titmuss (1968) argued that the experience of fifteen years of National Health Service had shown that higher-income groups know how to make better use of the Service than do low-income groups, especially the unskilled working-class families. Titmuss was writing about utilization of the National Health Service in general; his view did not pass unchallenged, and there is an ongoing debate on this issue. However, data showing the differential utilization of preventive services by social classes are very convincing. Michael Alderson (1970) reviewed research data relating to social class variations in the use of particular services, and found that Social Classes IV and V make less use of the preventive services, especially in relation to their needs, than do higher social classes. The studies he reviewed showed that women in upper socio-economic groups responded best to cancer screening services (cervical cytology); that Mass Miniature Radiography was much under-utilized by working-class people in relation to pick-up rates; that Infant Welfare clinics were used less by working-class than by middle-class mothers; and that regular visits to dentists were much more a middle-class habit. In a study of family planning services Ann Cartwright (1970) found that a higher proportion of middle-class than of working-class mothers had an ante-natal examination and attended family planning clinics; others have shown that middle-class people are much more likely to consult chiropodists and are more likely to keep their own teeth.

Thus, there is considerable evidence of a middle-class bias in the utiliza-tion of preventive services; why this should be so is not obvious and several explanations have been put forward. One is that different attitudes to prevention reflect underlying cultural differences, i.e. that variations in health behaviour as between social classes are associated with cultural values and norms. In this view, cultural background, the influence to which people are subjected from early childhood, guides health behaviour, and the value attached to the taking of preventive health measures reflects the value accorded to such measures by these cultural factors.

A variety of studies (e.g. Milio, 1975) have shown that traditionally, in fact ever since its emergence in the early days of industrialization, the middle class has had a future-orientation, i.e. that planning ahead has been stressed as important. Both in business and in private life, long-term planning and the postponement of immediate pleasures for more distant goals have been values associated with an industrial ethic. This ethic was internalized by generations of middle-class children through family and educational systems, and health behaviour reflects this orientation. Because much value is placed on the exercise of forethought, preventive health measures are similarly valued. The frame of mind that one should think of possible risks to health when one is healthy is future-oriented and is analogous to the way that an industrial enterprise caters for future risks. The popularity of regular health checks and other preventive precautions is a consequence of this value orientation of the middle class.

Conversely, the industrial working class is said to have a traditionally present-day orientation (Straus, 1962; Weeks *et al.*, 1958). Established in early industrial society, when economic forces affecting their livelihood seemed just as incomprehensible to the working man as the forces of nature which sometimes led to the failure of crops, their values emphasized present-day benefits and immediate solutions to their problems. (Indeed, long-term planning and future benefits make no sense if intervening forces are unknown and incomprehensible.) Occurrences in life were viewed as 'luck' rather than as the products of design. Limited education, a traditional feature of working-class environment, increased the difficulty of understanding economic forces; it also led to difficulties in communicating with people outside a fairly narrow group of family and workmates and to the reinforcement of traditional value orientations. Although these traditional values may well be changing, general value orientations do so only slowly, and successive generations have to be socialized according to new patterns before new orientations become freely established. Contemporary health behaviour is influenced by those traditional values, and the present-day orientation does not emphasize preventive measures as important. Under-utilization of preventive services is accordingly explained by the tendency not to cater now for future risks.

A related, but somewhat different, explanation of the under-utilization of preventive services by the working class concerns their alienation from the world of organized health care (Suchmann and Rosenblatt, 1964; Zola, 1964). The argument is that the low-income, unskilled worker, with poor education and a traditionally narrow life-style finds health clinics and hospitals an alien world. Bureaucratic rules, like appointment systems and form-filling, the unfamiliar speech of doctors and nurses, difficulty in communication with receptionists – all influence lower-working-class families against services, especially preventive services, where the need is not imperative.

Other explanations stress the differences between social classes in their knowledge of available services, their access to them and their familiarity with the health care system. Middle-class people are more knowledgeable about the availability, location and uses of the services; they know how to 'work' the system of health care. Lack of transport facilities and telephones and lack of money might well prevent some working-class families from reaching clinics or hospitals.

Finally, social-class variations in the use of the preventive services may also be attributed to their uneven distribution. There is considerable evidence to show that in Britain the areas with a high proportion of people in unskilled or semi-skilled occupations have poorer than average medical care (Noyce *et al.*, 1974). In such areas general practitioners have larger lists, health visitors have heavier case loads, there are fewer family planning clinics, more obsolete hospital buildings and less equipment. Tudor Hart (1975) called this situation the 'inverse care law: the availability of good medical care tends to vary inversely with the need of the population served'. If preventive services are less available in working-class areas and the people there are less inclined to use such services anyway, it is hardly surprising that there exists a general under-utilization of preventive services by working-class people.

An important point to bear in mind, though, is that differences in the use made of preventive services by various socio-economic groups do not indicate differences in the value put on health by these groups. Those who make little use of the services may value their health quite as much as do those who use them much more. Even if it is accepted that under-utilization reflects underlying cultural orientations and is not merely the result of practical difficulties or unfamiliarity, these cultural orientations, although incompatible with the use of available services or even with the notion of prevention, may nevertheless be entirely compatible with placing a high value on health.

Several researches have revealed differences in the health behaviour of men and women. Socio-medical studies have shown that women seem the more concerned about health matters, and are more likely to follow health recommendations and to have regular check-ups (Anderson, 1963). They are twice as likely to take tonics and vitamins and, individually, take them in larger quantities (Jefferys, 1965). These findings are consistent with another result of these surveys, that women are larger consumers of unprescribed medicines than are men (Dunnell and Cartwright, 1972).

Similar to the association of health behaviour with social class, the explanation for this difference between men and women is complex, several factors probably contributing to it.

In Western culture, women were traditionally regarded as the 'weaker sex'. It is possible that over-attention to health practices does not accord with notions of 'manliness', but savours too much of 'fussing' about oneself. Two studies by David Mechanic (1964; 1965) showed that sex-roles are important in health behaviour and in attitudes towards health risks. In one study of 350 mother–child pairs, he found that one of the best predictors of children's reports of 'fear of getting hurt' and 'attention to pain' was the child's sex: boys felt that they had to express tougher attitudes than did girls. In the other, he found that male respondents expected their mothers to be less stoical in illness and to bear pain less bravely than did their fathers.

Of course, women come into contact with preventive services during pregnancy and child-rearing; they are urged to take care of their health and that of their babies during these periods and this may well contribute to the difference in health behaviour. Their interest, once awakened in health matters, would continue. Women might come to feel that responsibility for looking after the health of their families rests with them – this would seem natural to their roles of mother and wife. This developed interest in health practices generally would be reflected in the utilization of services, the buying of vitamins and diet-consciousness.

It might be worth remarking here that women frequently do the family shopping and are consequently more exposed to advertising and displays in shops than are their husbands. They spend, on average, more time at home and they have more opportunity to attend clinics, etc. Perhaps the women at home may more readily turn to the aspirin or the medicine bottle than would the man at work, for whom such remedies are not so readily available. Practical considerations of this sort very likely contribute to differences in health behaviour as between the sexes.

Variations in health behaviour are a reflection of the very considerable interest that centres around health matters, resulting in a considerable exchange of views within groups. Freidson (1973, p. 289) argued that advice-giving and advice-seeking in health affairs among laymen organizes the direction of behaviour and called this the 'lay referral system'. According to Freidson, 'the organization of people into families and other kin groups, neighbourhoods, work groups, cliques and the like thus operates to enforce particular views of illness'. In all kinds of health matters, whether relating to immunization, family planning, diet, or the evaluation of symptoms, a social process of advice-seeking within social groups occurs. This process reinforces the tendency of individuals to act similarly to others in their immediate social group and assures people of the approval of their peers concerning health behaviour. This way women more than men and middle-class more than working-class individuals would be encouraged to use services or to take an interest in their health.

Earlier it was said that although great homage is paid to the ideal of preserving life and health in our society, in everyday life risks to health are evaluated in the light of other, competing priorities. Positive health measures are not universally popular: available services are not used by everybody. It can be further argued that to some people in certain circumstances, illness seems more attractive than health and that this will be reflected in the health behaviour of such people.

It was the psychoanalytic school which first introduced the notion of 'escape into illness': an individual may escape from personal problems, or social constraints, to illness, which is regarded, in this framework, as motivated. Later, Talcott Parsons (1951), developing the concept of the 'sick role', stressed the existence of motivational factors in illness.

Certainly, it is a rather common experience that on occasions, acquiring a minor illness may seem positively desirable. One may prefer to be sick rather than face a difficult examination, be called up for the army, or attend an unpleasant interview. Nor is the attraction of ill-health apparent only on such specific occasions; Micheal Balint (1964, p. 18) argued that 'some of the people who, for some reason or another, find it difficult to cope with the problems of their lives resort to becoming ill'. For someone with severe personal problems, an illness possibly necessitating removal from home to hospital, may seem an excellent even if temporary relief. In these situations less value would be placed on health. Parsons (1951) pointed out that abandoning social obligations, which a sick person is entitled to do, may seem attractive. Health represents the requirement to participate in society, to carry out social responsibilities.

Claudine Herzlich (1973, pp. 114, 116) also found that for some people illness appears as a kind of liberation. One man remarked: 'when I'm very tired, I often wish I were ill . . . illness is a kind of rest, when you can be free of your everyday burdens'. From another respondent in this research comes the remark: 'Health is what is required of you every day; that's why one isn't particularly anxious to get better.' Thus health may become identified with social constraints and problems while illness represents an escape from demands made on the individual.

Being ill may seem attractive not only as an escape from personal problems and from the responsibilities attendant on being healthy but also because it may provide an individual with some positive good things he values: a chance to stay in bed, to have his meals put in front of him, his comforts attended to and so on.

In these circumstances, there is a motivation to become ill, and some positive health measures may be neglected. In Balint's words (1964, p. 226), 'there is the type to whom any semblance of an illness is more than welcome, who goes out of his way to "catch" diseases'. Furthermore, if one enjoys the hospital stay, and is not anxious to return to health and all it represents, then one will not make much effort to get healthy; hospital staff are very familiar with patients who develop symptoms before discharge.

It is not being suggested, of course, that illness is attractive to everybody; only that some people, in given situations, find it so. In Herzlich's study (1973), while some people regarded illness as a 'liberator', others thought of it as 'destructive' and very undesirable.

THE MEDICALIZATION OF HEALTH

Lay conceptions of health are not static; they undergo changes and so do patterns of health behaviour. In contemporary Western societies new trends in both lay attitudes and lay behaviour are becoming apparent. Briefly, health expectations are rising, increasing areas of daily life are considered to be health issues and many personal problems are becoming reclassified as health problems.

Changing expectations of health

Higher standards of living, better hygiene and advances in medical knowledge have combined to improve the health of Western industrial nations during this century. The infectious diseases, formerly major threats to the lives of children and young adults, have been dramatically reduced. Most children are better nourished and able to resist infection. Many previously incurable diseases are prevented, cured or modified today. Much of the damage caused by organic malfunctioning can be repaired.

These many improvements have not, however, resulted in the 'good health' of the population which the optimists of earlier days expected. Instead, new disease patterns have emerged. With the virtual elimination of epidemics, people live longer and experience the diseases of middle age and old age, which tend to dominate the health scene today. Medical advances have enabled the handicapped and the chronic sick to survive. Technological and social changes have brought road accidents and obesity.

Epidemiologist J. N. Morris (1967, p. 14) has described the situation as the 'onion principle': when one set of predominating diseases is brought under control (for example, diphtheria and tuberculosis), another 'layer' comes into prominence (such as the degenerative diseases of middle and old age). Morris argued that 'with the decline of crowd diseases, other infectious and non-infectious diseases predominate. Lessen physical deprivation, and widespread emotional impoverishment and social incompetence are exposed. Reduce physical disease, and problems of mental health can no longer be ignored. When environmental casualties are controlled, genetic failures receive more attention.' Indeed, after each success the attention of medicine becomes focused on the next problem to conquer.

Similarly do lay people concern themselves with each unfolding layer of illness, becoming preoccupied with the threat of heart attacks and the problems of ageing now that the more immediate threats of infectious diseases have receded. Additionally, with improved health, once minor problems assume importance.

As well as this constant refocusing of attention on newly emerging problems, a recent important development is the enormously improved technology for the detection of abnormalities. Previously, diagnostic tools consisted of the thermometer, the stethoscope, optical instruments and the simple X-ray machine. Advanced technology has brought highly sophisticated instruments, e.g. automatic machines which carry out twenty chemical analyses on a single specimen and scanners which can screen the whole body for early signs of cancer. Before, the aim of medical diagnosis was to look for gross pathological signs; today abnormalities in biochemical patterns can be sought. Widening of the scope of technical investigations has led to an enormous potential increase in the detection and discovery of previously unknown abnormalities. If medicine is to advance in this direction, a situation may ultimately be reached when, instead of an apparently healthier population, very many individuals will have one or more diagnosed conditions and be possible candidates for treatment.

An indication that such a trend may be developing comes from the popularity of the 'clinical iceberg' notion (Last, 1963). This refers to recognized and treated abnormalities as being the tip of the iceberg, with the unrecognized and untreated ones being the much larger, submerged, part. The implication of this notion is that those who have no diagnosed condition and are thus far regarded as healthy, have not been properly investigated, but were they to receive medical attention much potential illness would be discovered.

Certainly, repeated health surveys of populations have found that only a small proportion of each sample is free of symptoms which doctors would consider suitable for treatment. For example, in a study of a London borough, a number of tests were administered to 1,000 adults and only 6.7 per cent of the persons screened were found to be symptom-free (Epson, 1969).

It has been estimated that in an average British general practice, for every eight persons treated by the doctor for diabetes, there are a further 69 who have undiagnosed 'latent' diabetes which would be detected by investigation; for every five persons known to the doctor to have ischaemic heart disease, a further 15 would be discovered by investigations (Morris, 1967). Studies in the United States and in Britain have shown that only a small percentage of various sample populations are considered by doctors to be free from any condition which could benefit from treatment (Pearse and Crocker, 1944; Schenthal, 1960; Hinkle *et al.*, 1960).

Advances in techniques of treatment along with the many new pharmaceutical preparations now available make the discovery of abnormal conditions seem worthwhile: many people might have improved health and longer life if such conditions were brought to light.

Developments in medicine, new discoveries relating to causes and cures, are of great interest to the public and are much discussed by the media. News of spectacular transplant operations and of the latest research successes are of news value and receive wide publicity. It may well appear to lay people that there is no limit to future achievements and that longer life and better health are becoming increasingly available to everyone.

Rising expectations of health together with confidence in continuing achievements in the medical field make it seem worthwhile for people to turn to doctors with an ever-widening range of health problems.

Extension of medicine into health

Much has been written in recent years about the increasing medicalization of life. Zola (1972, p. 487) describes this as 'an insidious and often undramatic phenomenon accomplished by "medicalizing" much of daily living by making medicine and the labels "healthy" and "ill" relevant to an ever increasing part of human existence'. In contemporary medical thinking a great deal of emphasis is placed on the influence of social factors in the causation and course of disease. Indeed, there has been a change from the specific etiological disease model to the multi-causal one and Zola (1972, p. 493) argues that this change has 'enormously expanded that which is, or can be, relevant to the understanding, treatment and even prevention of disease'.

In recent years, the importance of the prevention of disease has gained wide acceptancEh professionals, and public alike. It is often repeated that, as with crime, prevention is better than cure. The very notion of prevention means a shift of medicine into the lives of the healthy. The formal goals of prevention are the early discovery and treatment of conditions that, neglected, would have serious consequences, the encouragement of habits that promote good health and the discouragement of habits prejudicial to it. If the aim of prevention is to catch the illness before it starts, or at any rate before it becomes apparent, it is necessary to intervene in the lives of people who regard themselves as healthy. High standards of personal hygiene and cleanliness, good housing conditions and adequate, balanced diet have long been accepted as relevant to the prevention of disease. As medical research brings to light more causal factors, other aspects of daily living also become relevant. The amount of exercise taken acquires significance and influences choice of leisure activities, especially of those in sedentary occupations. Modification of specific dietary habits, e.g. eating animal fat and dairy produce, is advocated in the light of their alleged association with specific diseases. The extent and type of domestic heating has a bearing on health and so has the type of clothing. Air pollution, cigarette smoking, alcohol consumption also come under scrutiny – the list is a very long one. One is left with the impression that under certain conditions virtually any human activity can lead to medical problems and that as a consequence all the habits of the population are becoming medical concerns.

Only semi-frivolously Zola (1972, p. 494) remarks 'and what will be the implications of even stronger evidence, which links age at parity, frequency of sexual intercourse, or the lack of male circumcision to the incidence of cervical cancer, can be left to our imagination'.

Thus, in the name of prevention, doctors are involved, not just with the sick but increasingly with the healthy. This process is spelt out in medical writing on the role of doctors. For example Backett (1961, p. 541) says, of the future of the family doctor, that increasingly he will 'switch his attention from sick people to the habits and behaviour of healthy people'. The result is, according to Ivan Illich (1975), that 'people have become patients without being sick'.

Prevention of disease is not the only medical activity that reaches into the lives of healthy people. The development of new techniques has made possible many procedures which take medicine far beyond its original concern with disease. As an example, Zola (1972) considers the case of plastic surgery: once its concerns were the restoration of damage caused by accidents and disease and the correction of congenital deformities; today, plastic surgery is also engaged in changing the shape of the nose or breasts for cosmetic purposes and in re-creating a youthful appearance by concealing signs of ageing. There is no question of illness or the threat of it here; healthy people are able to take advantage of medical skills for purposes unconnected with sickness.

Or, to take another example, research into congenital diseases has advanced knowledge about congenital deformities, and predispositions for disorder, and has enabled people to turn to doctors for genetic counselling in an attempt to improve the quality of subsequent generations of human beings. It is certainly possible that, in the future, couples will be ever more ready to seek advice regarding the suitability of marriage partners and the desirability or otherwise of producing children, and will want to predetermine the sex of their offspring.

Family planning and pregnancy is an area of healthy life that is rapidly becoming very much a medical concern. Before modern methods of birth control existed, the avoidance of unwanted pregnancies was a matter for lay discussion and advice. Today, medical advice is sought; the fitting of contraceptive devices is carried out by medical personnel; sterilization, both male and female, is a surgical matter; and the popular contraceptive pill is prescribed by doctors. In a survey of mothers and family planning by

Ann Cartwright (1970) nearly 1,500 married women were interviewed; two-thirds of them had discussed methods of birth control with a professional, i.e. doctor or nurse. Although a good deal of informal advice about family planning was sought and given amongst friends and relatives, the general practitioner was mentioned most frequently by these mothers as the most helpful adviser. This survey was carried out in 1967–8 and at that time 48 per cent of the women said that they had discussed birth control methods with their general practitioners, besides which they, and others, had consulted doctors in hospitals and family planning clinics on the matter. In an attempt to assess changes taking place, additional interviews were conducted in 1970 when 57 per cent of the women in the sample said that they had discussions on this subject with their general practitioners. This higher percentage indicates that medical advice is increasingly being sought about family planning, a trend very likely to be related to the wider interest in the contraceptive pill, which is considered as a drug, or medication and the need for women to seek medical advice regarding possible health hazards involved in using it. Confirmation of increasing professional consultations came from doctors who took part in the survey: four-fifths of them said that they spent more time discussing family planning with patients than they did five years previously.

Pregnancy, too, is increasingly a matter for health professionals: antenatal clinics ensure that pregnant women are examined, instructed, tested in a clinical setting. Yet only a few generations ago pregnancy was regarded as a natural process and such advice as seemed necessary was gleaned from older women, experienced in such matters.

A great many members of the lay public, it appears, are eager to medicalize their lives. This must be also the conclusion drawn from an examination of the changing pattern of the consumption of drugs.

The consumption of medicines in Britain has grown considerably in recent years. Not only has the number of prescriptions increased during the 1960s and 1970s, but, also, the sales of medicines bought over the counter have gone up (Office of Health Economics, 1968). The majority of people in Britain are regular consumers of medicine. This appears from the result of more than one research. According to the previously mentioned survey by Dunnell and Cartwright (1972), 80 per cent of the adults in the sample had taken some medicine during the previous fortnight, and other studies, in two London boroughs (Wadsworth *et al.*, 1971) and in a working-class housing estate (Jefferys, Brotherston and Cartwright, 1960), produced similar results. Moreover, all these studies found that the bulk of this consumption was self-medication: Wadsworth (1971, p. 41) says that 'for every medicine prescribed by a doctor, two were taken either on the respondent's own initiative or on that of some other lay person'. It was further reported by these surveys that a large number of medicinal preparations are bought and taken by people who, at the same time, describe their health as good or excellent; by individuals in whom no particular condition has been diagnosed. It can be argued then that medicine-taking has become part of the everyday behaviour of healthy people.

The nature of the medication consumed confirms this argument. The types of medicine most often taken by adults in Britain are aspirin and other pain-killers. Dunnell and Cartwright (1972) found that 41 per cent of their sample had taken at least one of these in the two weeks before their interviews, and in Wadsworth's (1971) study 38 per cent of the adults had taken analgesics. The other 'popular' medicines, according to these studies, are indigestion remedies, skin ointments or antiseptics and throat or cough remedies. Thus, a great deal of self-medication goes on with the aim of treating or relieving symptoms such as headache, colds and coughs, indigestion, and cuts and bruises – in other words, the types of symptoms which people regard as compatible with good health. It appears that although such ailments are regarded as part of normal health, to buy medication for them is part of accepted behaviour. This may be the result of rising health expectations: possibly, there is an increasing unwillingness to tolerate even minor symptoms. Growth in the consumption of medicines might also be attributed to the much increased availability of a wide range of preparations pushed by the vigorous advertising policy of the pharmaceutical industry. However it came about, the current pattern of drug-consumption is another sign of the growing medicalization of health.

Seeking medical answers to personal problems

Many medical and non-medical writers have considered, in recent years, the role of the family doctor in Britain, and especially the tendency of patients to turn to their general practitioners with a range of problems which would not previously have been regarded as medical matters (Office of Health Economics, 1974; Royal College of General Practitioners, 1970). These include marital strife, trouble with children, financial difficulties, dissatisfaction with work, sexual problems, feelings of loneliness and deviant behaviour like violence and alcoholism. Family doctors' advice-giving activities are described as their 'counselling' or 'pastoral' role.

There is a certain amount of evidence from studies that this trend towards seeking advice from doctors is growing. Ann Cartwright (1967), in a survey of patients and general practitioners in the 1960s, asked respondents whether they would discuss with their doctor a personal problem which was not strictly medical but which worried them. This question was asked again in a study conducted by her and a colleague five years later (Dunnell and Cartwright, 1972), and the comparative figures revealed that during that time the proportion of adults who said that their doctor would be a good person with whom to discuss a personal problem rose from 28 to 41 per cent. Other studies show that the family doctor is considered to be the appropriate person to consult on drinking problems and family planning (Robinson, 1976; Cartwright, 1970). In various researches, of those respondents who said that they would not go to the general practitioner with personal problems many gave as their reason that they thought the doctor too busy, too overburdened with sick patients, to find time for their difficulties, and not that it was inappropriate to turn to medical men with non-medical problems.

It is also quite possible that people go to the doctor when they wish to talk about personal problems, but that in the first instance they present a health problem, perhaps a minor symptom, which otherwise they would not have consulted him about, and hope that the worrying personal problem will be brought up in the consultation. Moreover, there may not be a definite, formulated personal problem: feelings of loneliness, isolation or inability to cope with daily life are examples of underlying reasons for some people visiting the doctor's surgery. In one investigation, a general practitioner in Hampshire found that about two out of five patients who went to the surgery for treatment (not counting those who attended for services, like inoculation, cervical smears and the pill) showed no evidence of physical or psychological illness (Thomas, 1974). He concluded that 'these patients are not ill in the accepted sense of the word, they are temporarily dependent and want only reassurance and support from their doctor'. This does not seem to be an isolated finding; indeed the Research Committee of the College of General Practitioners (1963), when conducting a study of eleven practices, found that the average 'firm diagnosis' was 55.5 per cent.

Michael Balint drew attention to the type of person who visits the doctor often, with a variety of symptoms; such frequent attenders at the surgery may, in Balint's words, 'propose various illnesses' and if the doctor does not find anything wrong, they will go on proposing new illnesses. Balint (1964, p. 13) cited, as an example:

A woman, aged sixty ... she comes regularly with three complaints: headaches, pumping in the stomach and giddiness. When I give her medicine for her headaches, she complains next time of her stomach, and when I give her something for her stomach she complains next time of giddiness. ... I brought her to tears one day when I pointed out that all these medicines did no good.

Balint argued that such people have an underlying emotional problem which the doctor could bring to light by talking to them about their personal lives and relationships. However, not many doctors today would do so; a much more common response of the doctor is to examine the patient, consider the symptoms presented by him and if all is well, tell the patient that nothing is wrong with him.

It does appear, then, that among the general public there are certain people who turn to doctors with personal, emotional troubles; some in a straightforward manner, openly stating the problem, others ostensibly seeking help with a health-complaint; in certain cases the problems are unacknowledged by the persons concerned, to be brought to light only by skilful questioning.

There are a number of social reasons which foster this trend. Previously, many people turned to members of their families and kin-groups, to neighbours and friends, for guidance with personal problems. People who lived in long-established communities and had strong kinship and community ties with others around them, found little difficulty in talking about their worries and obtaining advice.

With today's greatly increased mobility many people find themselves living in places, far from their former familiar surroundings, where these kinship and community ties are largely absent. Opportunities to consult the family are much reduced and neighbours hardly known; nor, in an increasingly secular society do individuals look to the parish priest to anything like the same extent as before. In these circumstances it is not surprising that people turn to the doctor for the comfort and counselling they once obtained from community and Church.

Moreover, the general practitioner is always to be found. Many would not know how to contact a social worker, would not know of the existence of marriage guidance counsellors, but the locations and times of the surgery are easily discovered.

Another factor could be the greater social acceptability of health problems rather than emotional or personal ones. High blood pressure or kidney disease are regarded as unavoidable and thus are not likely to carry implications of blame or responsibility as might desertion by a husband or delinquency in one's children. Some, unwilling to admit failure in careers or social ambitions or in the attainment of a well-adjusted family life might well be glad of a health explanation for such inadequacies. To go to the doctor rather than, say, the social worker is to opt for the socially acceptable explanation.

Thus, there appears to be a dichotomy of attitudes towards social inadequacy and ill-health, the latter being the more acceptable. Of course, this is itself a social evaluation: there are no inherent reasons why personal problems, more than ill-health, should be seen as someone's 'fault'. The Office of Health Economics (1975, p. 16) argues that 'Ill-health is at present too often incorrectly seen as being an unavoidable and wholly excusable consequence of exposure to external challenges. It should instead perhaps be seen as a failure of the mind or body to adapt and to cope with the physical, psychological and social challenges which every human being must experience.'

The ability of the general practitioner to provide tranquillizers and sleeping pills is another reason why personal problems are taken to the surgery. It may seem to some that although the doctor cannot find a solution to their problems, he can provide relief in the form of drugs. To be able to sleep with the help of sleeping pills, to be less anxious and tense as a result of medication, may enable one to cope better with problems – and in any case even temporary relief from worries may seem worth having. The variety of psychotropic medicines available today is a recent development and one very likely to influence lay behaviour. When writing about the medicalization of society, Zola (1972, p. 495) says that:

> any observer can see, judging by sales alone, that the greatest increase in drug use over the last ten years has not been in the realm of treating any organic disease but in treating a large number of psycho-social states. Thus we have drugs for nearly every mood:
> to help us sleep, or keep us awake
> to enhance our appetite or decrease it
> to tone down our energy level or to increase it
> to relieve our depression or stimulate our interest.

Further he says: 'Recently the newspapers and more popular magazines, including some medical and scientific ones, have carried articles about drugs which may be effective peace pills or anti-aggression tablets, enhance our memory, our perception, our intelligence and our vision.'

A recent study by Cartwright (1976, p. 27) suggests that the very form of the patients' illness depends on the remedies available. According to her, patients 'are likely to emphasize the aspects of their ill-health to which they feel the doctor is most sympathetic and to stress the symptoms which they regard the doctor as most able to treat.'

Thus, many factors combine to produce an increasing tendency to reclassify as health problems many troubles and worries previously regarded as the problems of life and outside the sphere of medicine: the free availability and accessibility of doctors, the relative lack of help from community and kin-groups, the secularization of society, the relative social acceptability of health problems compared to that of social problems, and the availability of psychotropic drugs. In effect the tendency is to look for medical answers to social and personal problems, in other words, to medicalize life.

Several difficulties are created by this situation and these are becoming increasingly apparent. If a variety of social and psychological problems are viewed by lay people as medical concerns about which it is suitable to consult the doctor, the call upon medical care is potentially unlimited. Increasingly more problems and difficulties of life may come to be regarded in this light, building up a virtually inexhaustible demand for additional doctors and more medical facilities, thus exacerbating a situation already made difficult by the new diagnostic techniques discussed earlier which detect more and more abnormalities. It is not expected that economic resources in the foreseeable future can be made available to cope with such an enormous demand being made upon them.

The consulting of doctors about personal problems raises questions as to their ability and qualifications to handle such matters. Most doctors receive very little, if any, training in counselling patients regarding their social and psychological problems and are ill-equipped to do so. Of course, family doctors over the years may gain much experience and be able to give sympathetic understanding and valuable advice; but for a doctor to develop such counselling skills is a personal achievement, not based on his medical training which is the main reason for lay people to consult him. In other words, some doctors may be very effective counsellors, as are some members of the lay community and the Church, but this is largely unrelated to their professional medical knowledge.

Difficulties of another type arise if people go to the doctor with ostensible health problems and the doctor, disinclined to look for underlying personal problems, sets out to investigate the reported medical symptoms. Indeed, doctors' training and orientation will incline them to this course rather than to acting as counsellors. Many of them would, in any case, feel it safer to look for disease than to risk missing it; Scheff (1972), in an interesting essay called this the 'medical decision rule', guiding the activity of doctors: it is safer to impute illness than health. The layman's various presenting symptoms, then, may be taken seriously and be investigated by doctors. If some abnormality is found and the individual is informed, a hitherto healthy person becomes a sick one; wished for or not, he acquires a medical label.

The Office of Health Economics (1975, p. 8) describes this situation as 'conferring' illness on people.

> When a doctor, by his diagnosis, translates an 'ordinary smoker's cough' into 'bronchitis' he has probably created a lifelong chronic illness. Similarly, he can do so with a case of dyspepsia caused by persistent dietary indiscretion if he translates it into a 'suspected peptic ulcer' or a 'grumbling appendix'. In both situations the first was an irritating condition with which the patient had formerly expected to live as best he could. The second has become a specific, if hypothetical, medical condition which will be regarded as a justification for continuing health service care and perhaps repeated absences from work.

As said earlier, a medical label can be used as justification for discontinuing social roles and responsibilities.

To summarize this discussion: there appears to be a social trend which has been described as the 'medicalization of life'. It can be seen in the expanding frontiers of medicine, with medical activities reaching into many aspects of the everyday lives of healthy people, it can be seen in the rising expectations of good health, in the lesser tolerance of minor symptoms and in the demand for medical labels for personal problems.

CONCLUSIONS

What is health then and who is healthy? In this discussion an attempt has been made to demonstrate that the lay conception of health has a dual character. On the one hand evidence shows that laymen are able to accept a given level of health as 'normal' and can define whether an individual is healthy or not according to prevailing standards; on the other hand there is evidence of a general wish to extend the frontiers of health and of an unwillingness to accept the level currently obtaining, which is expected constantly to rise.

Health is both a norm and an ideal and in this lies the duality of the lay conception of it. As a norm health is socially defined and people tend to accept symptoms as part of normal health so long as they come within that social definition, the more so if the symptoms are minor, do not arise suddenly and do not disrupt everyday activities. Individuals are able to see themselves and others as healthy without experiencing, in the words of the World Health Organization, 'a state of complete physical, mental and social well-being'. Perfect health, as an ideal, similar to perfect happiness, implies a goal towards which people may strive but never quite attain. A 'mirage' in the words of René Dubos (1959).

Nevertheless, recent social trends involving the medicalization of the healthy, reaching into many areas of daily life previously outside the sphere of medicine, may indicate that people are coming to regard the ideal of perfect health as an attainable goal. It is possible, owing to 'cultural lag' which so often delays the acceptance of new ideas, that the W.H.O. conception of health is only now acquiring social importance. The assumption of this conception as a realistic goal capable of attainment is likely to prove dangerously misleading if people come to believe that all life's ills can be resolved by the application of medicine in its widest sense. The adoption of the W.H.O. definition as an attainable objective must lead inevitably to a constant escalation of health expectations and of demands for health care services, which available resources would never be able to meet. From this exploration of the lay perspective it would appear better to distinguish clearly and to keep separate the concept of health as a norm from the concept of health as an ideal.

CHAPTER 2

Health Care Policies

The National Health Service, established by the National Health Service Act 1946 and implemented in 1948, represented an important development in the collective provision of health care, but was not really a revolutionary measure. Aneurin Bevan, who scored a considerable personal success in negotiating the terms under which the majority of the medical profession was prepared to support the health service measures, was overstating his triumph, when he claimed the National Health Service as a victory for socialism. He was jubilant that health measures had become part of the system, but insisted: 'But they do not flow from it. They have come in spite of it. . . In claiming them, capitalism proudly displays medals won in the battles it has lost' (Bevan, 1952, p. 74).

In fact, the development of public responsibility for health was a gradual process, like so much else in society, and while the National Health Service Act 1946 marked the most comprehensive statement until then made on the subject of public responsibility for health care, and represented a great improvement in provision, it introduced no radically new principles, nor any radical redistribution of health opportunities. Collective concern for health had been explicitly expressed before the middle of the nineteenth century. In 1842, Edwin Chadwick, secretary to the Poor Law Commission, published his report on the sanitary conditions of the working people of Britain (Chadwick, 1842), and although the mass of disturbing information which he published was less influential than Chadwick hoped, the report did contribute to the setting up of the Central Board of Health under the Public Health Act 1848.

Chadwick, in his report, noted not only the squalor of many of the rapidly growing industrial towns, which encouraged disease and the spread of infection, but also the economic cost to the country of a high rate of illness

38

and death, and he urged the acceptance of public responsibility for promoting healthy conditions. He pointed out, for example, the enormous loss of productivity resulting from the 'appalling fact that, of all who are born of the labouring classes in Manchester, 57 per cent die before they attain 5 years of age, that is before they can be engaged in factory labour [children were not normally employed before the age of 7 or 8] or in any other labour whatever' (Chadwick, 1842, p. 158).

Chadwick and his co-worker on the report, Dr Southwood Smith, discovered that over half the paupers claiming public relief had lost their work (or in some cases the breadwinner for a family had died) owing to disease promoted and spread by the insanitary conditions of the mid-nineteenth century towns. Once again Chadwick pointed to the good economic sense of the state accepting responsibility for promoting a healthy environment, and thus saving on pauper relief.

A Central Board of Health, charged with promoting a healthier environment, was set up in 1848. None of the original three members of the Board was medically qualified, and it was only later in the year, when an epidemic of cholera broke out in Britain killing 53,000 people in a few months, that a doctor (Southwood Smith) was added to the Board. The omission of a medically qualified person was not as surprising in 1848 as we, in the 1970s, might think. The medical profession had not then developed the knowledge and technologies which today enable it to play such a vital part in health care. In 1848 anaesthetics (ether and chloroform) had only just been discovered, and the development of internal surgery (as distinct from amputations which had been carried out without anaesthetics) as a basic part of medical care was just beginning. It was still many years, however, before an understanding of the importance of antisepsis was widely disseminated throughout the medical profession, and until then some three-quarters of the patients undergoing internal surgery died of post-operative infections and complications (Woodward, 1974). The pharmacopoeia available to physicians for the treatment of medical conditions was limited to pain-killing products such as opium and its derivatives (aspirin and barbiturates were not in use until the end of the century), digitalis, quinine, laxatives, and very little else.

The medical profession, therefore, did not have much to offer in the form of a personal health care service, and the fact that the majority of people could not afford to retain the services of a personal physician when they fell ill probably did not amount to very great hardship. When a person became ill, the family could usually give all the comfort and care that the existing state of medical knowledge indicated was appropriate. If, owing to poverty, the family was unable to provide such care, then the Poor Law institutions supplied the necessary food and shelter for the sick. (Chadwick, the architect of the Poor Law Amendment Act 1834, had seen the Poor Law Workhouse as a sort of correctional institution for able-bodied paupers who would thus be encouraged to find work and solvency. In fact the workhouses took in increasing proportions of elderly and chronically sick destitute people, leading in the 1860s to legislation to establish workhouse infirmaries.)

The public of the 1840s did not look to the medical profession for any major improvements in health. In any case, the diseases which scourged the population and accounted for the majority of deaths – cholera, enteric fever, diphtheria and other infectious diseases of childhood, tuberculosis, smallpox – were all amenable to public health control and environmental improvement. The introduction of pure water supplies, efficient sewerage and refuse disposal, adequate nutrition due to cheap imported foods, improved housing standards, and reduction of overcrowding, plus, in the case of smallpox, vaccination which was developed by Jenner around 1800 and practised increasingly after 1840, together made a tremendous impact on the average expectation of life at birth.

When so much could be achieved by environmental control, it is not surprising that the history of collective provision for health in the nineteenth century is a history of public health acts. Personal health care did not become a matter for state intervention until the National Insurance Act 1911, which introduced cash benefits and access, without payment of a fee, to a general practitioner, for most workers. By that time there had been a rapid development of medical knowledge and profound changes in the social structure of society.

SOCIAL CHANGE AND MEDICAL DEVELOPMENTS

The hundred years after 1848 saw an acceleration of the changes which had already begun in Britain in the eighteenth century. The improvements in agricultural production which accompanied the movement to enclose common lands, led to an increased supply of food. This was further augmented during the nineteenth century by trade with America, which burgeoned after the end of the Napoleonic wars.

It was probably the improvements in diet, giving greater resistance to disease, which accounted for the upswing in population from the end of the eighteenth century. There was no obvious increase in the birth rate, nor was there any significant immigration, so that the population increase must have been attributable to a decline in the death rate. Any such decline is not explicable in terms of medical intervention to cure disease, since knowledge of therapy was extremely elementary in that period. It seems to indicate a greater resistance to illness on the part of the population generally (Mc-Keown, 1965).

The growing population, however, was not needed on the land, where developments in agricultural techniques had reduced the labour force required, and where competition from overseas produce was forcing the abandonment of cultivation of less fertile fields. There was, therefore, a pool of labour available for the factories which were growing up in the new urban centres of the North and Midlands.

These towns grew rapidly and with no concern at the beginning for planning or standards of hygiene. In 1800 a quarter of Britain's population lived in towns. By 1851 one half did so, and by 1901 two-thirds. Today, over 80 per cent of our population live in urban surroundings. Such rapid concentrations of population, especially in the insanitary conditions which prevailed until late in the nineteenth century, facilitated the spread of infectious diseases and constituted a threat to the economy, as Chadwick noted, by wiping out productive or potentially productive members of society. The public health measures, as have been said, were developed to counter these problems.

As more complicated productive techniques developed there was increasing interest in keeping fit, or in restoring to health, the working population. Sickness absence of a skilled and experienced worker represented a production loss that was not remediable simply by taking on any other pair of hands that happened to be available. It was far better for the individual and his employer if prompt medical treatment could avoid or minimize sickness absence. The National Insurance Act 1911 was devised to make such care available, free of charge at the time of need, to all manual workers, and to all others earning, in 1911, £160 per year or less. The families of insured workers were not covered. By 1938, the earnings ceiling had been raised and roughly two-thirds of the employed population was covered by the provisions of the Act.

Pressure to extend the coverage of the 1911 Insurance Act, and especially to include the families of insured workers, grew during the period between the two wars, and came not only from those members of the public denied cover, but also from the British Medical Association. By this time, medical knowledge was considerable when compared to the middle of the nineteenth century, and the value of access to a doctor at times of sickness was correspondingly much greater. General practitioners had benefited considerably from the insurance scheme. Ninety per cent of them took insured patients and although this did not preclude their taking private patients as well, by 1938 the bulk of their time was spent on their 'panel' (i.e. insurance panel) practice, and they derived a comfortable and secure income from the capitation fees in respect of these patients. The general practitioners were more than willing to see the families of insured workers included in the scheme and added to their 'panel' rather than lose them to the hospital out-patient clinics.

Perhaps some self-interest was a factor in the B.M.A. pressure for extension of insurance cover but one must also recognize the changed circumstances brought about by new medical knowledge. In the nineteenth century, medicine in the community was limited basically to environmental health measures, with some general vaccination programmes. Personal health care was largely confined to institutions, except for a small minority of people who could afford to retain personal physicians to attend them in their homes. Even in the institutions – the workhouse infirmaries, public fever hospitals, mental asylums and the voluntary hospitals – it was only when the nineteenth century was considerably advanced that the personal attention given in them assumed a therapeutic as distinct from custodial or caring role. By the 1920s, however, the medical profession had much greater therapeutic skills and was able, and anxious, to offer a personal health service in the community, rather than leave such services to institutions. The 1911 Insurance Act put personal health care in the community within reach of many. It was logical, humane, and eminently practical to extend this facility to all. Recommendations to this effect were the substance of reports published by the British Medical Association (B.M.A., 1929, 1938), but neither report resulted in any action.

A committee, chaired by Lord Dawson, was asked by the government to make recommendations on future health provisions. The Dawson Report, appearing before either of the B.M.A. proposals, suggested state provision of an integrated health service, funded out of general taxation (Dawson, 1920). Although given a good press, and initially welcomed by the B.M.A. (but later rejected in favour of their own proposals for an extension of the insurance scheme) the Dawson Report was simply shelved during the economic and political crises of the 1920s and 1930s. Dawson, and the B.M.A. proposals, were ahead of prevailing opinion of the inter-war years.

THE NATIONAL HEALTH SERVICE

There are a number of books which describe the National Health Service, its origin, inauguration and structure (e.g. Willcocks, 1967; Stevens, 1966; Forsyth, 1966). Not one sees the National Health Service Act 1946 as other than a stage in a process which had begun long ago of increasing public concern with health care. This chapter has tried to indicate some of the reasons for this increasing concern and has suggested that a number of factors were important. Firstly, the dangers of ill-health, at least of the infectious kind which then were the most common diseases, were greatly increased by the changes from a scattered rural population to a concentrated urban one. Secondly, the necessity of sound health among workers and potential soldiers assumed greater weight as the productive technology became more complex and as international competition provoked political crises and wars. Lastly, at least chronologically, the development of medical knowledge of effective preventive and curative techniques that could really contribute to the maintenance or restoration of health, made the organization of medical services a much more important matter for the community than it had been in the past.

The deficiencies of the existing hotchpotch of health services had become increasingly apparent in the 1920s and 30s, and when war again threatened, the government, remembering the near collapse of medical services under the avalanche of First World War casualties, was concerned to ensure as efficient a service as possible, at least for war-wounded. The strategy adopted was to form the Emergency Medical Service in 1938, which grouped together all the 1,000 voluntary and 2,000 public hospitals in eleven administrative regions – the forerunners of the health regions of today.

The Emergency Medical Service assumed direct responsibility for about a third of all non-mental hospital beds, with the intention of having these beds available for war-wounded and civilian air-raid casualties. To staff these beds, the Emergency Medical Service employed consultant and other specialist doctors on a salaried basis, and a number of nurses. In effect, the Emergency Medical Service took over the financing and control of about

1,000 hospitals, mainly the large voluntary hospitals and the better local authority hospitals. For the former it meant a solution to the financial problems which had bedevilled them for years, since their income from bequests and flag days could not keep pace with the costs of hospital care, increasing with every advance in medical techniques of investigation and therapy. For the latter it meant a rise in standard of equipment – 1,000 new operating theatres were installed between 1938 and 1939 – and an influx of progressive medical ideas from the salaried specialists who were posted to the hospitals under the terms of their contracts with the Emergency Medical Services (Abel-Smith, 1964).

As the war years progressed, and the numbers of Service wounded and air-raid casualties mercifully failed to reach the heights pessimistically anticipated, the Emergency Medical Service beds began to be used for the civilian sick. By the end of the war many people – doctors, nurses, administrators and patients – had experience of a nationally organized hospital service and, apart from minor deficiencies, had found it a vast improvement on the pre-war hospital system. It was unthinkable merely to dismantle the Emergency Medical Service and return to the pre-1938 arrangements. Indeed, this was never contemplated.

At intervals throughout the war there were reports and proposals concerned with the future of the health service. In addition, the influential Beveridge Report of 1942, echoing the Chadwick Report of a hundred years earlier, identified sickness and disease as major and largely preventable causes of poverty and destitution. The government finally responded to professional and public pressure and accepted responsibility for planning a post-war health service. The National Health Service Act 1946 was the culmination of a series of plans, modified by discussion and negotiation, and reflecting the experience gained during the operation of the war-time health services.

The structure of the health service which emerged was a compromise. To say this is no criticism, since reorganizing hospital, family doctor, preventive and environmental health services, all with varying traditions over different periods of time and with sectional interests, within the limits of the available resources of manpower and money of post-war Britain, necessarily involved compromise. Even if better arrangements could have been made, which is by no means certain, the structure which was agreed proved sufficiently satisfactory to last substantially unchanged for a quarter of a century, during which it facilitated considerable development in medical techniques and services.

It is not the place here to give a detailed account of the National Health Service structure created in 1948. It is, however, appropriate to examine the areas of stress in the health service which became apparent as the years went by, together with the changing pattern of health need, and which culminated in the reorganization of the health services in 1974.

PROBLEMS AND CHANGES AFTER 1948

The National Health Service began life in 1948. Some of the early doubts faded as the Health Service became established, but the objections to the tripartite nature of the administration continued and gathered weight. The voluntary hospitals and general practitioners had been adamant that they would not accept local authority administration. On the other hand, hospital doctors, who had experience of the Emergency Medical Service, were not averse to a salaried service. The local authorities, for their part, had lost control of their hospitals to the Emergency Medical Service and had no hope of regaining them, so they were particularly defensive of their other health functions – maternal and child welfare, environmental and preventive health.

As a result, a tripartite system was instituted, of hospital boards, general practitioner executive councils, and local authority health departments. These divisions, dictated by factors other than the rational organization of health care, were criticized at the time of their creation and were seen increasingly over the years to limit the coordination of the three branches of health services. In the field of maternal health, for example, a pregnant woman could attend her general practitioner, a local authority maternity clinic, and a hospital maternity unit. Each service could act in ignorance of the interventions of the other two. As a move to overcome this potentially dangerous fragmentation, the professional who first confirmed pregnancy in a woman was, after 1962, required to issue her with a 'cooperation card' which was supposed to be taken to every ante-natal appointment to be completed by the general practitioner, midwife, hospital doctor, etc., with details of any action taken. Because of lack of uniformity in the use of these cards (Topliss, 1970), they did little to overcome the divisions in the organization of services.

Apart from the above specific example of lack of coordination between the three branches of the health service, there was increasing concern about the division between primary and specialist services. The gulf between the specialist hospital doctor and the generalist family doctor in the community had been growing in the inter-war years, but at least in that period the general practitioners had retained access to and virtual control over the 800 or so cottage hospitals in which, in the one year of 1938–9, general practitioners carried out 2½ million surgical operations. Furthermore, the income and conditions of general practitioners had then compared favourably with most hospital doctors other than the consultants, who were few in number.

In 1948, however, the cottage hospitals came under the control of the regional hospital boards, and although the general practitioner still had access to some of the smaller cottage hospitals in rural areas, his opportunities for hospital work were greatly curtailed. Moreover, the junior hospital staff gained far more in pay and conditions from the introduction of the National Health Service than did the general practitioner, and opportunities for promotion to senior and consultant grades increased rapidly with the expansion of hospital specialisms. In addition, popular respect for specialist skills and esoteric technologies in medicine meant that the general practitioner, with his humble surgery boasting little more than a couch and a stethoscope, and a bag of prescription pads to carry from house to house on his calls, lost status heavily in comparison with his hospital colleagues. Increasingly the view prevailed that hospital medicine was the peak of professional achievement and that only those doctors unable to make the grade in a specialism would become general practitioners. This was expressed very clearly by Lord Moran, a former President of the Royal College of Physicians and subsequently Chairman of the National Advisory Committee on Distinction Awards for Consultants, who said, in defending the differentials of pay between consultants and general practitioners: 'How can you say that people who get to the top of the ladder are the same as the people who fall off it?' (Pilkington, 1960a).

Despite the blows to the status of the family doctor, however, the National Health Service Act 1946 had given a key role to the general practitioner. He was to be the point of contact for the sick individual, and in the vast majority of sickness episodes he would give all the treatment and medical advice necessary. In the minority of cases, where the general practitioner decided that further intensive investigation or specialist treatment was necessary, he was to direct the patient through the proper medical channels. Except in cases of extreme emergency, no direct access to a consultant was envisaged under the National Health Service: patients were to be referred by their general practitioner. In addition, the general practitioner was expected to be aware of and able to contact other forms of community help as appropriate for his patient, such as the district nurse or the school health service, which were run by the local authority.

The part to be played by the general practitioner achieved even greater prominence as the years went by, owing to the changing pattern of health care need, but his status did not increase commensurately. In 1946 the architects of the National Health Service still thought in terms of the patterns of ill-health of the past – the acute illnesses with a kill-or-cure outcome. They concentrated on providing a framework of services that would treat minor illness immediately, thus avoiding serious complications or, if necessary, pilot the patient expeditiously through to the specialist curative facilities of hospitals. But the triumph over infectious diseases won by higher standards of living and better hygiene, followed by the development of antibiotics and the sulphonamide drugs, meant that the whole pattern of need for health care was changing, and further developments in medicine only intensified the trend. Increasingly the general practitioner was being called upon to deal with a growing volume of chronic and degenerative illness and permanent disability among his patients. This added up to a heavy increase of demand for community-based, rather than hospital-based, health care and yet the proportion of doctors in general practice fell over the years (Hicks, 1976; D.H.S.S., 1976a).

The image of the over-worked, under-valued general practitioner was a disincentive to newly qualified doctors to enter the community field, thus intensifying the problem. The founding of the College of General Practitioners in 1952 (which was not made a Royal College until several years later) did not remove the discontents. By the late 1950s, dissatisfaction among general practitioners had assumed considerable proportions. It focussed on issues of pay and hours, and led to the appointment of a Royal Commission, under the chairmanship of Sir Harry (later Lord) Pilkington, to review doctors' and dentists' remuneration. The Royal Commission's report (Pilkington, 1960b) made recommendations for a marked improvement in the level of remuneration of general practitioners, and for the encouragement of the growth of group practices. These measures were aimed at improving the status of the general practitioner, stimulating recruitment, and improving the primary health care service available to the public. Apart from the direct incentive of higher remuneration, the encouragement of groups of general practitioners rather than the traditional single-handed doctor was an attempt to improve the status and conditions of general practice more indirectly. A large group practice, whether in premises controlled by the member doctors themselves, or in local authority-provided health centres, offered the opportunity to employ clerical and administrative staff, and a practice nurse on an expense pooling basis. This range of supporting staff, wider than a single-handed practice could afford, would free the doctors to concentrate on those tasks which really needed medical skills.

Moreover, by working in cooperation with each other, there would be greater professional stimulation and opportunities for each doctor to develop his special area of interest. The existence of a group was also expected to facilitate regular off-duty, holidays and study leave, since other doctors would be available to cover for the absence of each one in turn.

It was hoped that the combination of better pay, more regular hours, a wider range of supporting staff, and opportunities for refresher study and the development of specialist interests, would greatly increase the satisfactions of general practice, thus attracting into it enthusiastic, able and committed young doctors, leading to an overall improvement in the status of general practitioners.

The measures which followed the Pilkington recommendations undoubtedly increased the earnings of general practitioners, and stimulated the development of some larger group practices and health centres. By 1973, however, a fifth of general practitioners were still operating single-handed practices, and a further quarter were in partnership with only one other doctor. A mere tenth of all general practitioners were operating in groups of five or six doctors – regarded as the optimum size of group in a report by a sub-committee of the government's Standing Medical Advisory Committee (Harvard-Davis, 1971). It is doubtful whether, after all, the image of general practice was much improved by the changes, and certainly little had been done to bridge the gap in the health service between primary and specialist services. They still operated in virtual isolation from each other. For example, hospitals could increase their bed occupancy rate by reducing the length of stay for certain cases, thus transferring the burden of convalescent care to the community, without any joint planning or consultation.

Even within the hospital service, the National Health Service Act 1946 had left divisions. Not all hospitals were under unified administration, as the teaching hospitals (twenty-six of them in London) retained their individual and separate identities under Boards of Governors, and were outside the Regional Boards which controlled all the other hospitals. This division was undoubtedly dictated by the determination of the teaching hospitals to preserve the standards of excellence and progress for which they were famed and which their previous privileged and independent position had fostered. On the other hand the separation of the teaching hospitals from the main body of the hospital service may have impeded the dissemination of the new ideas and techniques in health care which were developed by research and advanced study in medical schools. Conversely the development of medical education was probably also impeded by the division. The report of the Goodenough Committee, issued before the inauguration of the National Health Service (Goodenough, 1944) had envisaged universities (each hospital region in the National Health Service was centred on a university medical school) becoming centres of medical education and development for the whole region. Under the separate system of administration, however, the university medical schools were directly linked only with the specially designated teaching hospitals, and this may have discouraged the development of regional medical training programmes – certainly there were few really new developments in medical education for some years after 1948.

Another problem which persisted after the inception of the National Health Service was that of the disparities in provision between Regions. The Royal Commission on Doctors' and Dentists' Remuneration had noted, when considering the way in which special merit payments were distributed among hospital doctors, that it would be desirable for conscious efforts to be made to use the merit award system in order to spread consultant services (and high earnings) more evenly throughout the country (Pilkington, 1960b). A little later, a working party, set up by the Royal Colleges and other professional organizations, under the chairmanship of Sir Arthur Porritt, to review the medical services of Great Britain, reported that there were wide variations in the standards of service given (Porritt, 1962).

The Labour government again referred to disparities in health care provision in the Green Paper on the National Health Service issued in 1970, saying: 'In the twenty-one years since the National Health Service was created, there has been some (though not sufficient) levelling up of those areas which were medically impoverished before 1948' (D.H.S.S., 1970, para. 1 (ii)).

The need to effect a redistribution of health care resources was one of the aims of both the Labour and Conservative proposals for reorganizing the health services. Indeed, there was considerable consensus in all quarters as to the problems of the National Health Service after some twenty years of operation, and a good measure of agreement, but by no means complete, on the general principles of any reorganized service.

THE REORGANIZATION DEBATE

The first official indication that a reorganization of the health services was being contemplated came in 1968 when the Minister of Health in the Labour government, Kenneth Robinson, produced a Green Paper for discussion, outlining the problems of the National Health Service and suggesting possibilities for a new structure (D.H.S.S., 1968). The Green Paper stressed the need for unification of the three branches of health care, and for greater centralization of control necessary because of the large resources in money and skilled manpower which the health services absorbed.

In order to achieve the required efficiency and integration, the document suggested that all health services in a given area should be administered by area health boards of some fifteen persons. The health boards could, the document tentatively suggested, be a committee of the new, larger local authorities then in process of creation. Alternatively, the area health boards could remain outside the local government structure and be responsible directly to the Minister.

Considerable discussion was generated by this first document on reorganization. The idea of putting all health services under local government administration was soon abandoned. The sharp reduction in lay participation that would result from the new structure also came in for considerable criticism. In the second Green Paper, produced by the Labour government in 1970, the possibility of local government administration of health services was formally rejected because the cost of health care was far too high to be met by the system of local authority funding, and anyway the health professions were resolutely opposed to such an arrangement. The second Green Paper also included suggestions for increasing the lay element in administration by the creation of district health committees responsible for all health services in a locality, on which half the members would be appointed from people living or working in the district, and the other half by the area health board. This latter body would in turn have one-third of its fifteen members nominated by the relevant local authority. In addition to the district committees, and area health boards, a third tier was mentioned, the Regional Health Councils, but the functions of these bodies were left rather vague, except that they would not supervise or control the area health boards.

When the Conservative government came to power in 1971, Sir Keith Joseph was made Secretary of State at the Department of Health and Social Security. He briskly produced a further consultative document in which he firmly declared an intention to limit the period of discussion, which he considered had been too protracted already, and to introduce legislation for reorganization on the basis of three principles (D.H.S.S., 1971). Firstly, there should be a unified service; secondly, the primary responsibility for planning and resource allocation should be at Regional level; and thirdly, the Area Health Authorities should have boundaries coterminous with the newly created local authorities. Sir Keith Joseph made it plain that his government's proposals differed from those of the Labour government chiefly by placing greater emphasis on effective management. In the interests of efficiency, the Conservative proposals not only strengthened the role of the Regional tier as part of a line of control from the Department, through Regions to Area Health Authorities, but they also rejected the idea of district committees. On the other hand, mindful of the storm of protest which had met the first proposals in 1968 to reduce lay participation in the administration of the health services, Sir Keith Joseph proposed an alternative to district committees in the form of community health councils, which would represent local opinion but would not be part of the management structure. He even argued that the views of the public would be voiced more directly and effectively through these councils than they could be by greater lay membership of health authorities (D.H.S.S., 1972a).

In rejecting attempts to introduce democratic control of the health service by means of an increased representational element in the members of health authorities, Sir Keith Joseph was being consistent with his avowed intention to create maximum devolution downward matched by maximum accountability upward. Each level in the health service was to be answerable to the next level up, and this accountability could not, in his view, be diluted by the dual accountability of members to some outside body which had elected them to the health authority. He therefore insisted that members of health authorities should be chosen for their personal qualities of ability, drive and judgment, and not as representatives of groups or interests in the general public.

Despite Sir Keith Joseph's arguments in favour of the structure which he created, fears persisted that democracy had been subordinated to, or even eliminated by, the interests of administrative efficiency. Such fears were reinforced by the fact that a working party, including a team of management consultants, which was set up to work out the details of the operational mechanisms of the new health service structure, ignored the role of the community health councils altogether (D.H.S.S., 1972b); yet these councils were the main channel by which public opinion was supposed to influence the working of the health services.

The legislation for reorganization on the lines Sir Keith Joseph had outlined, was introduced and passed by Parliament with only minor amendments. The lack of alteration did not, however, mean that the arrangements were universally acceptable.

THE REORGANIZED STRUCTURE OF THE NATIONAL HEALTH SERVICE

Before the National Health Service Reorganization Act 1973 could come into effect in 1974, there had been a change of government, and Barbara Castle, the new Secretary of State at the Department of Health and Social Security, promptly issued some proposals for changes, aimed chiefly at increasing what she saw as the inadequate democratic element in the new structure (D.H.S.S., 1974).

It was too late to effect any radical changes in the organization Sir Keith Joseph had moulded, but in any case, as the long discussion period prior to legislation had made obvious, both sides of the House of Commons were agreed on many of the major issues. Both sides wanted a unified health service, efficiently managed by a more centralized administrative structure, which, while independent of local government, would parallel the boundaries of the new local authorities at Area level. Both sides had also agreed on which of the functions previously discharged by local authorities as part of their health duties should be transferred to the new Area Health Authorities, and which should remain as part of the personal social services administered by the social services departments of the local authorities. The criterion for division of these duties was to be that, where the principal skill of the primary providers of the service was medical or nursing, responsibility would pass to the health authorities. Where, however, the principal skill was that of personal or domestic help, or social work, the service would remain with the local authority. Concern over this division of responsibility between the health and personal social services has grown over the years since 1974, but it was not a matter of dispute in the Labour and Conservative proposals for reorganization.

The main area of difference lay in the way in which the democratic influence on health policies, which both agreed was a necessary influence, was to be assured. The changes which Barbara Castle envisaged in this respect were not such as to need major revision of the structure created by the National Health Service Reorganization Act 1973. Under this Act, the geographical boundaries of the old Regional Hospital Boards were retained as the boundaries of the new Regional Health Authorities. These bodies plan, in conjunction with the Department of Health and Social Security, the overall strategies and priorities for health care for the whole Region, providing guidelines for the lower tier, the Area Health Authorities. They also directly control some services for the whole Region, such as the Blood Transfusion Service.

The Areas, of which there are 90, have, on average, populations of about half a million. They have responsibility for the whole range of health services within the Area, and for coordinating health services with the services (such as the personal social services) of the relevant local authority. To facilitate this coordination, the new Area Health Authorities have, as far as practicable, geographical boundaries coterminous with the new local authority boundaries created in the 1974 reorganization of local government.

The Area Health Authorities, with a few exceptions, are further subdivided into Districts, considered to be the smallest size unit for which the full range of general health services can be provided. A typical district would have a population of about 250,000 with a district general hospital and district community medical services. The services of the district are run on behalf of the Area Health Authority by the district management team, comprised of officers of the National Health Service, and without lay membership.

This brief outline of the reorganized structure is given in order that the ensuing discussion of points of continuing controversy may be comprehensible. For a more detailed description of the reorganized service, readers are referred to the Office of Health Economics Pamphlet no. 48, *The N.H.S. Reorganization.*

THE CONTINUING CONTROVERSY

The immediate bone of contention when the new system of organization was introduced in 1974 was over the degree to which democratic participation could be increased without impairing efficiency. Barbara Castle's proposals concentrated on strengthening the role of community health councils, and increasing the representational element on Area Health Authorities, because, she argued, a clear-cut distinction between efficient management and representation of consumer interests was impossible to sustain.

The community health councils, bearing as they did the main burden of democratic participation in the reorganized health services, excited a good deal of interest apart from Barbara Castle's encouragement. Their role had not been clearly worked out in the Act of 1973, and exactly how they were to represent public opinion and needs, and the ways in which they might influence health service policy, were left very open. A D.H.S.S. circular, (H.R.C. (74) 4) sent out in 1974, listed a whole range of possible interests and activities for community health councils, but the uncertainty about their role meant that the councils got off to a very slow start (Klein and Lewis, 1976).

As these councils have no management function, it seems reasonable to argue that the extent to which they can influence health services policies will depend on whether their views, presented in their annual report to the Area Health Authority, or publicly reported, command attention. This in turn makes the membership of the councils of crucial importance; members must be willing and able to devote a considerable amount of time and energy to developing an expert understanding of the National Health Service in general and the local services in particular, before they can hope to present views and recommendations with the force and precision that will ensure serious consideration by Area Health Authorities. It is too soon, in view of the very slow start of community health council activity, for there to be any conclusive evidence that these councils will play a significant role in enabling the consumer to have a voice in policy determination. What evidence there is does not encourage optimism (Topliss, 1975; Klein and Lewis, 1976; R.C.N., 1977).

Another strand in the continuing controversy over the reorganized service has been the argument that, in creating such a strongly centralized structure, too much power has passed to the Secretary of State. Politics have thus been brought into the arena of health care, an intrusion condemned by many as inappropriate and contrary to the best interests of the patient.

The counter-argument is that the new structure rightly *intended* to bring politics into the determination of National Health Service priorities and policies. There had been strong pressure from both sides of the House of Commons for a unified health service structure which would be more responsive to the social issues in health needs. In a democratic country such as Britain, the elected government is commonly regarded as the institution most responsive to, and best able to interpret, social concerns, and this therefore indicated governmental involvement in the ordering of health care priorities and the administration of services.

The growing conviction that government has a duty not only to ensure that health care services are available, but also to play a part in determining the type of health care to be made available, reflected an increasing understanding that the need for health care was by no means unchangeable, or even clearly definable. In the past hundred years, for example, the death rate from tuberculosis, enteric fever and the childhood infections of scarlet fever and diphtheria has been reduced by 99 per cent or more. An effective vaccine against whooping cough and another against poliomyelitis have also been developed and widely used to protect children and young people. One history of medicine claims that before long the scientist will be able to provide a vaccine to protect man from most of the common virus diseases (Poynter and Keele, 1961). Even if this claim is somewhat optimistic, Britain already lives with the far-reaching consequences of previous medical innovations. As survival chances have improved for the younger age groups, so a greater proportion than in previous generations have lived to grow old. This is reflected in the fact that while, in 1901, only six per cent of the population was over retirement age (65 for a man and 60 for a woman) in the 1971 census the proportion had risen to 16 per cent. Over nine million people in Britain are elderly, and associated with increasing age are increasing frailty and ill-health. Nonetheless, the vast majority (over 90 per cent) of these millions of elderly people live in their own homes, many thousands of them entirely alone, and they call upon the community health services to meet their needs for medical care, rather than on hospital or other residential provisions.

Just as the elimination of infectious illness as a major cause of early death has brought into prominence the chronic and degenerative conditions

associated with old age, so other medical successes have had their unanticipated consequences. For example, the improved facilities for treating
victims of serious accidents has resulted in the saving of many lives which in
earlier days would have been lost. Some of these survivors however are
permanently disabled and in need, if not of continuous care as in the tragic
cases of massive brain damage, at least of more health service attention
than the average able-bodied person. Again, the highly skilled obstetric
and paediatric care which has improved maternal and child health generally, has also meant that even seriously malformed babies more often survive
than was the case in the past. The increase in the numbers of school children
and young adults handicapped with spina bifida reflects not so much an
increase in the numbers of babies born with this condition, but a development of techniques which, from the mid-1950s, permitted surgical intervention to keep such babies alive.

In other words, the successes of medicine have not led to a reduction in
the amount of sickness and ill-health, as the advocates of the National
Health Service, including Aneurin Bevan and Sir William Beveridge, had
confidently expected. Instead they have resulted in a changed pattern of
disease – eliminating much acute illness which was typically of short
duration with either complete recovery or death as the outcome – and
substituting the chronic and degenerative conditions associated with permanent disability and old age. This has shifted the main volume of health
care very decisively away from hospitals and into the community, but
without a matching massive reallocation of resources.

Moreover, medical techniques are increasingly powerful, elaborate and
expensive. Not only does this raise the question of how best to allocate
resources on health care in order to get the maximum return in patient
benefit, but it also raises with increasing urgency the issue of what is to the
patient's benefit. Is it, for example, justifiable to use the whole armoury of
medical power and knowledge to keep alive a person whose prolonged
existence will be of questionable quality? Is it justifiable to devote resources to developing more sophisticated techniques to excise an unwanted
life by termination of pregnancy? These are not questions susceptible of a
clinical answer, but rather matters which raise moral and economic issues
that must be reviewed away from the immediate pressures of delivering a
service. They call, in other words, for an organizational system which
provides for a centralized review of policies and objectives in the light of
society's changing circumstances and values.

Any attempt to review the objectives of the health services and determine how best to match available resources to need, necessarily involves a consideration of what is meant by *need* for health care. The standard of 'good health', the goal of health service provision, has proved to be relative to the prevailing conditions in society. As the hazards of premature death have receded, so public expectations have been adjusted so that health is no longer equated with merely being alive, but involves increasingly such things as absence of discomfort, capacity for active effort, sense of emotional well-being, etc. Nearly all medical treatment is elective in the sense that it is not given as the result of some emergency which involves the patient in submitting to treatment he has done nothing consciously to initiate. Much more typically an individual decides when his health is below the standard which he is willing to accept as normal, and he then solicits medical advice (see chapter 1 for a fuller discussion of the factors involved). If public expectations rise with every improvement in health – in much the same way that every step of economic progress apparently stimulates yet higher material ambitions – then potential demand for health care is unlimited and can never be wholly satisfied.

When the National Health Service was first introduced in 1948, it was believed that the removal of the need to pay for medical advice and treatment would enable all individuals to obtain the health care they needed. Implicit in this view is the assumption that any demand on the health services was a reflection of a health need – the assumption, in other words, that need and demand were essentially the same thing. That assumption has been challenged in two major respects. Firstly there has been a growing tendency to refer to irresponsible use or even abuse of the health services (Porritt, 1962, para. 35b; B.M.A., 1977), suggesting that not all demands for consultation or treatment are the result of genuine need for health care. Secondly there have been a number of studies of populations using objective measures of disease, such as hearing or sight loss, crippled joints, etc., which have shown that there is a considerable amount of need for health care (according to the measures of ill-health used) which never reaches the point of making a demand on the health services (Goldberg, 1970; Rutter *et al.,* 1970).

Taken together, these two strands of criticism make it impossible any longer to assume that demand and need may be treated as synonymous. In any case, since demand on the health services increases as health expectations rise, it is no longer politically or economically feasible to equate demand with need and attempt to increase provision to keep pace. Consequently there has been a fairly recent but growing concern to identify need as distinct from demand (Bradshaw, 1972; Manson and Taylor, 1976), and to establish some scale of needs which would serve to fix priorities for the health services and facilitate the distribution, or redistribution, of the massive resources now involved. This problem was acknowledged by the Resource Allocation Working Party, set up by the Department of Health and Social Security to consider how resources might more equitably be distributed between Regions. The Working Party, which reported in 1976, (D.H.S.S., 1976b), para. 1.1), made two initial points before outlining their proposals for the allocation of resources among health service Regions:

(1) 'the resources available to the N.H.S. are bound to fall short of requirements as measured by demand criteria . . .'

(2) 'supply of facilities has an important influence on demand in the locality in which they are provided. . . .'

Therefore the Working Party proposed a formula for resource allocation which attempted to define need independently of demand for services. In the past the two had been confused, and had meant that the Regions with the best facilities had been able to demonstrate the greatest demand (i.e. greatest use of services) and therefore the greatest need for resources, thus perpetuating Regional inequalities. The Working Party proposed that in future the measure of need should be based on the population size and structure of a Region (since the different sexes and age groups have very different health needs). Evidence of disease in a Region was to be derived from mortality statistics, rather than from the numbers of cases treated, which was rejected as a measure too closely related to facilities provided to serve as a reliable indicator of need. When the formula developed by the Working Party was applied, it showed that some health Regions, such as the four metropolitan Regions, currently had a resource allocation in excess of the amount indicated by using the formula, while nine health Regions, including the four in the north of England, all had a lower allocation than their need, measured by the formula, would indicate.

The government accepted the new system for allocating resources, but in order not to create undue difficulties for the Regions which had in the past been over-endowed, it was decided that a policy should be adopted whereby the 'deprived' Regions would receive increases in resources at a faster rate than others until they had caught up to the target figure, i.e. an exact match of resources received to needs as measured by the formula. On the other hand, the over-endowed Regions would receive allocations which allowed for no increase in provision of services, although no overall cutbacks should be needed.

There have, of course, been criticisms of the way in which the Working Party devised its formula for resource allocation, but it does represent an attempt to establish an objective standard of need for health care resources which is independent of demand. Nonetheless, a formidable amount of work needs to be done before an agreed standard of health can be established in any community against which to assess priorities for types of health care provision.

There are many who, while agreeing with the foregoing analysis of the reasons making it essential to reach a more objective determination of health priorities than at present, will still argue that the reorganized structure which came into being in 1974 will inhibit rather than promote such a development. According to this argument, the strongly centralized structure is dominated by management efficiency experts who are not well equipped to undertake a fundamental reappraisal of the aims and objectives of the health services. Furthermore, the diminished democratic element in the management structure is seen as insulating the experts from pressures to change, so that, far from creating a service which will be more adaptable to the changing health scene, reorganization may have produced streamlined inflexibility, impervious to public opinion.

The role of public participation in the management of the health services has certainly been considerably reduced numerically. Before 1974, every Hospital Management Committee had its lay members, and the local authority health services were subject to the control of a committee comprised of elected councillors. After 1974, lay influence in the management of the health services is restricted to the members of the Regional Health Authorities and the Area Authorities. In the former case the Secretary of State appoints all the members, and these in turn appoint the members of Area Health Authorities, so that the Department of Health and Social Security exercises considerable control of those members of the lay public who are selected to play a part in health service management.

This formal control over appointments, however, is exercised within certain constraints. Approximately one-third of the membership of every Health Authority is nominated by the relevant County and District local authorities, and one member is nominated by the university or universities in the Region. Further places on each Area Health Authority are reserved for a hospital consultant, a general practitioner, a nurse or a midwife, and a trade unionist. For each of these vacancies the relevant professional or trade union organizations recommend a few names from which the Regional Health Authority chooses. Two further places have, since 1977, been reserved for persons elected by National Health Service employees. Only the remaining places, usually some five or six, are unspecified and are filled at the discretion of the Regional Health Authority.

The plans and policies formulated by the Department at the top, and communicated downwards, are supposed to be the result of information on needs and availability of services fed upwards from the District (where there are health care planning teams to consider the needs in, for example, geriatric or mental deficiency services), via the Area and then the Region. At all these stages, however, critics claim that there is little opportunity for a really open discussion of alternative policies, and community health councils, as has already been argued, seem unlikely to play a major role in the determination of policy.

Nonetheless, there are signs that wide discussion of the issues concerning the health service is officially encouraged, for example by publishing the report of the Resource Allocation Working Party for discussion, and also by issuing, as a consultative document, the government's proposals for priorities in health care (D.H.S.S., 1976a). It is true that in the Department of Health and Social Security circular HC(76)29 of May 1976, which set planning guidelines for health Regions for 1976–7, the proposals in the consultative document on priorities, which had only just been issued, were taken as the basis of the Department's policy. It was, however, pointed out that 'the national strategy it proposes may be modified in the light of consultation'. In addition, in 1976, the government appointed a Royal Commission under the chairmanship of Sir Alec Merrison, to review the National Health Service. The Commission early declared an intention to enquire into hospital and community health services, private practice, the relationship between the health services and the personal social services, environmental and occupational health services, and the management structure and financial matters in the National Health Service. This represents a very broad interpretation of the Commission's terms of reference: 'To consider in the interests both of the patients and of those who work in the National Health Service the best use and management of the financial and manpower resources of the National Health Service' (Royal Commission, 1976, p.1).

In fact the occupational health services, the environmental health services, and the personal social services are not part of the National Health Service. The Commission's announcement that their review will nonetheless take in these areas, suggests a determination not to limit their concern merely to commenting on the operation of the health services as determined by their current form and structure.

In general, there is certainly no evidence that public debate of health issues has been inhibited by the management-orientated structure of the new health service administration. On the contrary, the media have devoted considerable space and viewing time to National Health Service matters. It is, of course, arguable that such public debate may serve only as a safety valve for people's concern, but may have little or no effect on health service policies.

This, however, is fundamentally a criticism of the operation of democracy in general, rather than of the organizational structure of the health services in particular. It is, in effect, an argument that the Secretary of State at the Department of Health and Social Security – a member of a government elected by majority vote – is unresponsive to public opinion to the extent that policy guidelines issued by his Department will take no account of the wishes of the people.

In fact, in the history of health care provision, there is ample evidence that government policy has taken account of the views made known (Willcocks, 1967). On the whole, however, these have been the views expressed by organized groups, notably the medical professional bodies. In the present situation of a reappraisal of the aims of the health service, it may again be that the views which reach the government most clearly, cogently and forcibly, will be the views of the medical profession, rather than the views of the consumers of health care. Both groups have a vital concern in the matter of priorities, but for the professionals it is a concern of life-long duration, informed by long experience and expressed with the collective weight of their professional organizations. For the consumers, concern with health care is intermittent and based for most of us on fortunately limited episodes of ill-health, and there is no powerful organization to coordinate the diverse individual experiences and comments into a cogent argument for policy which must be heard. This situation, however, is not new, and has not been exacerbated by the reorganization of the health service. It could indeed be said that while the reorganized structure does nothing either to promote or inhibit wide public discussion of the fundamental aims of the health services, it does at least give a rather better assurance than the previous organization of the National Health Service that such policies as are agreed will be efficiently implemented.

FUTURE TRENDS

What has surely been made unambiguously clear in all the welter of discussion about the health services, is the fact that good health standards are not simply an individual or family matter, but are a concern for the whole society. In other words, health care is ever more clearly seen not only as a response to individual need, but also as a part of the total social pattern. Changes in the order of priorities for care are frankly argued in terms of costs and benefits to the community as well as on grounds of individual need – indeed, the latter criterion for care is increasingly ambiguous, being inextricably confused with demand, which is itself now seen to be heavily dependent on supply of services.

This, of course, is echoing the theme of the beginning of this chapter, when it was argued that the development of collective provisions for health had from the beginning been seen as contributing to national as well as individual well-being. To some extent the link with the national interest had been more clearly visible in the nineteenth century, when the major health measures were those of environmental control and improved living standards to eliminate early death from infectious disease. The development of medical technology in this century, which has enormously increased the range of therapeutic measures available in the health care of individuals, tended to obscure the close connection between health and national interests. This link, never broken although ignored, has now once again been openly acknowledged.

It is, perhaps, significant that in the period after 1948, when health care was thought of chiefly in terms of meeting individual needs, there was a widespread tendency for British people to think of a health service as unique to Britain, reflecting a peculiarly British ideological commitment to equalizing health opportunities irrespective of income. This was a totally erroneous view, since the governments of all other advanced industrial countries, including the United States, have been deeply involved in making provisions for health care. All societies characterized by complex technologies, a high degree of division of labour and interdependent productive processes, and with concentrated urban populations, have followed the same path of control of infectious diseases, increased expectation of life giving rise to a reduced birth rate and an increased proportion of elderly in the population, and changing patterns of disease. The actual mechanisms for administering health care services vary from country to country (Maynard, 1975; Hyde, 1974), but state intervention in one form or another, and to an ever increasing extent, is common despite considerable variation in the political outlooks of the countries concerned. The convergence in the matter of health care provision is more striking than the dissimilarities, and can be explained in terms of the common health problems facing industrial nations. These problems have promoted changes in the organization of health services in all the countries concerned, and the path for the future is a matter for debate in all.

As far as Britain is concerned, the current situation suggests that questions about future policy involve not only deciding priority groups to receive health care, but also a major review of the role of health care professionals. Nowadays nearly three-quarters of all deaths occur among people over 65 and diseases that strike heavily with advancing age – heart disease, cancer and strokes (in that order) – together account for two-thirds of all deaths in England and Wales. Of the 25 per cent of deaths occurring to people under the age of 65, the vast majority are of people aged between 45 and 64. In this age group male deaths preponderate, and by far the most important single cause of death among the men is ischaemic heart disease, followed by cancer (especially lung cancer). Among the females aged 45–64 cancer is the main cause of death, with breast cancer chief among all cancers, followed by heart disease, but the death rate from all causes among females is much lower than that of men of the same age group. Only about four per cent of deaths, amounting to some 30,000 deaths a year, occur to people under 45 (excluding deaths in the first year of life which are mainly due to congenital abnormalities and other perinatal causes). In this age group, accidents are a major cause of death.

The implications for the health services of this pattern of mortality are significant. There is little scope for reducing overall mortality among the elderly, whatever medical resources might be devoted to such an aim. In any case such efforts are only doubtfully justified, having regard to the quality of the life likely to be thus extended. In other words, for the elderly population, the future emphasis must be on care and optimum management of residual capacities, rather than on cure.

As far as mortality among younger people is concerned, it has been estimated that if deaths from heart disease could be eliminated among those under 65, it would do more to avoid loss of productive years than would the elimination of any other single cause of death. There is, however, considerable evidence that the prevention of ischaemic heart disease is largely in the hands of the individual himself, since it is associated with life-style, such as cigarette smoking (as is lung cancer, another significant cause of death among men aged 45–64). Similarly, the elimination of accidental death and injury would make a major contribution to improved survival and health among the younger age groups. Many road accidents are due to recklessness often associated with drinking. The fact that the accident rate fell after the introduction of the breathalyser test without any noticeable reduction in road traffic, shows that prevention of accidents is largely in the hands of the individual drivers.

Major gains in survival for those under 65, therefore, are heavily dependent not on specialist medical services, but on a change of life-style among younger men and women of today so that they do not in their turn fall victim to accidental death, coronary attacks or lung cancer. Medical research and expertise has a much bigger part to play in the prevention or cure of cancer (other than lung cancer where the chief causal agent and the appropriate preventive measures are known), which is an important cause of the deaths occurring to those under 65. In the first year of life, also, survival rates may be considerably improved by the reduction of congenital abnormalities. Screening tests of pregnant women have been developed which can identify the foetus likely to result in a spina bifida or Down's Syndrome baby, and the expectant mother is then able to choose whether to go ahead with her pregnancy or accept termination. Although such screening is not routine for all pregnant women, it is offered to those known to be at risk of having a defective child. This procedure should result in fewer births of babies suffering from these conditions – both of them major causes of congenital abnormality – and therefore to a reduction in the number of infant deaths due to congenital abnormalities.

In general, however, the health services are in the paradoxical situation of having greater expertise and better equipment than ever before, but being able to do less than ever before to increase survival rates. This could be taken as an indication that the emphasis of the health services has turned full circle and is now, as in the nineteenth century but for different reasons, on care rather than cure. It is certainly true that in the excitement of impressive medical developments earlier this century, which greatly enhanced the capacity to cure, the health services developed a lop-sided emphasis on treatment of acute cases, leading to a neglect of provision for care of chronic or degenerative conditions.

The predominance of the current need for care rather than cure, however, is argued almost entirely on the basis of mortality figures – and death is a poor criterion of health and health needs! There are a number of conditions which, while they do not threaten life, can greatly limit or even extinguish enjoyment of life. Such conditions as hernia or varicose veins need cure rather than care, and modern medicine can offer cure, but usually only at the end of a long waiting list which may get even longer. Unfortunately, we still do not have a workable definition of good health, such that departure from an agreed standard would represent a 'need' for treatment. If we did, we could decide our priorities for health care in terms of promoting or restoring good health, and then the cure of conditions such as hernia and varicose veins might figure as vitally important aspects of the health services. Without such an agreed definition of good health, however, we have little option but to rely on *absence* of health, as measured by death, to indicate health needs. And, as has been shown, few of the major causes of death among people below retirement age are susceptible to medical cure, so the inevitable conclusion is reached that, on this basis of priorities, the health services will need to develop an overwhelming emphasis on care rather than cure.

It may be an inevitable stage in the development of health services that care rather than cure, with all that this entails in the role and training of health care professionals (Todd, 1968; Briggs, 1972; D.H.S.S., 1976a), should be the dominant theme in the 1970s and 80s. We may still hope that cure will return to prominence; not so much life-saving cure which, unless there is an unanticipated breakthrough, has probably had its heyday, but cure of the physical and mental conditions which leave life itself un-threatened, while severely diminishing all the enjoyment and enthusiasm which makes it worthwhile. When this happens, the National Health Service will indeed become a service for promoting health. Until then, health service policies will be geared to minimizing the consequences of ill-health.

CHAPTER 3

Primary Health Care

To understand the concept of primary health care one may imagine the structure of the medical care system as composed of a number of different levels (Fry and Farndale, 1972). The first level of medical care is self-care. People deal with the majority of their symptoms on their own, or with the support of family, friends and medication bought over the counter. However, once the individual or family decides that medical attention is needed, some trained person has to act as 'the doctor of first contact', 'the primary physician'. The features of health care at this primary level are: that it is the point of entry for individuals to the health care services, involving functions of assessment and of mobilization and coordination of further medical services; and that it provides personal, continuing and long-term care for individuals and families in a local community. Distinguished from the level of primary health care are the levels of general specialist care (for example, surgery and internal medicine), providing services which fewer people in a population will need to use; and super-specialist care (for example, neurosurgery), serving very large population units since the clinical problems are relatively rare.

In Britain a general medical practitioner has traditionally been the provider of primary health care, but this is by no means a universal pattern. The 'primary' medical worker is not always a doctor (as in parts of the Soviet Union, Sweden and Canada) and, where he is medically qualified, he is not always a 'generalist'. In the United States, for example, the vast majority of clinical practice is specialized, while in many Eastern European countries primary health care is provided through district specialist polyclinics. In these countries patients have direct access to specialists without apparent need for the referral system characteristic of health care in

Britain, where one of the underlying considerations in the continuance of the general practitioner has been the need for a single point of entry for the individual patient, in order to guide him to the appropriate specialist services and coordinate the totality of his medical care.

As has been outlined in chapter 2, the general practitioner service was a prominent feature of the health services in Britain before the creation of the National Health Service, when its importance as the pivot of the delivery of the personal health services was clearly established with the principle of providing a personal service for families and individuals. Unfortunately, it has not been until very recently, in the 1970s, that general practice has been given the priority and support to begin to make its position of importance something of a reality. Nevertheless, throughout the life of the National Health Service there have been numerous official reports which have concerned themselves with the general practitioner services, all usually concluding that the development of such services in a comprehensive and organized manner was vital to the effectiveness of the N.H.S. In addition, there has been a consensus that in the future primary health care should be provided through health centres, staffed by multi-disciplinary teams of workers in addition to general practitioners, and that the single-handed general practitioner working from a room in his house or a small lock-up shop was an obsolete and ineffective form of organization. Indeed, as early as 1920 the Dawson Committee recommended a comprehensive network of health centres as the basis of an effective health service (Ministry of Health, 1920).

In considering the importance of the position of primary health care within the National Health Service it is pertinent to mention that 98 per cent of the population is registered with a general practitioner, while 90 per cent of all illness episodes are dealt with by general practitioners without requiring the specialist hospital services (Central Health Services Council, 1963). Over the last decade general practice has been changing in important ways, not only by becoming better organized and equipped, in custom-built premises, but also by moving towards sophisticated forms of team-work. The quality of primary health care now depends on the skills of a number of professionals, such as nurses, administrators, health visitors and social workers, as well as on those of the physician.

This chapter will discuss the reasons why there is a need for a strong and effective system of primary health care and consider some problems which have hindered development. The functions of members of the primary health care team will be considered, with the problems and opportunities created by forming a team of different professionals committed to working together.

THE NEED FOR A COMPREHENSIVE COMMUNITY-BASED HEALTH SERVICE

'The whole man'

It has long been recognized that the individual in society must be seen in the context of his environment and the influences this brings to bear on him. This was clearly accepted in the realm of health during the nineteenth century, when the sanitary reforms began to have an impact on the epidemics of contagious diseases. However, a further refinement is the acceptance that the environment also includes the past and present family and social relationships of the individual, and not only the physical conditions of his occupation but the psychological stresses and strains that may accompany it. In addition, man must be seen not merely as a biological machine, but also as having a mind which influences the body. It is the interplay of these three factors of body, mind and environment which is responsible for the manifestations of disease. René Dubos (1968) summarizes this concept succinctly: 'Whatever the complaints of the patient and the signs or symptoms he manifests, whatever the medical problems of the community, diseases cannot be understood or successfully controlled, without considering man in his total environment.'

Such a concept suggests that the health needs of individuals are complex and demand the skills of a range of professionals, both medical and non-medical. Furthermore, the individual must be seen in the context of his family, job and the local community. This is a different concept of health and disease from that of a purely technical medicine which, in the extreme, views the individual as a machine, parts of which break down at times and need repair or replacement. Indeed, the health needs of an individual may be viewed in terms of his having to face and overcome various challenges in the environment. These challenges may be physical, psychological and social, and in overcoming them the individual may need sustained supportive help, which may of course involve medical technology. It is argued that a locally based, continuously attentive primary health care service is able to provide for health needs considered in this way.

The concept of 'the whole man' suggests that the social and psychological components of physical and mental illness and handicap are vital and sometimes more important than the biological components. Individuals often present psycho-social problems disguised as physical illness to general practitioners, as well as overt social problems which have no medical content. Indeed, the Report of the Committee on the Local Authority and Allied Personal Social Services recognized that general practice was in touch with a higher proportion of those in social difficulties than any other social service (Seebohm, 1968).

Perhaps the survey completed by Jefferys in Buckinghamshire remains the most useful in demonstrating the psycho-social content of a general practitioner's work. A random sample of 70 general practitioners was asked to give systematic information about every patient seen on a certain day. Replies from 50 of them, concerning 1,367 patients, revealed that just over one-third were believed by the doctors to have or cause some social or psychological difficulty. Four main social problem areas were isolated, constituting 71 per cent of the total social problems identified: those associated with mental illness and handicap; those associated with the care of the elderly; those associated with the chronically ill or physically handicapped; and those associated with marital and sexual relationships (Jefferys, 1965).

The changing pattern of disease

It was shown in the last chapter that a number of influences have resulted in a change in the pattern of disease, particularly in this century. The general rise in the standard of living which began at the end of the eighteenth century, and the environmental health measures of the nineteenth century have been followed by immunization programmes and the advances of modern medicine. At the beginning of this century the major health hazards were infectious diseases, which accounted for the majority of deaths and to which children were particularly vulnerable. Now some of these diseases are almost unknown. The dramatic decline in infectious diseases, however, has not resulted in a healthier nation, requiring less in terms of health services. Instead they have been replaced by a different set of major health hazards. Besides accidental injury (particularly road accidents), the major health hazards are now those experienced by the unborn foetus and the degenerative diseases of middle and old age. Medicine has been less successful in preventing or treating congenital and degenerative diseases of middle and old age. Medicine has been less successful in preventing or treating congenital and degenerative diseases and this, together with the reduction of the fatal effects of infectious disease, has increased the chances of survival, often with handicap, and the consequent need for long-term provision of health services. The emphasis has shifted from the needs of the acutely ill to those of the chronically sick and disabled.

These changes have clear consequences for the pattern of care provided. The emphasis has changed from 'cure' to 'care', which may involve slowing down the degenerative processes, minimizing their effects and sustaining individuals and their families, possibly over years. An effective primary health care system is best placed to mobilize and coordinate medical services for individuals and families over these long periods.

Demographic changes

In addition to the demographic changes described in the previous chapter there was during the earlier decades of this century a substantial surplus of single women who filled a particular role in caring for children, the sick and the elderly. There is no longer such a surplus. Changes in the pattern of family life have also been significant, particularly the increase in the number of women in paid employment. During the first decade of this century about 10 per cent of married women were in paid employment, whereas the figure is now nearer 40 per cent. Increased social mobility linked to redistribution of industry, rehousing policies and increased educational opportunities have all contributed to a reduction in the supportive network of extended families.

Within the changes one can see both an increase in the proportion of those who are likely to be dependent on others, together with a diminution of the possibility of this caring being done within the family network. Different ways, therefore, have to be found of supporting dependent people in need within the community.

Preventive medicine

It is widely accepted that the earlier a disease is detected the greater is the chance of cure, both for physical and mental illness. The belief has grown that the N.H.S. has spent vast sums on elaborate and expensive technology, often to provide patching-up, because preventive measures have been relatively neglected.

Much concern has been expressed about the amount of preventable ill-health which is not seen by doctors, and many surveys have indicated a huge amount of undiagnosed illness. The British Medical Association has suggested that less than half of all cases of diabetes, epilepsy, rheumatoid arthritis and mental illness were known to general practitioners, and only one in eight cases of anaemia (B.M.A., 1970). Last (1963) put forward similar ideas in his article, 'The Iceberg', seeing great areas of unmet need and the existence of these as a clear indictment of the health service.

The primary health care system is in the best position to provide preventive services because of its accessibility to the individual and his family and its ability to provide continuing care in the local community. From this base, for example, it is possible to arrange screening programmes for populations at risk. There are a number of conditions, such as high blood pressure and diabetes, which can be detected fairly accurately through relatively simple procedures. However, although the arguments for preventive medicine are not particularly contentious, the efficacy of large-scale screening and also the possibility of it releasing large areas of demand for service which cannot be met, are arguments to be considered. An Office of Health Economics pamphlet (1975) also argues persuasively that although the 'iceberg' may exist, the subjective social and psychological factors in the definition of illness and the process of becoming ill must be taken into account. Through relying on questionable 'statistical' definitions of disease, the paper suggests, we will continue to be blinded by an irrational belief in perfect health and consequently to squander resources on ineffective and often unnecessary treatments.

Hospital care and community care

A period of hospital care is generally only an episode or series of episodes in a much longer process of medical care, which begins at the stage of initial consultation and diagnosis and continues with the rehabilitative process. The success of each of these stages is dependent on the availability and efficiency of the others. A study in 1954 produced disturbing evidence of the therapeutic achievements of hospital care being destroyed or seriously diminished by a failure to provide adequate community care and through poor housing provision. Of the patients surveyed in four general hospitals in Scotland, it was estimated that one-quarter deteriorated seriously within three months of discharge and that this deterioration was due as much to preventable factors as to the inevitable disease process (Ferguson and McPhail, 1954).

It has long been recognized that many people who become hospital in-patients do not require the full specialist facilities of the hospital, but could be adequately cared for at home, given the appropriate level of medical and social community care. In recent years the increased provision of adequate health centre facilities for general practitioners, and their improved access to the diagnostic, pathological and X-ray facilities of the hospital, have enabled a reduction in inappropriate referrals and an increase in the range of treatment available at the primary level. There has also been a development of day attendance at hospitals, particularly for the mentally ill and for geriatric patients, and innovations in day surgery for a range of complaints which formerly involved in-patient care. The latter possibility has depended heavily on the increasing recognition and use of the expertise of the community nurse.

All these trends clearly imply the need for a well-developed system of medical care based in the local community. The personal social services have shown a parallel development in that the emphasis of recent legislation and policy, for example in relation to the elderly, the mentally ill, disturbed and difficult children, has been on enabling individuals to retain their place in the community and within their own homes for as long as possible.

Despite the general agreement on the desirability of developing local medical (and other social services) outside institutions, progress has been slow in creating a secure foundation of community care. It is now, however, generally recognized that the efficient use of the acute hospital service is dependent on an effective system of continuous and continuing primary health care. The government's Consultative Document on Priorities for Health and Personal Social Services (D.H.S.S., 1976a) is an attempt to define a strategy to allocate scarce resources to those with the greatest need. This will involve giving a clear priority to the development of community care in both the health and personal social service sectors.

THE DEVELOPMENT OF PRIMARY HEALTH CARE

Three major areas of difficulty will be discussed which have hindered the development of a strong and effective primary health care system, but which, in recent years, have begun to be resolved.

The relationship between general practice and hospital medicine

The interdependence of hospital and primary health care has already been mentioned. The failure to develop an effective relationship between the two and to give sufficient priority to primary health care arose partly out of the historical development of the health services. The problems of general practitioners since 1948 have often been related to differences in status between them and hospital doctors and to consequent concern over pay differentials. The distinction between hospital doctors and general practitioners can be traced back to the seventeenth century. Physicians and surgeons were usually of high social status and well-to-do compared with apothecaries. Physicians were legally entitled to practise all branches of medicine, whereas apothecaries were not. The 1815 Apothecaries Act gave apothecaries defined status, independent from that of the Colleges of Physicians and Surgeons, and the formation of the forerunner of the British Medical Association in 1832, whose membership consisted mainly of apothecaries, was a further landmark in the development of general practice. Following the foundation of the General Medical Council in 1858 a unified pattern of medical education was introduced, but the divisions remained. Hospitals began to develop special interests (the origin of 'consultants'), and the development of nursing standards and of techniques such as antisepsis increased the importance of the hospital. The interdependence of the two systems was established by the referral of patients to hospital physicians by general practitioners, the former relying heavily on the income derived from these referred patients.

The coming of the National Health Service in 1948 took away the financial dependence of hospital doctors on general practitioners, since hospital doctors now received salaries. The divisions between hospitals, general practitioners and the public health services of local authorities were, if anything, formalized and strengthened by the 1946 National Health Service Act which set up a tripartite system of administration, unified only at the summit in the Ministry of Health. General practitioners' part-time involvement in hospital medicine was also drastically reduced, except in rural areas. The general practitioners now also often felt themselves to be the recipients of everybody's demands for twenty-four hours a day, unlike hospital consultants. The general practitioners had chosen an 'independent contractor' status, being paid by a system of fees, because they feared the position of being salaried employees would threaten their clinical freedom. Ironically, the salaried status of hospital doctors proved far from being a handicap.

Following 1948 the acute hospital services received priority in the allocation of finance and resources, and until recent years their share was growing relative to that for general medical services. In the 1930s about three-quarters of the medical profession were general practitioners, but by 1970 they constituted less than one half. More alarming was the absolute decline in the number of general practitioners between 1963 and 1968, due partly to mistakes in planning which led to a cutback in recruitment of medical students, but partly to the relative unpopularity of a career in general practice.

A clear turning point in the modernization of general practice came with the British Medical Association's 'General Practitioners' Charter' (B.M.A., 1965), whose proposals became the basis for successful negotiations with the government on pay and conditions of work. Besides introducing increased basic levels of remuneration, the Charter also became the basis for improvements in practice organization, through the introduction of special payments for group practice, and direct reimbursement of ancillary help. A body was established to make loans for the improvement or building of practice premises (Practice Finance Corporation). Additional allowances were also introduced for vocational training and postgraduate education and for seniority.

One of the principal aims of the reorganization of the health service in 1974 was to overcome the divisions between the hospitals, general practitioners and the preventive medical services (see chapter 2). With reorganization, general practitioners retained their independent contractor status so that, unlike hospital doctors, they are not salaried but are paid by basic capitation fees and a complicated system of over twenty different kinds of payment. However, closer integration of general practitioners into the system was sought in various ways. The Family Practitioner Committees, which succeeded the old Executive Councils, are responsible for administration and payment of general practitioners. They are closely linked with Area Health Authorities, who appoint up to one-third of members and provide administrative services. In addition, general practitioners combine with other doctors in the district medical committees which elect two members, one a general practitioner, to serve on District Management Teams.

Health centres

The failure to provide satisfactory premises with the necessary range of other professional skills and administrative services also held back the development of primary health care. The health centre has long been considered an essential element of good primary medical care. More than fifty years ago the Dawson Report (Ministry of Health, 1920) advocated setting up a national network of such centres, and in 1942 the B.M.A. gave further clear support to their development. Most importantly, clause 21 of the 1946 National Health Service Act made it a clear responsibility of local health authorities (now Area Health Authorities) 'to provide, equip and maintain buildings for general services, medical, dental, pharmaceutical, local authority services . . .'. Nevertheless, even since the creation of the N.H.S. the development of health centres has been remarkably slow. The spiralling of building costs has played its part, making it difficult for general practitioners to provide their own premises, while local authorities faced competing demands on their resources – for schools, new roads and other new buildings. The general practitioners themselves were also long used to providing their own private surgeries, and retained some fears of local authority control.

However, general practitioners have been encouraged to work together in group practice (as distinct from in health centres) since 1967 by financial support and incentives, and health centres have multiplied in the last decade. In the first 18 years of the N.H.S., only 33 health centres were opened. Between 1967 and 1972 there was a tenfold increase in the number of health centres. There were 365 centres by the end of 1972, housing 10 per cent of all general practitioners. By the end of 1975 this figure had increased to 17 per cent (representing 3,500 general practitioners), and there were 634 health centres in operation. It was estimated that by the end of March 1976 building work would have begun on a further 146 schemes (D.H.S.S., 1976b). The government's suggested plans for the future development of the health and personal social services (D.H.S.S., 1976a) gave a degree of financial priority to the development of primary health care higher than for any other group of services of a comparable size. Special attention was given to the building of new health centres on the basis of certain criteria, which also aimed to ensure the development of primary health care in areas where it was poorly developed and where standards of health were low. Economic developments have overtaken some specific plans, but outline strategy remains unchanged.

Professional education

There has been, until recent years, a lack of suitable medical education for primary health care at undergraduate and postgraduate levels. Traditionally doctors and nurses have been trained in hospital medicine. The only preparation required for doctors to enter general practice has been the statutory basic medical education of an undergraduate course followed by a year of supervised hospital experience before registration. The Royal College of General Practitioners was established in 1952 and has done much to enhance the professional development and education of general practitioners. A voluntary trainee scheme for general practitioners was introduced in 1948, which consisted of a year of in-service training with an approved general-practitioner principal, but the numbers were always small, and even declined in the 1960s. A number of local schemes providing training both in hospital and the community also developed. However, although many were providing a good standard of training, they attracted only small numbers. Training was not obligatory and until 1967 there was no financial inducement to participate in training schemes. The Royal Commission on Medical Education, which reported its recommendations in 1968, proved to be a landmark in the development of specific educational provision for general practitioners (Todd, 1968). It came at a time of increasing concern about the decreasing numbers of young doctors entering general practice, and the belief that an undesirable proportion of those who did enter, did so because they had failed to obtain posts in chosen hospital specialities. The Todd Report considered the whole range of medical education, and recognized that, until that time, teaching about the 'behavioural sciences' had been only sketchy. Recommendations were made for an integrated approach to the teaching of sociology and psychology to medical students. The continuing need for a general practitioner service was clearly underlined (paragraph 41), but for a service very different from that of the past: 'The kind of general practice we see in the future will be based on proper premises, good equipment, and well-trained and well-organized staff. . . . the most obvious and natural setting is the health centre. . . .' The Report envisaged a three-year general professional training, including both hospital and community experience, and recommended experience in certain fields of medicine, such as obstetrics, paediatrics and psychiatry, for intending general practitioners. It was hoped that successful completion of this training would provide eligibility for admission to the Royal College of General Practitioners. This would be followed by a further two years of supervised general practice, with opportunities for further education outside the practice. The Royal College of General Practitioners also envisaged a five-year vocational training period, although of a slightly different nature. The proportion of voluntarily vocationally trained doctors entering general practice has increased in recent years, and they now account for about one-third of new entrants. There are over 90 training schemes. However, it was only in 1977 that a Bill to make vocational training compulsory for admission to general practice came before Parliament. The National Health Service (Vocational Training) Bill gives 1980 as the year by which it is hoped to make this mandatory.

On the other hand, since the mid-1960s there has been a development of postgraduate medical centres to provide continuing postgraduate education. Over 90 per cent of general practitioners now attend recognized courses and lectures each year.

The Todd Report suggested that medical schools should provide some undergraduate experience of general practice to all medical students, whatever their eventual chosen speciality, and that there should be senior academic appointments in this field. In 1969 Edinburgh was the only medical school with an independent department of general practice, and it was the first university to create a chair in this speciality. Byrne's survey of all medical schools in 1972 demonstrated a rapid improvement in the situation. There were by then 11 departments of general practice and six chairs, and 22 medical schools were providing general practice experience for all undergraduates (Byrne, 1973).

There have also been some developments in the training of other professionals for work in primary health care, although progress has not been rapid. Training of district nurses is now provided at 47 different centres (D.H.S.S., 1976b) leading to a recognized national award both for registered and enrolled nurses. However, it is not obligatory to obtain these qualifications before practising in the community. An option in community nursing is now also available during initial training for nurses. The Briggs Committee (D.H.S.S., 1973) recognized the continuing demand for district nurses and health visitors, but also made recommendations for a higher level of skills and qualifications for already registered nurses, a Higher Certificate for 'community preventive nursing'. These recommendations have so far not been implemented. The Association of Medical Secretaries has also laid down standards for the training of secretary/receptionists, who hold a key position in the functioning of a primary health care team, and courses are increasingly being offered in various technical colleges. Health visitors and social workers have traditionally been trained for work in the community, although in social work education little attention has been devoted to primary health care.

THE PRIMARY HEALTH CARE TEAM

The Working Party on the Field of Work of the Family Doctor (Central Health Services Council) suggested in 1963 that

> ... the general practitioner's field of work has no formal limit. ... The other health and welfare services depend on him for their effectiveness and he is in a position to influence their development by his identification and interpretation of the patient's needs. Above all, he has unique opportunities to husband the health of his flock, to detect incipient disorder at the earliest point and to give advice that can reduce the risk of its occurring, postpone its onset, or lessen its impact.

It has come to be increasingly recognized that the general practitioner needs the cooperation of other professionals in carrying out these functions. In this section the development of primary health care teams will be discussed, bearing in mind the organizational obstacles to such developments already mentioned. The opportunities created by working in this way will also be considered, along with some problems that may be encountered. It is all too easy to assume that simply putting a group of professionals together in appropriately equipped premises will create a satisfactory working team.

Nurses

Long before the possibility of reimbursement of up to 70 per cent of a nurse's salary from central funds, created by the 'General Practitioners' Charter' in 1965, some general practitioners employed their own practice nurses to help in their surgeries. Local authorities provided domiciliary nursing care for defined geographical areas through district nurses. The attachment of local authority nurses to particular practices grew out of the initial employment by general practitioners of practice nurses. Attachment schemes have developed rapidly in recent years. The Health Services and

Public Health Act of 1968 enabled district nurses to work in the surgery treatment room, insofar as it made possible 'the attendance of nurses on persons who require nursing elsewhere than in their own homes'. There was a dramatic increase in the numbers of attached district nurses between 1968 and 1969, and by 1972 the figure had grown to about 80 per cent. Moreover, since 1959 the absolute numbers of district nurses steadily increased, whilst home nurses employed by health authorities, but working in collaboration with family doctors, were singled out as a priority for growth in the government's Consultative Document 'Priorities for Health and Personal Social Services in England' (D.H.S.S., 1976a). Since the 1974 reorganization of the N.H.S., home nurses have been employed by Area Health Authorities and, in theory at least, the reorganization should permit greater flexibility in their use. Some general practitioners continue to employ their own practice nurses, as in some places there are still no attached home nurses, and in others, although they may exist, they do not perform treatment room work. However, some difficulties have been experienced in the working of attachment schemes.

A study by Lisbeth Hockey (1966) revealed disturbing problems in the links between district nurses, and general practitioners and health visitors. Contact between them seemed to be minimal. The nurses frequently lacked information on patients' conditions, and treatment, and often did not know what drugs had been prescribed. Furthermore, much of the nurses' work did not require their professional skills, and doctors were generally ignorant of the help they could offer. By 1969, a government-sponsored study by Ann Abel began to reveal some positive implications of attachment schemes, both of home nurses and health visitors to general practice, which contrasted markedly with some of the findings of Hockey in 1966. Abel (1969) found that, where nurses had been attached to general practices, there was greater appreciation of respective roles, and more effective utilization of the nurses' professional skills. The patients also benefited from a more coordinated approach to their care. The recognition of the professional skills of the State Registered Nurse has enabled her to perform numerous procedures formerly only undertaken in the community by doctors, whilst the less qualified State Enrolled Nurse has been able to carry out a proportion of the tasks previously the domain of the S.R.N. Several official reports in recent years have recommended an increasing delegation of work to different levels of nursing personnel including S.R.N.s, S.E.N.s, nursing auxiliaries and bath attendants (D.H.S.S., 1970; B.M.A., 1974). The more extensive use of nursing skills may not only save the doctor time, but improve the quality of the care given, partly by allowing those with the appropriate professional skills to devote their time to better clinical medicine.

Home nurses may play a valuable role in making follow-up visits and in the long-term supervision of the chronically ill and elderly, a function previously carried out to a large extent by general practitioners. Perhaps most revolutionary have been schemes in which nurses have been the first point of contact for patients, both in the surgery and on home visits, and it is they who decide whether the patient needs to see a doctor (Weston Smith and Mottram, 1967; Kuenssberg, 1970). This is still an experimental organization of work, about which there remains some contention, not least because it goes far beyond the traditional relationship between patients and their 'family doctors'. Clearly, if such a way of working is to be effective, it must depend upon appropriate training for the nurses, and good and regular communications between them and general practitioners.

Midwives

The future place of the midwife in the primary health care team is less clear. Her traditional role has been in providing care during labour and delivery, but over 90 per cent of deliveries now take place in hospital, and it is likely that eventually almost all will do so. The average length of confinement in hospital has declined, and very early discharge home is increasingly common, the stay in hospital being sometimes as short as six hours. Because of this there is an important part to be played by midwives in providing a continuity of ante-natal and puerperal care from a primary health care base. If this were integrated with the hospital confinement, the midwife could be involved at this stage also.

Health visitors

Health visitors attached to primary health care teams are also identified as a priority growth area in the government's Consultative Document (D.H.S.S., 1976a). As with home nurses, the attachment of health visitors to general practitioners has increased markedly in recent years and about 80 per cent are now attached. To some extent this may seem surprising, as there had traditionally been a much greater gulf in the understanding and appreciation of the health visitor's role by general practitioners. This may partly have arisen out of the breadth of the health visitor's responsibilities and the fact that she was originally a registered nurse (with additional training) who no longer performs practical nursing procedures. Her activities are also predominantly preventive and educative – activities which are usually less visible and less easily measurable.

The original health visitors, in the last century, were appointed to educate families in the necessity for cleanliness and good living for health. Their role developed with a particular emphasis on advising mothers about the care of young children, with the aim of reducing malnutrition and the spread of infectious diseases. The 1946 National Health Service Act made it a duty of every local authority (now of Area Health Authorities), 'to make provision in their area for the visiting of persons in their homes by visitors, to be called "health visitors", for the purpose of giving advice as to the care of young children, persons suffering from illness and expectant and nursing mothers, and as to measures necessary to prevent the spread of infection'. The health visitor's training gives her a combination of knowledge of medical and psycho-social matters. Clark's survey (1973) of attached health visitors in Berkshire revealed an immense variety of problems dealt with, while in addition they contacted a wide range of different agencies on behalf of their patients. The role of the health visitor still appears somewhat diffuse, and one may speculate as to how it may develop. There could perhaps be a re-emergence of the concentration on maternity and child welfare, particularly in the wake of the recently published Court Report (D.H.S.S., 1976c) with its emphasis on what the media have called the 'scandal' of Britain's high infant mortality rates when compared with many other Western European countries, and its recommendation for an integrated child health service within general practice. Alternatively, the need for health education and prevention of the major health hazards of today, and the existence of the already discussed 'iceberg' may indicate a broader, but specific, preventive role, perhaps in screening programmes. Then again, the increasing incidence of chronic illness points to a need for more attention to be given to sustaining the ill and the elderly over long periods.

Different practices and areas, of course, have different needs; some practices will have many more elderly people or young children than others. This may indicate that the role definition should be left as wide as possible. The Council for the Education and Training of Health Visitors identified five main aspects of work.

(1) The prevention of mental, physical, and emotional ill-health or the alleviation of its consequences.

(2) Early detection of ill-health and the surveillance of high risk groups.
(3) Recognition and identification of need, and mobilization of resources where necessary.
(4) Health teaching.
(5) Provision of care.

The health visitor is the only professional worker whose training is specifically and predominantly concerned with the interplay of medical and social factors. The integration of the health visitor into the primary health care team, and her original nursing training, may suggest the possibility of her assuming a dual home nurse/health visitor role, particularly with the chronically ill. However, the Briggs Committee (D.H.S.S., 1973) firmly came down on the side of retaining the existing division.

Social workers

It could be thought that the inclusion of the health visitor in the team would obviate the need for a social worker, as it may appear that there are many similarities in their roles. However, there are also distinct differences in their method and approach to problems, and especially in the powers and responsibilities carried by social services departments. Over the years, various official reports have underlined the need for social workers in the primary health care team. The 1946 National Health Service Act, in its concept of the health centre and its staff, strongly implied the inclusion of social workers. Similarly the Seebohm Committee (1968) had no doubt this was a desirable trend, although they felt that general practitioners were generally not yet ready to embark positively in such cooperative ventures. The B.M.A. (1974) saw social workers as members of the essential 'nucleus' of the primary health team.

The gaps in understanding between social workers and general practitioners have been much greater than those previously mentioned between general practitioners and nurses and health visitors. Although much written support has been given to the inclusion of social workers in the primary health care team, actual developments have been slow and there is still considerable doubt about the appropriateness and/or necessity of including them. The personal social services and the health services have both been reorganized during the 1970s, but separately, the former being a local authority responsibility and the latter now wholly a central government responsibility. In the main, the geographical boundaries of Area Health Authorities and local authorities are now coterminous, and machinery has been established for coordination at local level between the two. The introduction in 1976 of joint funding arrangements has also begun a policy of coordinated provision of personal social and health services. The responsibilities of social services departments are in themselves very wide, and it is sometimes argued that much of their work does not require close collaboration with primary health services. Whether and how these two services should and could be brought together organizationally are complex questions. But certainly the need for close collaboration for a significant proportion of the work of both social services departments and primary health care teams is undeniable. It is likely that primary health care is the single biggest source of referrals to social services departments. Theophilus (1973) found that primary health care accounted for 11.5 per cent of referrals, but Mead (1975) obtained a figure of about 25 per cent.

Some studies have indicated that general practitioners made little use of existing social services, and were often uncertain of the provisions. Jefferys (1965) observed this in her Buckinghamshire study. Harwin *et al.* (1970) undertook a survey of 129 general practitioners in an inner London borough, with well-developed community services. The striking finding was the apparent lack of contact with the local mental health department; only five per cent of general practitioners recorded any regular contact. Only one-third of the general practitioners surveyed recalled any direct contact with the then existing child care officers, and probation officers. The problem seemed to be a lack of awareness rather than hostility, and whilst 46 per cent were in favour of some form of collaborative work, one-third firmly rejected the idea of teamwork.

There are no official statistics which indicate the numbers of social workers attached to primary health care teams. Ratoff *et al.* (1973) surveyed all directors of social services departments by postal questionnaire in April 1972, one year after the creation of social services departments, in an attempt to measure this. Their findings concluded that only 178.6 wholetime equivalent social workers were employed in attachment to general practitioners, and these constituted only 1.5 per cent of social workers in post. There was no obvious association between those areas with most social workers and those with more attachments. They felt that outside hospitals this form of medico-social liaison was negligible, and that development had been hampered by the absence of a firm central directive. To some extent this is fair criticism, and perhaps this issue has been submerged in the mass of complex unresolved problems facing social services departments since their creation.

There have been various positive accounts of attachments of social workers to general practice, the most notable being Goldberg and Neill's (1972) description of a four-year attachment to the Caversham group practice in Kentish Town, London. The role of the social worker was considered to have been threefold: the psycho-social assessment of patients, provision of a casework service, and linking with other service-providing agencies. In such attachment schemes, the social workers were more likely to deal with problems at an early and more treatable stage. Attachment also changed the nature of referrals to social workers, tending towards a greater use of the workers' therapeutic skills, as distinct from a predominance of referrals for practical and material help. However, these accounts are of situations existing before social services departments were established. The social workers involved were also very experienced specialists, and therefore not necessarily representative of the typical younger, generically trained social workers of today's social services departments.

Good collaboration can be achieved by other methods than attachment and these could be more appropriate in some situations. In many areas liaison schemes operate between social workers and general practitioners, which involve designated social workers having primary responsibility for communication between their own department and a specific group practice and may or may not involve the social worker dealing with the referred cases personally (Mead, 1975). The Derby scheme (Cooper, 1971) which operated during the 1960s is an interesting example of close collaborative work between general practitioners and linked, local authority-employed social workers. On a much more informal basis, the creation of local discussion groups of health visitors, social workers, and general practitioners as described by Payne (1976) is an example of what can be achieved through a willingness to cooperate and learn from each other. It is unfortunate that there is no collated knowledge of the multiplicity of collaborative schemes which exist, and of their strengths and weaknesses.

While much positive collaboration exists between social workers and primary health care teams, albeit generally unknown outside its own locality, there are numerous possible reasons for the all-too-often poor relationships. Social services departments are frequently short of professionally qualified staff, have quite inadequate resources to meet the demands they encounter, and experience rapid staff turnover. In such circumstances it is likely that other professions will be dissatisfied by failures to meet their expectations. Often the relative youth of the social work profession, compared to that of medicine, is suggested as a reason for the distance between the two. Certainly there is a difference in emphasis and perception, but this must be so if the two are to have different roles. The doctor's primary focus has been upon the biological aspects, and the social worker has been principally concerned with the behavioural aspects of the individual's problems. There are also differences in method; doctors tradi- tionally have been authoritative and decisive, whereas the tradition of social work has been to make a relationship and listen to the patient/client over a period of time in the hope of helping him find his own solutions. Such an apparent polarization of methods is tailor-made for the creation of misunderstanding and follows from a lack of clear knowledge about each other's training. Social workers, too, may fail to recognize the pressures that general practitioners work under and, like society at large, also have magical expectations of medicine and doctors, which are unrealistic. Likewise, general practitioners often fail to understand the breadth of responsibilities of the social services departments, or expect social workers to supply practical help which may not always be realistically possible. To a great extent all these problems arise out of myths held by each profession about the other, which are created and continue to survive, where there is inadequate communication. Payne's description (1976) of the initial meet- ings of a general practitioners', health visitors', and social workers' study group reveals almost farcical myths held about each other.

Other team members

To include all the possible remaining members of the primary health care team in a section entitled 'other team members' has no significance other than organizational tidiness. It should not be construed as a lack of appreciation of, for example, receptionists and secretaries. The keeping of adequate records is vital for the efficient functioning of a multi-disciplinary health care team, whilst the receptionist staff are at the front line of contact with patients. The importance of their knowledge and skills for the smooth running of the practice will not be underestimated by anyone who has worked in a primary health care team.

The B.M.A. monograph 'Primary Health Care Teams' (1974) also suggests various other team members, including dental surgeons and pharmacists, and possibly, in larger practices, radiographers. The prevalence of chronic disease and the need for long-term management in the community perhaps indicates a place for physiotherapists and occupational therapists. As diet plays an important part in the management and treatment of many diseases there is also a case for the inclusion of dieticians. However, the monograph suggests that there is a nucleus of members whose presence is vital in the team: namely doctors, nurses (home nurses, midwives and health visitors), social workers and medical secretaries. The activities of other members are important but it is not vital that they be permanent members.

The success of the team

As previously stated, it is not enough to assume that merely putting a group of professionals together in a health centre with appropriate facilities will create a team in the sense of cooperative working. The importance of communication and appreciation of the roles of others has already been stressed. The need for regular team meetings to discuss frankly joint responsibilities and problems is widely recognized as vital, but all too often they are never held. We have no clear idea of how big the primary health care team should be. There have been various estimates of the numbers of general practitioners who can work together successfully, and how many nurses and health visitors are necessary to support them, but virtually nothing is known about the appropriate amount of social work time. In some health centres general practitioners have continued to function largely as one-man practices, whilst in others there are several groups of general practitioners. A deterrent to cooperation at times has been an apparent fear by some general practitioners that the intervention of others in the care of their patients will interfere with their special relationships with individuals. Concerns about confidentiality are also often mentioned. However, the evidence of studies generally reveals that patients feel that their doctor has been able to provide them with a better service, and the anxieties are perhaps more related to a lack of knowledge of, and confidence in, the skills of the other professionals on the part of the doctor.

Although a clear definition of respective roles is necessary for team members, this does not deny overlap between various roles. There is generally considerable overlap in the perceived roles of the various members of the team. For example, many general practitioners see the psychotherapeutic treatment of those with minor psychosomatic symptoms as their domain, whilst many social workers would feel it to belong to them.

There are many varieties and combinations of such role conflicts in the team, which must be met openly, with maturity and good humour, if the team is to work successfully. It is also important that there should be some role flexibility, for at times a particular team member may be the most appropriate to deal with a particular problem because of an existing relationship with the patient rather than primarily because of his or her professional designation. For such flexibility to exist, the personalities must be compatible and consequently trusting of each other. Lamberts and Riphagen (1975) concluded about their own team that business meetings were slow and ineffective 'because of the large number of personal problems between members of the group practice'. They decided that most decisions were made ineffective by personal differences.

Finally, the question of leadership of the team is particularly important and often contentious. Rightly the doctor is the clinical 'leader' of the team, but leadership in this situation involves democratic management and delegation. It is likely that leadership will change at times depending on the nature of the problem and who is most skilled to help. Brooks (1973) surveyed seven teams in the later 1960s and produced some interesting findings about the leadership problem. Half the 16 general practitioners surveyed saw themselves as the leader, and the nurses and midwives unhesitatingly saw the doctors as leaders. Some health visitors agreed with the nurses, but others saw the issue as one of partnership. The social workers were strong in their emphasis on a shared responsibility. Brooks suggests that different styles of leadership may be necessary, depending on the personalities involved, and that the important factor is that the members should agree about the leadership, rather than that all teams adopt a common pattern. The fact that the various professions have different lines of professional accountability is yet another element complicating authority and leadership.

FUTURE TRENDS IN PRIMARY HEALTH CARE?

That primary health care and community care are to be key areas for development in the National Health Service is clear from the government's Consultative Document (D.H.S.S., 1976a). Although the level of anticipated development is likely to be reduced in view of economic considerations, the emphasis will undoubtedly remain. Inherent in these proposals is an attempt to achieve a more equitable geographical distribution of health services. It is wise to remember that this policy does not assume that too much, in absolute terms, has been spent on acute hospital services, although in places there is undoubtedly wasteful use of resources, but that we have now recognized the finite nature of resources available. It is, in any case, clear from the earlier discussions that demands for care, and expectations of health, may not be closely related to the resources available. Decisions on the optimum allocation of resources must be based on considerations of the balance of needs for care, cure, or treatment.

Specialization

Added together, the various developments point to a greater proportion of health problems being dealt with by primary health care teams. This involves, among other things, the practice of clinical medicine to a higher level of skill outside acute hospitals during an era when medicine is becoming increasingly complex. At the same time, it remains important for primary health care to provide a system of personal care, seeing the patient as a whole person and not as a collection of symptoms. McKeown (1965) produced a revolutionary concept to resolve this dilemma. He saw the solution in specialization, by general practitioners, in patient age groups. He saw each practice as requiring specialist primary physicians for obstetrics, paediatrics, adult medicine and geriatrics, in proportions relative to the practice population. McKeown postulated that the medical and social problems of each of these groups were relatively homogeneous. Each doctor would act as a personal doctor and also have responsibility for the patient in hospital within the bounds of possibility. One of the major criticisms of such a system is the possible loss of continuity of care for families (if this has ever existed to the extent we have believed). However, we do not yet know about the problems and possibilities of this type of specialization. An experiment in specialization along similar lines to those suggested by McKeown is currently under way in the Department of Primary Medical Care of Southampton University.

Community hospitals

The need to coordinate the work of acute hospitals and community medicine, particularly when chronic disability is a major and increasing problem, is now well recognized. The trend expounded in the 1962 Hospital Plan towards the relative concentration of hospital facilities in fewer and larger district general hospitals, has now been clearly modified in the government's policy of recent years to encourage the development of community hospitals (D.H.S.S., 1974). These are small local hospitals, which are part of the primary health care team's responsibility. Britain's first full-scale community hospital was opened in 1973 at Wallingford in Oxfordshire (Robinson, 1974). Community hospitals are particularly well-placed to provide care (in-patient, out-patient, and day-patient) for the elderly and chronically disabled, often on an episodic basis, thus allowing patients to remain for the optimum amount of time in their own homes. It has been estimated that up to half the geriatric beds necessary could be provided by community hospitals. They could also be used for minor surgical cases, and for those needing post-operative care from acute hospitals, where this is not possible in their own homes. It is recognized that community hospitals must be coordinated with district general hospitals, particularly as there will be a two-way flow of patients between them. It is also intended that hospital consultants should hold some out-patient clinics in the community hospitals. Besides being more accessible for the patients, this will also provide a setting where the different sections of the health services can come together. This is obviously part of a long-term plan for the health services, as is the redevelopment of some existing cottage hospitals as community hospitals. An important role for social services departments is also envisaged both in the planning and future provision of social work support for community hospitals.

Taken together, the policies for the development of health centres and their primary health care teams, and for the development of community hospitals, represent a recognition of the need for an accessible, continuously caring system of health care for the majority of needs, and the reservation of expensive acute hospitals for the highly complex medical technology less frequently required. However, little is yet known about the effectiveness of such new-style primary health care organizations and how they should best be established. In a survey of patients' attitudes towards the care delivered by a primary health care team Marsh and Kaim-Caudle (1976) concluded that well over 90 per cent of those questioned were satisfied or very satisfied with the care they received. Cartwright's study in the early 1960s, on the other hand, revealed that patients were generally satisfied with their 'old-style' general practitioner service, which contrasted sharply with the prevailing view within the profession that general practice had failed to keep pace with the medical and social needs of the community. Cartwright concluded that patients' acceptance of the status quo indicated 'an uncritical acceptance and lack of discrimination' (Cartwright, 1967).

CHAPTER 4

The Mentally Ill

The interaction between mental illness and the surrounding social environment is a large field for study and one that has lent itself to dogmatic assertions and conflicts of opinion not easily resolved by appealing to the evidence. For those who are concerned in providing (or using) social and medical services for the mentally ill, it is of immediate practical importance to decide how influential aspects of the social environment are in causing the appearance of mental illnesses and what kinds of social milieu seem most effective in promoting recovery and rehabilitation. Social attitudes to mental illness will be reflected in the development of legislation and social policy in this field and are important in determining the kinds of service provision that are feasible. The purpose of this chapter is to examine the evidence relating to the importance of social and environmental factors in the onset and course of mental illnesses and to discuss the organization and provision of services for the mentally ill in the light of this evidence. In this wide field the discussion is inevitably selective.

WHAT MEANING HAS THE TERM 'MENTAL ILLNESS'?

Although this chapter is not primarily concerned with clinical features of mental disorder it is important, in the present climate of confusion and controversy, to clarify the meaning that will be attached to the concept 'mental illness' in the following pages. There is at present very little consensus on the nature of mental illnesses: at one extreme are writers who argue forcefully for a purely physical conception of mental illnesses and pay little attention to the role of social factors either in their causation or

90

treatment; at the other extreme are those who explain all so-called mental illnesses as the result of social and interpersonal processes. Are individuals who deviate from normally accepted patterns of behaving, thinking and feeling to be categorized as patients with illnesses or as people with problems in living, victims of an alienating family and social order who are further damaged by being labelled as mentally ill? T. S. Szasz, for example, points out that scientific investigation has failed to demonstrate any physical abnormality in those regarded as mentally ill. Their abnormalities of behaviour are identified with 'problems in living', 'differences in personal needs, aspirations and values' which it is clearly absurd to attribute to abnormal biochemical processes (Szasz, 1972). R. D. Laing argues that the experiences and actions of schizophrenic patients are intelligible when seen in the light of their family situation: the apparently abnormal responses are the patients' only way of surviving the social and emotional pressures placed on them (Laing and Esterson, 1971). Sociologists have tried to show that 'mental illness' is not a property of individuals but is something ascribed to persons who perform certain kinds of deviant act. Attention is focused less on the deviant behaviour but rather on the circumstances in which 'labelling' takes place and the often adverse consequences for the individual so identified (see, for example, the collection of readings, all from the American literature, in Spitzer and Denzin, 1968). All these writers seem to suggest that there is no such thing as mental illness and that doctors, nurses and social workers, in treating disturbed people as 'patients', are at best ineffective and at worst actually harmful.

Since this chapter will make the assumptions that there are relatively objective criteria on which a definition of mental as of physical illness can depend, and that there are grounds for accepting the relevance and usefulness of a medical approach to mental illness; and since these assumptions no longer (if they ever did) go unchallenged, some time must be spent in attempting to justify them.

Attempts to define health or mental health as a positive attribute have proved extremely difficult. It seems better to agree with Lewis that in practice it is the presence of disease that can be recognized, not the presence of health, and so to consider healthy everyone who is free from evidence of disease or infirmity (Lewis, 1953). Once the patient has appeared in the doctor's consulting room, social criteria play little or no part in traditional medical determinations of what is or is not illness, which rest on the patient's subjective accounts of his state, together with a demonstration that he is suffering from the disordered functioning of some part of his body and has symptoms which conform to a recognizable clinical pattern. A medical diagnosis is usually able to go further than this in making a statement about the etiology of the disturbed functioning. Psychiatric diagnoses are, however, often only statements that a patient's symptoms cluster together in a recognized syndrome or pattern. Judging these patterns as evidence of illness involves measuring them against norms.

Are these norms, as Szasz argues, really ethical and social judgments about desirable behaviour, or can judgments of mental illness be distinguished from those of socially deviant behaviour? Lewis argued that mental illness can be aligned with physical in having as a common feature the disturbance of part-functions: perceptions, learning, thinking, remembering, emotion and motivation. Deviant, socially maladapted and non-conformist behaviour is considered to be symptomatic of illness only if it is accompanied by a manifest disturbance of some such functions. The psychopathic personality, defined by abnormally aggressive or seriously irresponsible behaviour, on these criteria could not legitimately be described as ill. Although we can try to exclude social criteria from definitions of mental illness in this way, our estimate of the efficiency with which psychological functions work must take account of the social environment in which the patient lives. Yet the criteria of health are not social and it is misconceived to equate ill-health with social deviation or maladjustment.

A government committee set up to consider the problem of the Mentally Abnormal Offender (the Butler Committee, 1975) proposed a definition of 'severe mental illness' which will have meaning in a legal context. In these proposals the basic characteristics of mental illnesses are set out in a form which stresses the disturbance of psychological functions in the way suggested by Lewis:

Mental illness means an illness having one or more of the following characteristics:
(i) More than temporary impairment of intellectual functions shown by a failure of memory, orientation, comprehension and learning capacity.
(ii) More than temporary alteration of mood of such degree as to give rise to the patient having a delusional appraisal of his situation, his past or future, or that of others or to the lack of any appraisal.
(iii) Delusional beliefs, persecutory, jealous or grandiose.
(iv) Abnormal perceptions associated with delusional misinterpretation of events.
(v) Thinking so disordered as to prevent the patient making a reasonable appraisal of his situation or having reasonable communication with others.

The aim in this approach to the definition of mental illnesses is to exclude social components from the definition itself, though fully recognizing their importance, possibly in the causation and certainly in the course and outcome of illnesses. However, it is recognized that psychiatric illnesses are particularly complex in their interweaving of biological or psychological symptoms and social handicaps. Three aspects have been distinguished: illness or injury recognized by biological or psychological abnormalities which sometimes persist as chronic primary impairments. In schizophrenia, for example, symptoms, such as a persistent feeling that thoughts are being inserted into one's mind by an external agency, are primary impairments, part of the illness itself. Secondary handicaps, such as social withdrawal, loss of confidence and apathy, are likely to be present but as consequences of the illness rather than an inherent part of it. Thirdly, more general social handicaps, such as poverty and lack of access to educational and work opportunities, may be present, perhaps increasing the chances of developing an illness or complicating its course, but not a part of the illness itself. The so-called 'medical model', therefore, by no means stresses physical causes of mental illnesses to the exclusion of other factors and has nothing in common with the crude organic approach which believes that physical treatments alone have value. The value of the medical approach to severe mental illnesses lies, as Wing argues, in the power of a careful, thorough diagnostic process to generate useful predictions about pharmacological and social treatments, rehabilitation and prognosis, and hence to relieve the suffering of patients and their families (Wing and Hailey, 1972).

To illustrate these general remarks a brief discussion of clinical features may be useful. Mental illness is normally described using the classificatory system of the International Classification of Diseases. The main distinction is that between *psychosis* and *neurosis*. A sufferer from psychotic illness tends to lose contact with reality and withdraw into a world of his own. The largest group of psychoses are the conditions known as *schizophrenia*. Recently, a study of patients diagnosed as schizophrenic by psychiatrists in nine different countries with widely differing social and cultural conditions showed that the presence of a small number of core symptoms was likely to lead to a diagnosis of schizophrenia being made, whatever the cultural background of the examining doctor (W.H.O., 1973). These symptoms were: *passivity experiences,* in which the individual feels that his thoughts, feelings or actions are under external control; that thoughts are being inserted into his mind from outside or that his thoughts are being broadcast to others; *auditory hallucinations,* in which the individual hears voices discussing him, referring to him in the third person; *primary delusions*, which cannot be explained in terms of previous abnormal perceptions or experiences – for example, a patient saw a dog lift his front paw and immediately knew that he was being persecuted. An example of a characteristic auditory hallucination is the following:

> A 41 year old housewife heard a voice coming from a house across the road. The voice went on incessantly in a flat monotone describing everything she was doing with an admixture of critical comments. 'She is peeling potatoes, got hold of the peeler, she does not want that potato, she is putting it back because she thinks it has a knobble like a penis, she has a dirty mind. . . .'

These symptoms seem to represent an abnormal way of experiencing reality and a disturbance of the normal functions underlying our ability to orient ourselves to the external world, to organize perceptions and experiences into coherent wholes and to distinguish what is inside ourselves from what is outside. In *affective psychosis* there are marked changes of mood in the form of either depression or elation. The sufferer may alternate between periods of extreme elation, irritability and overactivity and periods of deep sadness, self-reproach and retardation, sometimes with delusional ideas. It is thought that these groups of illnesses are partially genetically determined and that they have a biochemical basis. However, as we shall see, environmental factors are important as precipitants. In *organic psychoses* the physiological basis of the psychological disturbances is more obvious.

A person suffering from *neurosis* experiences unpleasant feelings and symptoms which may be socially disabling but which do not involve any loss of contact with reality. Depression, marked by changes in eating, sleeping and activity patterns as well as impaired thinking and depressed mood, and anxiety and tension are the most common manifestations. For example, a person suffering from phobic anxiety experiences terror in certain quite ordinary situations, such as shopping, accompanied by physical symptoms such as sweating, trembling and nausea, but is all the time aware that these fears are unrealistic.

In all these examples it is not socially unacceptable or deviant behaviour that leads to a diagnosis of mental disorder but the disturbance of psychological and physiological functions that accompanies the unusual behaviour. As Clare (1976) says, the housewife who is unwilling to leave her house is not necessarily mentally ill, she may merely have decided to withdraw her labour as a protest against the devaluation of women in our society. It is only if she is unable to leave without being overwhelmed by panic that her condition is viewed as a mental disturbance. The group of conditions known as *personality disorders* cannot be described as illnesses. People given this label are usually distinguished by their impulsivity, lack of consideration for others and a general propensity to get into trouble and be a nuisance to society. Such people have often experienced unsettled or traumatic early lives and may cause tragedy for themselves and those close to them. Yet they have no 'illness' and there seems no real reason why their problems should be seen as medical in nature. One particular form of personality disorder marked by abnormally aggressive or seriously irresponsible conduct (psychopathy) is however at the moment legally defined as a mental disorder. *Addictions*, harmful dependence on drugs or alcohol, are another grey area in psychiatry: not themselves mental illnesses but producing psychological and physiological changes which call for psychiatric aid.

Mental illnesses, however defined, are quite distinct from mental handicap, which is usually determined before or at the time of birth or soon afterwards and is an irreversible condition which limits the affected person's social and intellectual maturity. Mental handicap will not be discussed in this chapter.

PREVALENCE OF MENTAL ILLNESS

In studying the role of social factors in the onset, course and outcome of mental illnesses it would be very helpful to be able to point to valid counts of the amount of mental illness of various types among different social groups, and to changing patterns of mental illness at different points in time. If valid estimates of the prevalence of mental illnesses (the number of cases in a defined population at a defined period) and their incidence (the number of new cases appearing in a defined population at a defined period) were available, it would be easier to evaluate the role of social factors as causal agents in the appearance of mental disorders. At present, however, psychiatric epidemiology is in a relatively early stage of its history and there are few certainties to follow.

The psychiatric epidemiologist may wish to ask: what are the variations in prevalence and inception rates of, for example, schizophrenia, among subgroups of the population at risk? To answer these questions he will need a definition of the population at risk, a precise operational definition of the disease in question which will permit accurate case-finding and a method of identifying all cases in the population by a valid diagnostic technique. All these matters are fraught with difficulties, of which the most significant has probably been the problem of diagnostic unreliability. It is perhaps still true to say that the most striking lesson from reviewing prevalence surveys is 'the stern and endlessly repeated admonition that true progress toward a grasp of mental illness in the population . . . will not begin until the validation and universal acceptance of a precise diagnostic system' (Plunkett and Gordon, 1960). Recent progress has, however, been made in developing a standardized diagnostic interview, based on precisely defined symptoms, which investigators can be trained to use with a high degree of reliability. This approach has already borne fruit, for example, in the cross-cultural study of schizophrenia referred to above and should mark a significant advance in the application of epidemiological methods. But case-finding still remains an especially difficult problem in the field of mental disorder.

A great many factors besides severity of illness determine whether people receive psychiatric treatment for their complaints or not. The patients who attend a psychiatrist for help are only a proportion of all those in the community with similar symptoms, and social factors which are related to becoming a psychiatric patient are not necessarily related in a causal way to the appearance of mental illness itself. Unfortunately, most studies of the prevalence of mental illnesses use rates of admission to hospital, rates of referral to psychiatric services or, at best, rates in general-practice consultations as their measure of illness. It is possible that such studies are in fact measuring illness behaviour – the meaning the patient gives to his symptoms and the sources from which he seeks help – and the provision, accessibility and administration of services rather than the true prevalence of mental illnesses. Field studies of defined populations can overcome this problem but here the difficulty has been one of case definition: different investigators have adopted different criteria of what constitutes a 'case', and prevalence figures have varied accordingly. In the case of severe mental disorders, such as schizophrenia or manic-depressive psychosis, it is likely that psychiatric referral rates may approximate to the true incidence; with minor mental disorders this is not the case. Prevalence figures must therefore be viewed with reserve, but brief mention will be made of some of the evidence.

In recent years the development of psychiatric case registers, which systematically monitor all contacts with psychiatric services in and out of hospitals by the population living in a defined area, has enabled a more accurate picture to be formed of the prevalence of treated mental disorder. Table 1 shows the one-day and one-year reported prevalence in three different urban areas in Britain and one in the United States. The one-year prevalence figures are strikingly similar, suggesting that between one and two per cent of the population will consult a psychiatrist during the course of a year.

TABLE 1   *One-Day and One-Year Reported Prevalence in Four Urban Areas Covered by Psychiatric Case Registers. Rates per 100,000 Home Population Aged 15+*

	Aberdeen 31.12.64	Camberwell 31.12.64	Nottingham 30.9.67	Baltimore U.S.A. 30.6.63
One-day prevalence	854	861	838	1156
One-year prevalence	1775	2051	1964	1998

Sources: Wing and Bransby (1970); D.H.S.S. (1971).

A very high proportion of the total population of Britain is registered with a general practitioner, so that studies of the amount of psychiatric disorder among persons consulting him (but not necessarily referred to a psychiatrist) may come closer to a true prevalence. This is particularly so as neurotic and physical illness seem closely related, and people with neurotic symptoms have been found to be assiduous attenders at the doctor's surgery. It has not proved easy to enlist the cooperation of a random sample of general practitioners in studying the prevalence of psychiatric morbidity. The most comprehensive research is still that into 46 London area practices carried out by Shepherd and his colleagues. Table 2 gives the consulting rates for different psychiatric disorders in these practices, showing that approximately 14 per cent of all general practice consultations were for formal psychiatric illnesses or for psychiatric-associated conditions. After respiratory disease, psychiatric illness was the commonest reason for consulting the general practitioner. Severe mental disorder (psychosis) was seen comparatively rarely by general practitioners while minor mental disorders (neuroses) were fourteen times as frequent. All investigators agree on the much greater frequency of neurotic disturbances.

TABLE 2   *Patient Consulting Rates per 1,000 at Risk for Psychiatric Morbidity by Sex and Diagnostic Group*

Diagnostic Group	Male	Female	Both Sexes
Psychoses	2.7	8.6	5.9
Mental Subnormality	1.6	2.9	2.3
Dementia	1.2	1.6	1.4
Neuroses	55.7	116.6	88.5
Personality Disorder	7.2	4.0	5.5
Formal psychiatric illness	67.2	131.9	102.1
Psychiatric associated conditions	38.6	57.2	48.6
Total psychiatric morbidity	97.9	175.0	139.4

Source: Shepherd *et al.* (1966, table 14, p. 81).

Community surveys have tended to find a high prevalence of moderate and mild psychiatric symptoms and emotional disturbance in the populations studied: approximately half the population appears as psychiatrically disturbed in studies carried out in various parts of North America. Thus, emotional distress and some consequent impairment in social functioning is widespread and not necessarily best categorized as mental illness to be medically treated.

At all ages women are more likely to suffer from most forms of mental disorder than are men (schizophrenia, however, is an exception). For both sexes the incidence of mental disorder is highest among the divorced, separated and widowed with an extant marriage usually helping to protect against the appearance of mental disorder. However, young married women are a particularly high-risk group largely accounting for the peak in psychiatric referral rates that occurs in the late twenties and early thirties. Old age is the life stage most likely to bring psychiatric illness with the referral rate reaching its peak in the oldest age groups.

TRENDS OVER TIME

It is difficult to establish whether the pattern of mental disorders has changed over time since observed changes in, for example, hospital admission rates are likely to be due to administrative changes in the provision of services. However, there is little evidence that serious mental disorder (psychosis) has increased over the century. A famous study compared age-specific first admission rates to Massachusetts mental institutions in 1840–55 with rates a century later and found that first admission rates for people under fifty were as high in the nineteenth century as in the twentieth. The investigators concluded that there had been no long-term increase in the incidence of the psychoses of early and middle life (Goldhamer and Marshall, 1949). Other investigators have confirmed the stability of admission rates for functional psychosis over the years, in contrast to rates of treated neurotic disturbance which have fluctuated more and where there has been an overall increase. It is likely that social components enter more into the definition and recognition of minor mental disorders and that both sufferers and doctors are more likely to see a medical or psychiatric significance in emotional disturbance than they would have done in previous generations. In conclusion, then, there is little evidence to support the view that the greater complexity of contemporary life with its allegedly more stressful character is leading to an increase in severe mental disorder.

SOCIAL FACTORS

The discussion so far has tended to take the view that mental illness, though qualitatively different from an unhappy reaction to distressing circumstances and not to be explained merely as a result of interaction between vulnerable people and damaging social institutions, is yet inseparable from the whole social surroundings of the patient and depends very much on his relations with others. It has been argued that it is difficult to show that mental illnesses systematically vary in different national, social or occupational groups owing to unsolved methodological problems. Nevertheless there is some evidence to suggest that social situations can play a causative role in the onset of mental disorder. Social factors interact with each other in producing their effect but for purposes of discussion three sets of social influences will be considered separately: social status; social disorganization and isolation; life changes and life events.

Social status

Does a person's position in the social status hierarchy affect his chances of becoming mentally ill? A large number of investigators has attempted to answer this question which, however, remains a controversial one. A famous study of New Haven by Hollingshead and Redlich (1958) asked, firstly, whether prevalence of mental illness was related to social class, secondly, whether social class position affected the kind of psychiatric treatment that was received. A careful census was taken of all psychiatric patients in any kind of treatment who resided in New Haven, and a sample census was carried out on the general population. A social class scale was developed based on occupation, education and area of residence. The results were striking: the lowest social class has a much greater rate of treated psychiatric disorder than all other classes, and psychosis, especially schizophrenia, was most over-represented in it. The nature of psychiatric treatment received by a patient depended on his social class position so that upper-class patients were most likely to be receiving psychotherapy while lower-class patients were most often receiving custodial care.

This was a study of treated psychiatric illness and, as we have seen, treated patients are not necessarily representative of all mentally ill people in the community. However, a large-scale community survey carried out in New York (the Midtown Manhattan Study) also found a strong association between symptoms of mental disturbance and socio-economic status (Srole *et al.*, 1962). A large random sample of the population aged 20–59 was interviewed by professional interviewers, who obtained structured information about symptoms and social functioning. Psychiatrists then used this information and other records to classify patients into six groups, ranging from the well, with no evidence of symptom formation, through the mildly and moderately disturbed to the impaired, whose symptoms caused serious interference with social functioning. Less than a fifth of the population was classified as well and nearly a quarter was called impaired. These high prevalence figures have been generally criticized on the grounds that the study did not achieve a precise enough definition of what was to count as mental disorder. However the proportion rated 'impaired with severe symptom formation' and 'incapacitated' was significantly higher in the lowest socio-economic status group, and this finding held when father's and not subject's economic status was taken.

A recent community survey carried out by Brown and his colleagues in an inner London borough is less open to the criticism of over-inclusive definition of mental disorder. In this study a random sample of 220 women residents of the borough aged 18–65 was interviewed using a structured interview schedule tested for reliability (the Present State Examination). A high proportion, 16 per cent, were found to have had a definite psychiatric disorder, usually depression, during the three months before the interview. A measure of social status was developed taking into account occupation, education and prosperity level and, when rates of psychiatric disturbance in the different social status groups were examined, working-class women appeared significantly more disturbed than middle-class women – a quarter of the working-class women were rated as having had a psychiatric disorder in the previous three months compared to only five per cent of middle-class women. Working-class women were also more likely to develop chronic disturbances, lasting for over a year (Brown *et al.*, 1975). In a recent review of the literature relating to schizophrenia Kohn (1972) concluded that the evidence generally confirms that this condition occurs disproportionately in the lowest social classes. The majority of investigators, therefore, agree that there is a link between low social status and prevalence of mental disorder, especially schizophrenia, although there are negative findings which prevent complete certainty on the issue.

If it is accepted for the moment that there is an association between low social class and mental disorder, it is necessary to look more closely at the reasons for this observed association. Is there something about the conditions of life at the bottom of the social status hierarchy that actually causes mental illnesses to develop? Or is the association with low social status a result rather than a cause of mental disorder? In the case of schizophrenia, it is likely that the effects of the illness on the individual are such as to debar him from well-paid, high-status occupations and that he is likely to drift down the social ladder into unskilled employment and a relatively deprived living environment. A well-known study of schizophrenic men has shown that they failed to reach either the occupational level of their fathers at a similar stage in life or the level that might have been predicted from their own school performances (Goldberg and Morrison, 1963). Other researchers have demonstrated that schizophrenic patients drift downwards after their first hospital admission and cannot regain their former occupational and social levels. It must be concluded that low social class is not causally related to schizophrenia but is a result of it. However, as we shall see later, there are suggestions that stress, in the form of disturbing life events, occurs disproportionately often to working-class people who may also be less cushioned against it and more likely to react with strain, or mental disorder.

Ecological studies

Sociologists have approached the understanding and explanation of deviant behaviour, such as delinquency, crime or mental disorder, by examining the behaviour in its spatial context. Ecology, a term borrowed from biology, is the study of the relationships between a natural habitat and the species it contains: in social terms, the relationships between people sharing a local territory which are influenced by the characteristics of that territory. In studying a city, for example, it can usually be seen that there are natural and man-made features which determine the shape of the city's growth and divide it into areas or zones which exhibit distinctive socio-economic characteristics. The area surrounding the central railway or bus station, for example, will differ markedly in its housing facilities and inhabitants from an established residential area. In the 1920s, the Chicago School of sociologists described the city as divided into concentric zones: the central business district; a transitional zone – the rooming house and brothel district; a residential working-class zone; a district characterized by the high proportion of flats and residential hotels; the outer ring of commuting suburbs. The central areas were originally residential, then invaded by industry causing the wealthier inhabitants to move further out. As the central areas declined, rentals became depressed, and the area attracted newcomers, usually immigrants, who wanted low-cost housing. Families who could afford something better moved out so that the area could not reverse its declining character. In studying the spatial distribution of juvenile-delinquent residents in Chicago, Shaw and McKay (1939) found that high delinquency rates occurred in areas of the city with a declining population and physical deterioration, nearest to industry, and that these areas were also characterized by a mass of other social problems, such as adult crime, tuberculosis and mental illness, which diminished with distance from the centre of the city. The earliest ecological perspective on mental illness was provided by the work of Faris and Dunham (1939) who looked at differences in the prevalence of mental illness in the different Chicago zones. When they plotted all first admissions to mental hospitals and private institutions, they found a marked variation in rates for schizophrenia with high rates in the central and 'hobo' districts declining to the periphery. Admissions for manic-depressive psychosis, however, were randomly distributed through the city. Explanation of these findings as artefacts of poverty or mobility were considered but excluded, and the conclusion was that the living conditions of the inner city areas, which fostered breakdown in informal social controls and social isolation, caused people to develop schizophrenic reactions.

A community survey carried out in a rural area of Nova Scotia (Stirling County) attempted to study the relationship between the social organization of an area and the amount of mental disorder generated within it. A representative sample of over 1,000 people was interviewed, medical and other records were consulted, and the resulting material was rated by psychiatrists who made diagnoses using standard United States classifications. Over half the population was considered as 'probably' or 'almost certainly' having a defined psychiatric disorder, and the method of diagnosis is open to criticism on the same grounds as the Midtown Manhattan survey already mentioned. However, the social data are of considerable interest as these investigators attempted to develop an operational definition of 'disintegration' in a community. It was hypothesized that 'social disintegration generates disintegrated personalities', and ten indices of disintegration were developed: poverty; culture clashes between French and English values; secularization; broken homes; few and weak group associations; few and weak community leaders; few patterns of recreation; high frequency of violent and criminal acts. Local areas with high disintegration scores had high prevalence rates of mental disorder, leading these investigators to conclude that the level of social organization of the community in which the individual lives plays an important part in determining whether or not he becomes mentally ill (Leighton, 1959).

The ecological approach has been an especially fruitful one in studies of suicidal behaviour. Sainsbury's pioneering work in London tested the hypothesis 'that where social mobility and social isolation are pronounced, community life will be without order or purpose, and that this will be reflected to a greater or less degree in the suicide rates'. He found that the suicide rates of London boroughs differed significantly and the highest rates were to be found in boroughs with mobile, unsettled populations and many isolated people (Sainsbury, 1955). Subsequent work has confirmed that people living in environments characterized by high levels of geographic mobility and social disorganization are especially prone to suicidal behaviour (Morgan, 1975).

It may be that poor social conditions, in particular overcrowded houses lacking basic amenities, play an important part in causing people to develop these various symptoms of emotional distress and mental illness. It is also likely that vulnerable people drift into the central city areas and so are more likely to break down. However, it is also possible that cultural factors, such as attitudes, beliefs and patterns of interaction between people in such areas influence individuals towards increasingly deviant ways of expressing their distress. Whatever weighting is given to these various explanations of the observed findings of the importance of the social area in generating mental disorder, it is important to recognize the priority claims of areas with high levels of disorganization to resources for community involvement and improvement.

Life events

So far we have examined the role of broad social conditions – social status and living area – in the etiology of mental disorder. These are 'background factors' which may increase the chances of becoming ill but do not operate as immediate causal factors on individuals. We will now consider the individual's response to perceived social stresses. A stress is here defined as any factor in the environment which interferes with satisfaction of basic needs or threatens to disturb the individual's equilibrium. The individual reacts to stress by mobilizing adaptive mechanisms, physiological and mental, which can be protective but can become pathological if they persist too long or fail to resolve the threatening situation. A number of factors influence the individual's reaction to stress and the likelihood of his developing pathological reactions, including, for example, his genetic and constitutional endowment, age and marital status, social class and the balance of his previous positive and destructive life experiences.

In recent years a large number of studies has concentrated on unravelling the role of recent life events in causing an individual to become ill. American investigators have developed the Schedule of Recent Life Experience which lists 42 possible life events, each given a weighted score for the amount of social readjustment imposed by the event. Thus death of spouse receives a weight of 100, marriage scores 50, minor law-breaking scores 11. The Schedule has been given to different samples of the population and the investigators have been able to demonstrate its use as a predictive instrument: people who have recently experienced a number of life events leading to high scores on the S.R.E. are significantly more likely to become ill than those without such stresses (Holmes and Rahe, 1967). These investigations have not entirely overcome methodological problems (for example, the illness itself may influence the reporting of events) but other careful work inspired by Brown and his colleagues in England has found essentially similar relationships between disturbing life events and the onset of illness (Brown, 1976). The onset both of schizophrenia and of depressive illness has been found to be causally related to the occurrence of life events in the months before the illness. Different kinds of event which trigger depression are especially those which involve 'exits' from the patient's social field – losses by bereavement or break-up of relationships – and more threatening events. The community survey by Brown and his colleagues found that over three-quarters of depressed women in the community had experienced a severe event or long-term difficulty which was causally related to their illness, and that the experience of a threatened or actual major loss was the distinctive feature of the events. They conclude that 'events with severe, threatening long-term implications, most of which involve some major loss, play an important part in bringing about depressive disorders in women' (p. 243).

What accounts for the greater vulnerability of some people than others to stress and disturbing life events? The Midtown Manhattan investigators suggested that perhaps 'the self-esteem that comes with high socio-economic status, with loving but not over-indulgent parents, with acceptance by other racial, religious and status groups is what helps to stave off mental disturbance even in the face of great stress'. All their data pointed to a greater resiliency in the young and those of high status (Langner and Michael, 1963). The sources of this 'resiliency' call for further investigation. Brown, like the Midtown Manhattan authors, found that not only are working-class women more likely to experience stressful events but that working-class women, especially with a child at home, are more vulnerable to the onset of disturbance when they have a severe event or difficulty than are middle-class women. Nearly 40 per cent of working-class women in his sample having a severe event or difficulty developed psychiatric disorder, but only six per cent of middle-class women. Working-class women seemed more vulnerable because of a difference in the quality of their interpersonal relationships: they were receiving less support from a close, intimate and confiding relationship with a husband or boy friend. They are also more vulnerable in having larger numbers of young children at home and being unable to work. Thus an important source of 'resiliency' in women seems to be the heightening of self-esteem that comes from a satisfying marriage and the ability to work outside the home.

The experience of loss

It has been shown that events involving actual or threatened loss are particularly significant as triggers of psychiatric disturbance. Bereavement is of great importance in this connection and is also of interest in illustrating the difficulty in distinguishing between adaptive and pathological reactions to stress. Studies of 'normal' bereaved subjects suggest that there are different styles of normal grieving, of which the most common, and also probably the most healthy and adaptive, is a time-limited mourning passing through successive stages: an initial period of numbness and inability to realize the loss is succeeded by a subjective feeling of pining and yearning, pre-occupation with thoughts of the dead person and often illusions of his actual presence, with a loss of interest in other matters. The bereaved person often experiences psychological and somatic symptoms, such as tension, depression, weeping, insomnia, loss of weight, headaches and body pains. This period of intense grieving is normally time-limited and may last for no more than six weeks. It is painful but probably has an important function: the phrase 'grief-work' is often used.

The survivor was closely bound to the lost person by ties of affection, common habits and mutual need. He now has to release himself from these ties so that he is free to form new attachments. The 'work' of normal grief thus consists in the survivor's bit-by-bit detaching himself from the memories and bonds which bind him to the lost person so that he is free to move on to new relationships. Freud suggests that reality passes its verdict, that the object no longer exists, upon all the memories and hopes through which the mourner was attached to the lost object, so that the ego confronted, as it were, whether it will share this fate, is persuaded by the sum of its narcissistic satisfactions in being alive to sever its attachment to the non-existent object (Freud, 1950). Freud (1961) also suggests that although acute grief is time-limited the sense of loss may be permanent.

> Although we know that after such a loss the acute state of mourning will subside, we also know that we shall remain inconsolable and will never find a substitute. No matter what may fill the gap, even if it be filled completely, it nevertheless remains something else. And actually that is how it should be. It is the only way of perpetuating that love which we do not want to relinquish.

Grief therefore may be seen as a normal response to the loss of a love object which runs a fairly well-defined course and ends in recovery and the establishment of new relationships. In a minority of cases, however, bereavement is followed by pathological psychological or physical changes which may even bring about death. Studies of widowed people suggest that about a fifth develop a collection of symptoms (depressed mood; appetite and weight loss; sleep disturbance and fatigue; agitation or retardation; loss of interest and difficulty in concentrating; guilt; suicidal feelings) which would normally lead to a psychiatric diagnosis of depression and which are still in evidence one year after the bereavement (Bornstein *et al.*, 1973). Various studies have shown that recent bereavement of a spouse or a parent is significantly associated with entry to psychiatric treatment and with death by suicide (Parkes, 1964; Bunch, 1972). There is also a significant excess of deaths from natural causes in the year following loss of a spouse and this is mainly due to death from heart disease in the survivor (Parkes *et al.*, 1969). It seems clear, therefore, that bereavement can cause both mental and physical illness.

EFFECTS OF THE SOCIAL MILIEU ON ILLNESS

So far social factors having a causal relationship to the onset of mental disorder have been illustrated. The patient's social environment is also of great importance in influencing the course and outcome of an episode of illness and the chances of recovery or relapse.

The effect of institutions

It has long been known, and graphically described in works of literature, that institutions can have the most powerful effects on the personalities of their inhabitants. Mental hospitals are a particularly complex form of institution since they serve such a large number of different functions. Historically, mental hospitals developed as places of containment in which 'patients' were legally confined. However, at least in Britain, this custodial function has been greatly reduced in importance since less than one-tenth of patients are detained in hospital under any kind of legal restraint; the mental hospital now is more analogous to the general hospital with goals of active treatment and rehabilitation. Yet because of the historical circumstances leading to their erection, mental hospitals are particularly prone to develop a cultural pattern typical also of other communities whose inmates are segregated from the world around them. Erving Goffman has well described the features of these 'total institutions', so-called because of their all-encompassing character maintained by barriers to intercourse with the outside world, such as locked doors or high walls. The way of life inside such total institutions is marked by a destruction of the barriers that normally separate different spheres of social life such as sleeping, working and playing.

> First, all aspects of life are conducted in the same place and under the same single authority. Second, each phase of the member's daily activity is carried on in the immediate company of a large batch of others, all of whom are treated alike and required to do the same thing together. Third, all phases of the day's activities are tightly scheduled, with one activity leading at a prearranged time into the next. . . . Finally, the various enforced activities are brought together into a single rational plan purportedly designed to fulfil the official aims of the institution (Goffman, 1961, p. 6).

There is a basic split between 'inmates' and supervising 'staff', with great social distance between the two sides, who may perceive each other in narrow, hostile stereotypes. The staff keep control of all information and decisions affecting the inmate, who loses his autonomy and ceases to be seen, or to see himself, as occupying other social roles – father, employee, customer – outside the institution.

Some of these ideas have been tested in a study of different residential institutions for mentally handicapped children. The authors developed an index which was used to measure four processes of 'inmate management' most typical of total institutions. These were rigid, inflexible routines; regimentation of inmates; depersonalization of inmates; maintaining social distance between staff and inmates. All these processes were found in hospitals for the mentally subnormal but to a much lesser extent in non-medical children's homes or hostels for the subnormal, and the authors argued that this difference was due to the social structure of the hospitals themselves, which were hierarchical, over-departmentalized and too highly centralized, task-oriented rather than patient-oriented (King *et al.*, 1971).

Research has demonstrated the harmfulness to patients of those features of mental hospital life which resemble the culture of the total institution. A prolonged stay in such an environment will produce 'institutionalism':

apathy, loss of initiative and drive, dependence on the institution and unwillingness to think of leaving it. A case example may illustrate the plight of the long-stay psychiatric patient whose handicaps have been increased by prolonged residence in a total institution. Mr A was admitted to a mental hospital as a certified patient in 1940 when he was 31. He was diagnosed as schizophrenic, his reported symptoms being: 'He believes anyone has the right to take a piece of land if no-one else is farming it. He thinks buying and selling is wrong.' He was deluded that the hospital was full of Germans and 'probably has pyromanic tendencies'. There were no investigations into his social circumstances beyond the bare statement that he was a married farm worker. The case-notes observed that he was 'willing to talk about the theory of property and does so quite well in an unrealistic way'. In 1941 he tried to escape by jumping over the hospital wall but was docile when brought back; in 1942 he escaped from the railed Airing Court (now a thing of the past). No incidents are recorded in 1943 but there is one entry for each of the following two years recording that he was deluded, hallucinated and aggressive. In 1946 he again escaped briefly and the following year his wife divorced him. For the next thirteen years his life in hospital continued without incident. He remained in locked back wards and was assessed by a doctor about once each year. In 1961 the assessing psychiatrist found that he was 'near normality' and 'working well'. However he was reclassified and continued to be compulsorily detained under Section 26 of the 1959 Mental Health Act. In 1965 the notes record what seems to be a joke he was still able to make: when the doctor was called because he had been banging about in the ward he said, 'You must be hearing voices, I hear no noise'. In the late 1960s, he became increasingly aggressive and was sometimes involved in fights with other patients. The record ends in 1971 when he was given a thorough psychiatric assessment as he was to be included in a drug trial. There was no evidence of major psychiatric symptoms or abnormal thought processes but he had no wish to leave hospital. By this time he was 62 and had been detained in a locked mental hospital ward for 31 years.

However, a quite different form of social organization has also characterized mental hospitals. The principles of the 'moral treatment' movement in the eighteenth century were based on the conscious creation and use of a special social environment to ameliorate the effects of illness. The York Retreat, for example, founded in 1792 by William Tuke, a member of the Society of Friends, had only 30 patients and seven staff, giving a high staff-patient ratio which diminished the need for restraints and violent methods of control. The hospital regime laid great emphasis on social and religious activities which enabled patients to continue to play ordinary social roles and maintain links with the surrounding community. In this century the 'therapeutic community' movement has had a similarly beneficial and challenging effect on the custodial regimes of old mental hospitals. The main exponent of the therapeutic community has been Maxwell Jones. In this approach to the institutional treatment of mental illness the patient is not regarded as exempt from normal social rights and duties by virtue of his 'illness'. Rather, the distinction between staff and patients is blurred and both are seen as members of the community, sharing equally in the exercise of power in decision-making about community affairs. The climate is permissive, with all members tolerating a wide degree of deviant behaviour and communication being free and open. The medical staff are thus no longer seen as the only source of knowledge and treatment but the whole life of the hospital is seen as potentially therapeutic and utilized in daily group meetings where problems in living can be faced and worked through. There is little systematic study of the effects of this form of institution upon its inhabitants. The evidence suggests that attitudes of patients with neuroses or character disorders do change for the better while they are members of the community but that when they leave these attitude changes are not maintained.

Wing and Brown (1970) have studied groups of long-stay women schizophrenic patients in three large mental hospitals. They were interested in measuring the effects of different hospital regimes upon the patients' clinical and social state. Clinical condition was assessed by an interview which rated four symptoms (flatness of affect; poverty of speech; incoherence of speech; coherently expressed delusions) and by ratings of ward behaviour (social withdrawal and socially embarrassing behaviour). Institutionalism and dependence on the hospital were assessed. These clinical and social ratings could then be correlated with the social conditions the patients were experiencing in the hospital, as measured for example by the number of their personal possessions, how they spent their time during the day, occupation and contact with the outside world. These authors concluded that certain aspects of the social environment actually caused clinical improvement or deterioration: a social environment characterized by 'social poverty' – restrictiveness, lack of stimulation and interest – tended to cause social withdrawal, poverty of speech and flatness of affect. When social milieu was improved the clinical condition improved concomitantly. The most important single environmental factor associated with clinical improvement was a reduction in the amount of time spent doing nothing and especially increased participation in work or occupational therapy.

There seem to be two processes at work: an under-stimulating social environment tends to increase symptoms such as withdrawal, passivity and inertia; on the other hand social over-stimulation tends to cause breakdown with active hallucinations and delusions. The mental hospital unfortunately is liable to contain both sorts of noxious environment but it must be remembered that impoverished and over-stimulating social environments are also found outside the hospital and will have an equally damaging effect on schizophrenic patients.

Patients and families

The intimate social milieu of the nuclear family is far more pervasive in its influence on its members than the most encompassing of institutions. Families have been implicated as causal agents in the production of mental disorder, especially schizophrenia, and some of the research into the role of disturbed family patterns in the etiology of schizophrenic symptoms will now be mentioned. Two groups of American workers, both influenced by psychoanalytic insights, Lidz and his colleagues at Yale, and Bateson and his co-workers at Palo-Alto, have been most influential. Both groups start with the assumption that the family environment, the way parents interact with each other and their children, can explain the development of schizophrenic symptoms. Lidz viewed schizophrenia as a normal and understandable reaction to an abnormal family structure. Both fathers and mothers of future patients are described as grossly inadequate in their parental roles; their marriages are disturbed, characterized by patterns of 'schism' – open conflict between the partners and complete ignoring of each other's needs – or 'skew' – dominance by one abnormal and eccentric partner while the other plays a passive and subordinate role in the family. The child becomes involved in the parental conflict and learns from the parents the irrational thought patterns and abandonment of reality which will later become schizophrenic thought disorder. These theories, however, have been derived from the study of a very few, highly selected families, and subsequent empirical investigations have largely failed to confirm them (Hirsch and Leff, 1975).

In the work of Bateson and his colleagues (1956) the family is viewed as a social system with a pattern of reciprocal roles maintained by rules and prohibitions. Schizophrenic behaviour is seen as a specific pattern of communication which is integral to the functioning of the family. An example of the disturbed communication patterns which are believed to foster schizophrenic behaviour is the so-called 'double-bind'. In this kind of interaction one person, the speaker who is in a powerful position relative to the listener, expresses two messages which are incompatible with each other; an example is the mother who asks her son to come and kiss her while simultaneously stiffening and turning her face away. The recipient of this double message is prevented from exposing its inconsistencies and is unable to escape from the interaction. Thus he is presented repeatedly with intolerable conflicts from which he cannot escape except by leaning on schizophrenic 'strategy of behaviour' by which all his own communications are veiled, indirect and confusing. Although there is no research evidence to confirm the importance of the double-bind in the genesis of schizophrenia, later writers have systematically tested the hypothesis that abnormal communication patterns are characteristic of families with a schizophrenic child. Wynne and Singer argue that parents in such families communicate in obscure, vague and irrelevant ways that make it difficult for the listener to grasp the meaning of what is being said. This in turn affects the child's thought processes, interfering with his hold on reality and predisposing to schizophrenia. Under controlled conditions, some differences in communication patterns in families with a schizophrenic patient and normal families have been demonstrated (Hirsch and Leff, 1975).

The influence of family life on the course, as opposed to the genesis, of schizophrenic illness has also been extensively studied. It has been demonstrated that the emotional climate within the family where the patient is living has a decisive influence on whether or not he will relapse with a further flare-up of symptoms. When a patient leaves hospital after recovery and goes to live with relatives whose relationship with him has been marked by high levels of expressed criticism, hostility and emotional over-involvement, the chances of relapse are extremely high. In fact the best single predictor of a patient's relapse is the level of emotion expressed about him by a key relative at the time of his original admission to hospital. The practical implications of this finding for the planning of treatment and rehabilitation are obvious since, if there is no way of avoiding the patient's return to the unfavourable family environment and no way of modifying the relative's behaviour, at least protective measures can be instituted, such as limiting the amount of face-to-face contact and providing maintenance drug therapy (Vaughn and Leff, 1976).

What are the consequences for relatives of living with a mentally ill family member? First, there comes the confusion and distress caused by the initial stages of the illness, when the relatives must struggle to understand and cope with changes in a family member's behaviour and relationship with them. Relatives seem to try to 'normalize' strange and peculiar behaviour and put off recognizing it as symptomatic of mental illness. After the patient has entered treatment, relatives are often faced with problems in communicating with professionals such as doctors and social workers and may experience blame or implied criticism. The family may then have to care for a chronically handicapped person at home, and various studies have shown the serious effects that this can have on the relatives' mental and physical health, on their financial position and on social and leisure activities (Greer, 1975).

Attitudes to mental illness

Before discussing the provision of services for the mentally ill and their families we shall briefly mention research into public attitudes to the mentally ill and beliefs about mental illness. The amount of public tolerance and understanding is clearly an important determinant of what kinds of service organization are feasible and of how far 'community care' can become a reality. In spite of efforts to alter public attitudes, persons who are seen as mentally disordered tend to bear a stigma: the stigmatized person, and sometimes his relatives as well, feels insecure about how normal people will react to him, and may feel shame and inferiority as a result of having had psychiatric treatment. This may lead him to try to conceal his history or to restrict his contacts with 'normals' to avoid the pain of rejection.

Research into public attitudes and beliefs has been carried out by means of surveys, using hypothetical descriptions of people with mental disorders or statements designed to elicit negative and avoidance reactions, for example, 'I would rather not hire a person who had been in a mental hospital'. Findings suggest a rather pessimistic conclusion: that community attitudes to the mentally ill remain neutral so long as social distance can be maintained. It is when the ex-mental patient impinges directly upon the 'normal', as a potential neighbour or an employee for example, that unfavourable and rejecting attitudes are stimulated (Whately, 1968). Further, an experiment to test the effect of a health education campaign to alter attitudes to mental illness in a small community resulted in the unanticipated effect that community attitudes became more negative as the local inhabitants were bombarded with information and facts about mental illness (E. and J. Cumming, 1957). Thus stigmatizing attitudes still seem to be widespread and may not be responsive to traditional health education methods.

SERVICES FOR THE MENTALLY ILL

Services before 1959

The shape of services for the mentally ill has been largely determined by Victorian attitudes to mental illness and the institutions prompted by those attitudes (for an excellent historical account see Jones, 1972). The majority of the hundred-odd mental hospitals now in existence date from the Victorian era (none was built after the 1930s). Since the Victorians' belief was that mental disorder was incurable, their hospitals were built as custodial institutions. The aim was to provide a secure refuge for the patient but also to isolate him from the community, prevent escapes and provide constant supervision in an economic way. We have therefore inherited very large institutions, often in remote country sites, cut off from general medical services as well as from the local community.

The Victorian attitude to mental illness was enshrined in the 1890 Lunacy (Consolidation) Act, under which local authorities were compelled to provide asylums but treatment could be obtained only as an in-patient and with the agreement of a Justice of the Peace, and there were legal barriers to discharge from hospital. Not until 1930 did the Mental Treatment Act begin to reflect a more positive attitude towards insanity as an illness which could be treated, in its provisions that patients could be admitted to hospital on a voluntary basis, and for the establishment of out-patient clinics.

In the 1950s, however, important social and medical advances altered informed public attitudes and eventually resulted in a change in the law relating to mental disorder. In the early 1950s there were major pharmacological developments, in particular with the phenothiazene group of drugs which had tranquillizing effects on very disturbed patients. At the same time the attitudes of medical and nursing staff were changing and there was a more active approach to treatment and rehabilitation. These developments meant that after 1954, for the first time since the mental hospitals were built, there was a steady decline in the numbers of resident in-patients as discharge accelerated and duration of stay decreased.

However, three factors limited the extent to which these developments in mental health care could be fully exploited. Firstly, the mental health services were still operating essentially within the legal framework laid down by the 1890 Act, with its system of safeguards to prevent any sane person being detained in hospital, which also effectively prevented easy access to psychiatric treatment. Secondly, the hospitals had been designed for a custodial task, and very few resources had been allocated to replacing or updating them, even after the introduction of the National Health Service. Thirdly, although the 1930 Mental Treatment Act had authorized local authorities to make provision for out-patient clinics and after-care, no duty to do so had been imposed on them and very little provision had resulted. These three constraints – the legal framework, the allocation of resources, and the institutional emphasis – are still, in a modified form, operating on the development of the mental health services today.

The legal framework: The Mental Health Act, 1959

The innovations in psychiatric practice of the 1950s made it imperative to develop in response a new legal and administrative framework which would be more appropriate for the new aims of the services. The response was the establishment in 1954 of a Royal Commission on the Law relating to Mental Illness and Mental Deficiency (the Percy Commission) whose deliberations culminated in the achievement of the Mental Health Act of 1959 whose provisions are under review (D.H.S.S., 1976c). Under the Act 'mental disorder' is defined as meaning *mental illness*; *severe subnormality* – a state of arrested or incomplete development of the mind, which includes subnormality of intelligence, and which is of such a nature or degree that the patient is incapable of living an independent life or of guarding himself against exploitation; *subnormality* – a lesser state of arrested or incomplete development whereby the individual requires or is susceptible to medical treatment or other special care or training and is capable to some extent of living an independent life; *psychopathic disorder* – a persistent disorder or disability of mind which results in abnormally aggressive or seriously irresponsible conduct on the part of the patient and which requires or is susceptible to medical treatment. The Act, therefore, fails to provide a legal definition of mental illness as such, an omission which causes difficulties in situations involving a possible loss of liberty. The inclusion of 'psychopathy' as a category of mental disorder is also a contentious issue, owing partly to the difficulty of attaching a precise meaning to the term and also to the lack of any evidence to support the view that 'medical treatment' can influence this form of disorder.

The major importance of the Act was its removal of barriers which isolated the psychiatric services from other health and social services. The Act swept away the statutory limitation of treatment of the mentally ill in specially designated hospitals: any kind of hospital could now treat psychiatric patients and as much treatment as possible was to be informal and voluntary. However, various sections of the Act govern procedures for *compulsory admission to hospital.* To summarize briefly: Section 25 allows a patient to be detained in hospital for observation provided that he is suffering from mental disorder, as defined, and that his detention is necessary for his own safety or health or for other people's protection. Two medical opinions are required as well as an application from the patient's nearest relative or an approved social worker, and the period of detention lasts for 28 days. Section 29 allows for emergency detention for up to three days on the same grounds on one medical recommendation. Section 26 allows a patient to be detained for treatment for up to one year in the first instance with provisions for renewal. Section 30 allows a patient already in hospital to be detained for up to three days. Sections 135–6 allow the police to remove persons apparently suffering from mental disorder to a psychiatric hospital. Sections 60 and 65 govern compulsory admission of mentally disordered offenders through the courts, while Sections 72 and 74 relate to the transfer of mentally abnormal offenders from prisons to hospitals.

The decision to admit a person to hospital against his will rests on two broad criteria: first that he is suffering from a mental disorder; second that he is dangerous to himself or other people. Any interference with an individual's liberty raises difficult ethical problems. As Szasz (1974, p. xi) argues, 'If "mental illness" is a bona fide illness . . . then it follows, logically and linguistically, that it must be treated like any other illness. Hence, mental hygiene laws must be repealed. There are no special laws for patients with peptic ulcer or pneumonia; why then should there be special laws for patients with depression or schizophrenia?' This position sounds attractive but its consequences are perhaps less so. For example, people suffering from schizophrenia would be regarded as fully responsible for acts committed under the influence of delusional ideas and would be dealt with by the courts; again, the majority of people who kill themselves probably do so while in a mental state different from their normal one and usually given the psychiatric diagnosis of depression. Are they to be regarded as fully responsible people making a free choice or do they deserve some protection until they regain their normal functioning?

However, if people are to be deprived of their liberty in order to receive psychiatric treatment they have a right to be sure that procedures are not abused, that some effective treatment is available and that they are not worse off than they would have been as ordinary criminal offenders. Although only about 15 per cent of all psychiatric admissions involve any sort of compulsion it must be recognized that, for this minority, there are dangers of abuse. The rate of compulsory admissions varies widely between regions, suggesting that administrative practices rather than severity of illness are involved. The proportion of emergency admissions (the easiest to arrange and most likely to be abused) also varies widely – from one-third to three-quarters of all compulsory admissions in different regions. The MIND Reports on Patients' Rights and on the Mental Health Act have drawn attention to particular forms of abuse and called for a strengthening of safeguards (National Association for Mental Health, 1974; Gostin, 1977). One of the most important safeguards is the patient's right of appeal to a Mental Health Review Tribunal. These tribunals operate in each of the N.H.S. Regions and consist of a lawyer-chairman, a doctor and a lay member who are responsible to the Lord Chancellor's Office. The patient or his nearest relative, can apply to have a compulsory order removed. The tribunal, after meeting in the hospital and hearing from both sides, has powers to discharge patients detained in hospital (except for those under a Restriction order). About 14 per cent of all applications made result in a patient's discharge, a proportion which is greatly increased when the patient has a representative to help him prepare his case. The MIND Reports argue that provision of lay representatives for all patients and better channelling of information to patients about their rights are needed. However, even more important is the lack of resources, both for effective help in psychiatric emergencies arising in the community and for rehabilitation and resettlement of patients who have received hospital treatment, which ensures that many are unnecessarily admitted to hospital and remain there after the need for treatment is past.

The third important set of provisions in the Mental Health Act are those deriving from its expressed aim of reorienting mental health services away from hospital towards care in the community. Local authorities were given powers to provide a wide range of services: social work support, day care, employment and residential care. These powers, however, were only permissive and local authorities were not obliged to develop their services to provide a genuine alternative to care in the hospital.

Organization of services: the shift to 'Community Care'

Since 1959 the decline in the numbers of patients resident in mental hospitals has continued. In 1973 there were 94,185 resident in-patients, a fall of over 20 per cent in six years. Two groups of patients now dominate the resident population: those who remain in hospital for less than a year – nearly a third of the total; and those who have been continuously in hospital for five or more years – over half the total. This group, predominantly elderly and largely made up of patients admitted in the period before active treatment and rehabilitation were available, is declining but it will take at least 20 years to reduce it by three-quarters. A proportion of patients admitted under contemporary conditions still become long-stay but this too appears to be a declining problem. Thus, long-stay patients are gradually declining because new patients are not being recruited to replace those who die or are discharged.

The rate of *admissions* to psychiatric hospitals, which rose steadily until 1970, now appears to have levelled off. Indeed, first admissions (about a third of all admissions) are actually falling although readmissions appear to be still increasing. Thus fewer people referred to a psychiatrist are now admitted to hospital, and this downward trend is true for patients with psychotic as well as neurotic conditions. (However, admissions for alcoholism are rising sharply.) Over a fifth of admitted patients stay only a few weeks and are not readmitted, and another large group of mostly elderly patients remain for several years. The group who pass again and again through the hospitals' revolving doors are those, usually younger, given diagnoses of schizophrenia, personality disorder, neurosis and alcoholism, people who under the old regime would probably have stayed permanently in hospital (D.H.S.S., 1976a).

It is clear, therefore, that the reorientation of psychiatric care away from the institution, which the framers of the Mental Health Act hoped to see, is indeed taking place. Has this been matched by a growth of provisions in the community or, in the words of the Seebohm Report (1968, para. 339), is 'the widespread belief that we have community care for the mentally disordered – for many parts of the country still a sad illusion'?

'Community care' is still apt to be interpreted as separate from and antagonistic to hospital care, thus continuing the unwanted segregation of the hospital and its patients. In fact, of course, hospitals are part of a community's facilities for caring for its mentally disordered members, and what is needed is an integrated range of services for the mentally ill of a defined local community where the service provided is determined by the patient's needs and handicaps at any one time. The hospital is at one end of this continuum while independent living with support from family, friends and general practitioner is at the other. A chronic schizophrenic patient may need to move gradually from a fully supervised hospital ward, to a less supervised hospital unit and finally to a small group home in the community with support from the Day Centre; on the other hand the depressed young woman who takes an overdose of sleeping pills may need immediate but short-term help from a skilled counsellor who can help with relationship and practical problems. Either effort may be doomed to failure without a network of caring people and groups in the local neighbourhood to whom the 'patient' can be linked.

Reintegration of hospital care within the community

It has been official policy since 1961 to abolish the separate mental hospitals and replace them with psychiatric teams based on District General Hospitals. These new units will take all psychiatric patients (apart from the elderly) including the severely disturbed. The specialist psychiatric team will consist of psychiatrists, nurses, social workers, psychologists and occupational therapists. It should ultimately have at its disposal (rates per 100,000 population) 50 in-patient beds and 40 beds for the elderly mentally infirm, with special new units for patients, usually with schizophrenia, who need longer-term care. It will have rather more day-hospital places. In addition, the local authority social services department will provide some 30 residential places, both long and short-stay, and 60 day-centre places. An essential complement to the local district services will be regional facilities for disturbed young people and secure units for patients who cannot be contained on open wards. Linked with these specialized facilities will be the primary care teams based in general practice and the local authority social services Area teams (D.H.S.S., 1975).

How visionary it alls sounds to those who are experiencing the present services, whether as providers or consumers. At present three-quarters of all psychiatric admissions are to the old mental hospitals (D.H.S.S., 1976a); the average consultant psychiatrist is responsible for 154 in-patients at any one time and, if he is conscientious, has five minutes a week to spare for each long-stay in-patient (Clare, 1976); as recently as 1971, 40 per cent of local authorities had no hostel provision, two-thirds had no day centres and

60 per cent had no group homes or other subsidized living arrangements. The reorganization of the Social Services in 1971 may in the short term have worsened the situation of the mentally ill patient by limiting the development of mental health social work and perhaps as a consequence leading to a decline in social work interest in this field (Neill *et al.*, 1976). Nevertheless such a clear statement of official objectives is useful as a long-term strategy which can guide future developments.

The burden on the community

The trend towards a run-down in institutional provision without, at present, sufficient increase in compensatory non-institutional provision means that 'the community' has to assume caring and rehabilitative functions formerly performed by the hospitals. In some cases this means that ex-patients of mental hospitals are sleeping rough, or are in lodging houses or prisons. However, the people most likely to be taking up the hospital's role are the patient's family. How heavily are families burdened? A number of studies suggest that the burden may be a severe one and that the policy of admitting fewer patients and for shorter periods probably leads to more social hardship for their families, even though families seem to accept this burden without complaint (Grad and Sainsbury, 1968).

'Community care', therefore, is a vision of the future rather than a reality of the present. Yet, as we have tried to show earlier in this chapter, mental illness cannot be divorced from the social context in which it appears and is sustained, and so 'treatment' cannot be confined within the walls of the hospital. If social factors are important in the course and outcome of mental illnesses, then patients must be treated as far as possible in the local community in which they will have to find a role. Thus although it is sometimes easy to despair and accept that 'the sum of any patient's effective community is ... not more numerous than those paid employees of the institution which discharged him', it is important to ensure that community care can become more of a reality (Hawks, 1975).

Allocation of resources

There are two aspects to the problem of resource allocation in the field of mental illness: first, the balance between health resources allocated to mental illness as opposed to other specialities; second, the balance between spending on hospitals and that on social services for the mentally ill. Mental illness accounts for 29 per cent of all hospital beds (and mental handicap for another 15 per cent). Yet only 11 per cent of all consultants are psychiatrists and one-fifth of all nurses work in psychiatric units for the mentally ill (Clare, 1976). There are important disparities in resources between psychiatric and other hospitals, involving not only manpower but also expenditure on a patient's maintenance and even on his food. (This disparity reflects the general underprivilege of chronic as opposed to acute illness.) It is hardly surprising that scandals erupt in old hospitals, often still lacking basic amenities, that are chronically under-staffed. Psychiatry has a good claim to a rather larger share of health expenditure, recognized by governments over the years and re-emphasized in the Consultative Document on policies and priorities in the health field over the next five years (D.H.S.S., 1976b).

The imperative needs of the hospitals make it difficult, particularly in a time of economic stringency, to shift resources from them to social services in the community, and the difficulty is compounded by the separation of administrative responsibility between health authorities and local authority social services departments. If community care is to become a reality there must be a significant increase in local authority spending on services for the mentally ill, on hostels, day centres, group homes and trained staff, yet there seems little possibility of such an increase in the immediate future. The reality is that the old mental hospitals and institutional psychiatry will continue to have the major responsibility for the care of the most severely and chronically ill patients for a long time to come: fortunately these services, in spite of their disadvantages, contain innovators who will continue to move out into the community and develop their service in partnership with any interested people and groups they can find there. The reorganization of the National Health and Personal Social Services should ultimately facilitate more collaborative planning and resource transfer through the statutory coordinating groups – the Joint Consultative Committees at Area level and the Health Care Planning Teams in the Districts. However, for the next decade or more, the mental health services will be faced with problems of priorities, of scarcity and maldistribution of resources. In these circumstances some desirable community developments will have to be sacrificed so that the needs of the present patient population can be better met. Perhaps the specialized psychiatric services should at present be seen as mental *illness* services whose first responsibility is to patients with serious mental disorder and to the inherited chronic patient population.

CHAPTER 5

The Disabled

Few recent policy documents in the field of health and welfare have failed to mention the disabled (D.H.S.S., 1974, 1976a, b; C.C.E.T.S.W., 1976). The need to develop supportive services and train members of caring professions to meet the needs of the disabled is widely acknowledged, and there have been many developments in this field.

In the winter of 1968–9, the Office of Population Censuses and Surveys undertook a survey to discover how many disabled people there were in Britain, and even before the report of this investigation was published (Harris, 1971) the Chronically Sick and Disabled Persons' Act was passed in 1970, hailed as the disabled person's charter. It was followed in 1971 by the introduction of an Invalidity Pension in place of the previous indefinite Sickness Benefit, payable to disabled persons under the National Insurance Scheme, and an Attendance Allowance for very severely disabled persons being cared for at home.

Since then there have been a number of studies, reports and developments concerned with the disabled. There have been efforts, for example, to define the concept of disability, since any consideration of the needs of and provision for disabled people rests on the meaning attached to 'disablement' (Harris, 1971; Garrad, 1974; Topliss, 1975; Sainsbury, 1973). It is probably impossible to define disability adequately without reference to the individual's social context, since what is at issue is a person's capacity to perform the normal functions of life. The demands made on a person obviously vary according to the culture in which he lives and his social position within that society, so that his capacity or lack of capacity for life is related to his social context. In other words, disablement is not simply absence of perfect health (which itself cannot be unambiguously defined) but implies departure from standards of fitness and performance normal in the society, or strata of society, in which the individual lives. There is a

122

record, for example, of a society where the population generally exhibited very noticeable skin blemishes, or spots. This condition was therefore accepted as normal to the extent that young men and women who wanted to marry but did not show any spots, were deemed abnormal and unfit to found a family in that society (Dubos, 1965) – in other words, they were handicapped.

While it may be rare to find such reversals of what we in our society regard as normal, it is still true that the boundaries of what constitutes disability are blurred. Only in 1971, for instance, was alcoholism officially designated a disease, rather than moral deviance (Home Office, 1971) – and there still are many in our society who regard the alcoholic as a deviant but not disabled person. There is similar confusion about the boundary between those disabled for normal living by mental illness and those who are morally degenerate, as in the case of the psychopath, or the repetitive thief, or the unreliable and very intermittent worker. There is also disagreement as to the degree of physical limitation which can be accepted as 'normal' – over whether, for example, a rheumatic joint which limits a middle-aged woman's capacity for dancing or running up and down stairs constitutes disability or is merely part of growing older.

It is not surprising, therefore, that the attempts to define disability continue. In particular, there is a growing recognition that degrees and types of disablement need to be classified in a way that is related to the extent of the individual's handicap in life (Blaxter, 1976). This means that merely attaching the medical label for the condition causing disablement is inadequate, since a victim of, for example, cerebral palsy may have minimal brain damage, be able to walk and talk normally and be of normal intelligence, or he may be utterly helpless, incontinent and mentally defective. There is a need, therefore, for a generally accepted, simply operated, classification system which would identify the misfunctions or lack of functions consequent upon a given condition, which affect a person's capacity for what is accepted as normal living in such spheres as personal care, employment, family relationships, and social and leisure activities.

The present lamentable lack of such a system of classification is very apparent when one reviews the complex welter of provisions for the disabled. It is not, however, the intention of this work to undertake such a review, which could not be encompassed within one chapter, and which is in any case the subject of a recent book by the present writer (Topliss, 1975). It is instead intended to concentrate on the implications for family life of disablement in one of its members; on residential care for the disabled; and on the debate over the relative emphasis to be placed on integration rather than segregation of disabled people. These areas are believed to be of particular concern to those in the caring professions likely to be involved with disabled individuals and their families.

FAMILY LIFE AND DISABLEMENT

Although the precise impact of disablement on family life depends on the position within the family of the disabled person, a growing body of literature suggests that whether it is a handicapped husband, or wife, or child, or elderly parent, the disablement has an effect on the relationships and opportunities of the family as a whole.

One area in which disablement makes its impact is that of family finance. It must be remembered that disablement usually, if not always, involves extra expense – for heating, transport, domestic or maintenance chores, etc. – and therefore a below-average income for a family with a disabled member implies a greater degree of financial stringency than would the same income going to an able-bodied household.

Where the disabled person is the husband or breadwinner, and the disablement results in loss of employment, the family as a whole will in most cases suffer the deprivations of poverty. The National Insurance Invalidity Benefit, paid to some 465,000 persons in 1976, is at a rate little higher than the standard Supplementary Benefit level, which is itself tied to an officially determined subsistence level. This means that the 465,000 Invalidity Benefit recipients and their families will be living very close to the poverty line, and the extra expenses of disablement may push many families below it. Few of the Invalidity Benefit claimants will be married women, since these, even if they have been in paid employment, have not normally paid National Insurance contributions at a rate to qualify them for Invalidity Benefit.

There are also some 500,000 recipients of Industrial Disablement or War Disablement pensions, who will in general be rather better off than those receiving National Insurance Invalidity Benefit, because of the more generous rates and allowances payable, and because such pensions continue to be payable even if the recipient is in employment. Those unable to work, however, are still likely to have incomes below the national average household income. The General Household Survey of 1973 found that only

17 per cent of households where the couple were under 65 had an income of less than £40 per week, but in the same year a survey of disabled people under 65 in Southampton showed 85 per cent of such households to have an income of under £40 per week.

In addition to the above groups of disablement pensioners, totalling nearly a million recipients, there were in 1976 some 125,000 claimants of the Non-Contributory Invalidity Pension, which was introduced for the first time in November 1975. This is paid at a rate which is roughly equal to half the ordinary Invalidity Benefit. The N.C.I.P., as it has become known, is payable to people under retirement age, *other than married women,* who are unable to work owing to disability, but who have not got a National Insurance contribution record to entitle them to the National Insurance Invalidity Pension. These will mainly be congenitally disabled men and single women.

The introduction of the N.C.I.P. in November 1975 did not, however, really represent an increase in the incomes of 125,000 disabled people and their families to the full extent of £9.20 per week each. Nearly half these claimants were formerly totally dependent on Supplementary Benefit, which is reduced by the amount of the N.C.I.P. so that the net income of the recipients remained unchanged. This may be the reason for an estimated 60,000 disabled individuals who are eligible for the N.C.I.P. failing to claim it. A further 45 per cent of the claimants are patients in long-stay hospitals, the majority of them mentally handicapped people who have lived permanently in institutional care and who often had no personal pocket money at all. It had been planned to ensure that all such long-stay patients received a small sum weekly as pocket money, and the government had envisaged making this a charge on the Supplementary Benefits Commission. Instead, with the introduction of the N.C.I.P., such long-stay patients will each receive a standard amount of pocket money, the balance of the N.C.I.P. to which they are entitled being deducted at source as the patient is maintained without charge in a National Health Service institution. Only the pocket-money element of the N.C.I.P. for these patients in long-stay hospitals really represents an increase in government expenditure. For these 45 per cent of N.C.I.P. claimants, therefore, there has been a real increase in their financial well-being, but only at the rate of £3.20 per week pocket money. Furthermore, as all these pocket-money recipients are in institutional care, the improvement in their welfare, real and welcome though it is, cannot be counted as help to *families* caring for a disabled member in the community.

Only eight per cent of the 125,000 claimants of the N.C.I.P. really benefit at the full rate. These are people whose income from savings or private pensions was already at or above subsistence level and who therefore were not eligible for Supplementary Benefit. For these 10,000 individuals and their families, the introduction of the N.C.I.P., which is non-taxable, represents a very real increase in living standards. A further 10,000 claimants have, by receiving the N.C.I.P., raised their total income to a point where they do not need to claim any support from the Supplementary Benefits Commission, and so can avoid submitting to a means test. Among them, however, may be some who will find that by claiming the N.C.I.P. instead of Supplementary Benefit, they have lost their entitlement to discretionary allowances which go only to Supplementary Benefit recipients, such as special heating, dietary or clothing allowances. These disabled individuals and their families may actually be worse off by claiming the N.C.I.P. than they would have been by remaining on Supplementary Benefit.

From the government's own figures, which gave a net annual cost of £12,000,000 for the N.C.I.P. at the rates which applied in 1975–6, it is clear that the average recipient will benefit very little by the introduction of this new pension. A third of the £12,000,000 went to the eight per cent of claimants who benefit in full. The remaining £8,000,000 spread over the other 115,000 claimants represented an average net increase in 1975 of just over £1 per week – a negligible increase in a period of rapidly rising prices. Apart from this small cash advantage, recipients of N.C.I.P. are credited with National Insurance contributions. This enables them to build up a contribution record, which would mean, for example, that recipients could become eligible for a National Insurance retirement pension at 65 (60 for women) rather than apply for Supplementary Benefit which, although paid at the same rate as the Retirement Pension, is means-tested.

It is clear that the financial support measures in Britain for working-age people who are disabled and cannot work are such that, for the majority of these individuals and their families, the tragedy of disablement is compounded by the grinding hardship of poverty.

Even those disabled individuals who are able to continue in employment, are concentrated in the lower-paid occupational groups (Buckle, 1971). For many, disablement results in loss of occupational status. In 1974 a survey (data from which are incorporated in this chapter) of 1,095 physically disabled persons under retirement age and living in private households was carried out in Southampton, supported by the Social Science Research

Council and with the cooperation of the local authority. This survey showed that 40 per cent of the economically active disabled people claimed to hold some qualifications, but that, nonetheless, they were concentrated in the semi-skilled and unskilled jobs. Of the disabled men in employment who held some qualification, one-third had completed an apprenticeship for skilled manual work, but after their disablement only half of them continued to be employed as skilled workers.

Disablement then, even when it does not mean complete loss of employment opportunities, often results in a marked reduction of earning capacity. In the Southampton survey it was found that although 42 per cent of the disabled respondents over school-leaving age were in employment, 85 per cent of all the disabled were in households with an income which was below the average adult male earnings in that year, and half the households with a disabled member had an income at or below the poverty line.

It has, perhaps, been generally appreciated that disablement of the breadwinner, with consequent loss of employment, results in financial disadvantage. It has probably been less widely realized that a disabled person who managed to continue in employment is also likely to experience financial stringency. Even less obvious is the effect on family income of disablement not of the breadwinner, but of the housewife. Failure to appreciate this probably accounts for the fact that there was no pension for disabled housewives until 1977, when the N.C.I.P. was extended to married women who were unable to take up paid employment *and* unable to perform normal household duties. The Attendance Allowance is also available to those so severely disabled as to need continuous attention by day, or by night, or throughout the 24 hours, and a Mobility Allowance is payable to disabled adults under retirement age whose disability makes them unable, or virtually unable to walk. Valuable though these benefits are to those who receive them, it nonetheless remains that families with a disabled housewife appear to suffer financially almost as much as those where the breadwinner is disabled. In the Southampton survey, whereas 85 per cent of all families with a disabled member had an income below £40 per week, 79 per cent of those households where the disabled person was the housewife had an income below £40 per week. (The introduction of the Housewife's Non-Contributory Invalidity Pension may reduce the percentage of families with such low incomes.) It was not that, in most cases, the husband had given up work to care for his disabled wife, but many husbands spoke of being unable to do overtime because they were needed at home, and some thought that their domestic burdens had reduced their promotion opportunities. Above all, the disabled wives themselves were far less likely to be in paid employment than were able-bodied wives of the same age group. Families with a disabled housewife, therefore, are likely to lack the second income that is so common in most marriages, except for the years when the children are very young.

When the Non-Contributory Invalidity Pension was eventually extended to housewives, it was paid to disabled married women who were unable to take up paid employment and *also* unable to cope with their housekeeping duties. In other words, eligibility for the Housewife's Non-Contributory Invalidity Pension will be based on a more stringent definition of disability than is the case with men and single women.

The married woman is also excluded from benefiting from the new Invalid Care Allowance, introduced in July 1976. This is payable to those, other than married women, who give up work in order to care for a disabled relative who is in receipt of the Attendance Allowance. A husband who gives up work to care for his disabled wife may claim the Invalid Care Allowance, but a wife who cannot take up employment because she is looking after her disabled husband, will not qualify for the Invalid Care Allowance. Similarly, a single woman who gives up her job in order to care for an elderly parent will be eligible for the Invalid Care Allowance, but not a married woman who gives up her job to undertake a similar caring role for a parent. Up till the introduction of the Invalid Care Allowance, a man or single woman who gave up work to care for a disabled relative could claim Supplementary Benefit. Such people will now, instead, be eligible for the Invalid Care Allowance, which while it may not increase their total income, because Supplementary Benefit will be reduced accordingly, will mean that they are credited with National Insurance contributions while in receipt of the Invalid Care Allowance, thus safeguarding future National Insurance entitlements.

On the whole, a handicapped child in a family does not greatly affect the family's income level, at least at first, since most mothers with young children do not work, and accept a period of relatively low family income. Once the child is older and at school, however, the majority of mothers return to at least part-time paid employment. It is at this stage that the demands of a handicapped child are likely to have most effect on restricting the mother's ability to take up employment (Hewett, 1970; Anderson, 1973). This is particularly likely if there is delay in finding a school place or if, after leaving school, there is no place in sheltered employment or in an occupational centre for a severely disabled young person.

Although so far we have discussed mainly the financial stresses in a family containing a disabled member, this is certainly not because it is considered that money difficulties are the principal consequence of disability in the family. It is merely that the financial consequences can be quantified and objectively assessed. The deeper emotional impact of disability, both on the individual himself and on his family, is much more difficult to analyse. It is, however, likely to be of far greater significance than the material disadvantages.

There are some subjective accounts of the awareness of disability written by individuals incapacitated by various diseases (Hunt, 1966). There have also been attempts by sociologists and psychologists to describe the process of adapting to disability (Schontz, 1962; Goffman, 1963). Despite the fact that all these accounts of reactions to disability stress the significance for the disabled individual of how other people regard him, very little work has been done on the emotional impact of disability not only on the individual who is disabled, but also on the members of his family and on relationships between them. Most of the work that has been done is concerned with the husband/wife relationship (Fink *et al.*, 1968; Carpenter, 1974; Stewart, 1976). Vital though this is, it is not the only significant relationship, as those between parent and child, and between siblings, are also important, but have attracted little research (Hewett, 1970; Sanford, 1975).

It seems quite clear from studies so far carried out, that not only does the man or woman disabled after marriage have to reshape his or her marital role to take account of the disability, but spouses also have to adjust their roles correspondingly. One American study (Fink *et al.*, 1968) investigated the lives of 36 married women who had become disabled, to see how far their disability affected the satisfaction of their own needs and those of their husbands. The study concentrated on the disabled wife, rather than the disabled husband, because it was argued that:

> The wife-mother is usually the focal point of the family around whom most of the important activities in the home take place. When her health is impaired and she is unable to perform her usual role, the equilibrium of all family members, as well as the stability of the family as a social unit, is seriously jeopardized. [p. 64]

If this argument is accepted, it suggests that the wife's role, much more than the husband's, is centred around preserving and developing family relationships (Parsons and Bales, 1955). Her satisfactions, therefore, will depend upon her sense of achievement in these areas, whereas her husband, having a different role, regards such matters as less important. This probably explains the fact that the American wives who were studied were found to express far more satisfaction with the companionship they shared with their husbands, than did the respective husbands. For the disabled wives, the fact that their husbands had to spend more time at home looking after them only emphasized the home as a focal point in both their lives and was regarded as an increase in companionship. The husband, however, still wanted a wife who could accompany him on activities outside the home, and therefore registered dissatisfaction with the level of companionship remaining in marriage after the wife's disability.

On the other hand, a number of husbands in the study who were reasonably satisfied with life despite the severe disability of their wives, were found to derive considerable satisfaction from their work or social activities undertaken independently of their wives. The researchers recognized that they were looking at a biased sample, since they investigated the lives only of disabled married women whose marriages had survived the impact of disablement. The study is, however, very suggestive, since it indicates that satisfaction with the domestic aspects of marriage may be greatly reduced for an able-bodied husband having a disabled wife, though the same might not necessarily be true for an able-bodied wife having a disabled husband, since for her his dependence would merely intensify her home-centred role. In her capacity as a mother, also, she has experience of caring for children at all stages of dependence, from the totally dependent infant to the nearly independent adolescent, so that she has a ready made model on which to base her care of her disabled husband.

To the extent that the modern young woman is less home-centred than her mother, so her conception of her role may be changing, and it may prove almost as difficult for her as for a man to find satisfaction in the companionship of a disabled spouse. Apart, however, from the increasing tendency of successive cohorts of married women to take up employment outside the home, there is little evidence that women *are* becoming less home-centred. It is still a small minority of marriages which remain voluntarily childless, and most wives give up work altogether while their children are young, returning later only to such work (often part-time) as is compatible with their domestic duties. It would seem, therefore, that women continue to put heavy emphasis on their home-making and family relationships role. They may well, then, continue to be satisfied with the home-centred companionship of their husbands, whether this is imposed by their own disability or that of their spouse.

If this interpretation is correct, it would indicate that a marriage is at greater risk if the wife becomes disabled than if the husband does; and the risk becomes greater still if the husband cannot find success and satisfaction in his work role to compensate for the loss of the type of active companionship which his disabled wife can no longer give. The fact that several husbands of disabled women included in the Southampton survey expressed the view that their need to spend a good deal of time looking after domestic matters and caring for their disabled wives had interfered with their promotion prospects and earning capacity, suggests that for many husbands dissatisfaction at the loss of the active companionship of their wives is aggravated by their feelings of lost job opportunities. This may explain the high rate of breakdown of marriage among disabled women in the survey – 16 per cent of them were divorced or separated, compared with a national divorce rate of seven per cent. On the other hand, among the disabled men in the survey, only four per cent were divorced or separated. The sample of disabled people was, like disabled people in the population generally, disproportionately concentrated in older age groups, and divorce among older marriage cohorts is less common. It may be that the divorce rate for disabled men in the sample reflects the older average age of disabled people rather than any real tendency for marriages where the husband is disabled to be more stable than average. There is no doubt, however, that the marriage breakdown rate among the disabled women in the sample, who were also predominantly middle-aged, and might therefore be expected to have a low divorce rate, reflects the greater instability of marriages where the wife is disabled. (This corroborates Sainsbury (1970) who concluded that marriages were more likely to break up when the wife rather than the husband was disabled. A contrary finding was reported by Blaxter (1976), but her sample was very small.)

One area of companionship about which there has been increased concern lately is that of sexual relationships. In 1973, the National Fund for Research into Crippling Diseases set up a committee to enquire into the sexual implications and aspects of disability. This committee produced a report of its findings (Stewart,1976) but decided that the extent of the problem and the lack of help available to disabled people, warranted the continuation of the committee's work. The group, known by its acronym of SPOD (Sexual Problems of the Disabled), is therefore on-going, organizing conferences, promoting understanding, and offering help and advice, on the sexual problems of the disabled.

According to the committee's report, all severely handicapped people experienced sexual problems associated with their disability, and most disabled people, whatever the level of their handicap, at some time suffered some sexual impediment associated with it.

Yet only about a quarter of the disabled people included in the SPOD survey were impotent or partially impotent (in women this was defined as lack of clitoral/vaginal sensitivity). Another group of disabled people were found to experience difficulty in sexual relations because certain postures were uncomfortable or impossible, yet practically none had received any advice on how to overcome the difficulties. The majority of sexual problems, however, seemed to be rooted in the outlooks and norms of society in general. The report refers to the tendency of the general public to write off the disabled as sexual beings. Another writer (Lancaster-Gaye, 1972) has suggested that this is because the very idea of the sexual union of disabled people gives rise to disgust and revulsion in the minds of many able-bodied people, and they therefore choose to ignore the subject.

Such an attitude militates against the development of facilities and services to encourage the sexual development of disabled young people. The severely disabled, heavily dependent on others to organize their environment and social activities, find the opportunities to form friendships leading to courtship and marriage frustrated by lack of privacy. The less disabled who achieve greater independence to mix fairly freely are likely to form friendships with able-bodied young people, but when it comes to love, they may find that the modern emphasis on physical attractiveness and glamour as a basis for sexual relations militates against the acceptance as a sexual partner of anyone less than physically perfect. So far, however, there is little if any counselling available to disabled young people to help them cope with their awakening sexuality, in the context of an unhelpful, even unsympathetic, society.

For someone who becomes disabled after marriage, the impact of disability on the couple's sexual relationship may be far more severe than the actual degree of functional loss makes inevitable, because both the disabled person and the spouse will enter the new situation with the legacy of their able-bodied past and the norms which link sex with physical perfection and attractiveness. The problems are likely to be greater when the disability is the result of sudden trauma. In a slowly progressing disease, the couple have time to adjust their outlook gradually and to adapt their practices in order to give sexual expression to their affection in a manner compatible with the declining physical capacities of the disabled person. The couple must work out this adjustment for themselves, however, as again it is extremely rare for any counselling to be offered in such a case.

The ability to give such counselling is itself sadly lacking. For most medical students there is very little teaching on rehabilitation of the disabled. Even when it is taught, it tends to be limited to the rehabilitation of a disabled person as far as personal care and hygiene are concerned. Rehabilitation for the activities of employment is undertaken in some hospital settings, but rehabilitation for social life, including personal relationships and sex, is virtually absent from the teaching of medical students. It is not surprising therefore, if doctors feel themselves unable to give counsel in the sexual problems of disabled people.

No other professional group is any better trained than the doctors to give such help. The Spinal Injuries Association has been particularly aware of this issue since so many (about 80 per cent) of those disabled in accidents leading to permanent injury and paralysis, are young adults who before their accident were enjoying or were about to embark upon an active sex life. This Asssociation now tries to arrange for every newly paralysed patient to be visited while still in hospital by someone who has experienced such an accident, and learned to cope with disablement. From experience, the longer-disabled can reassure and advise the newly-disabled on aspects of living with paralysis, including living a sex life. This may, indeed, be the best possible source of advice, coming from experience. Nonetheless, there is a vital need for doctors, nurses, social workers and the general public to be as ready to raise the issue of sex with disabled people as they are with the able-bodied, in order to demonstrate to the disabled person that his sexuality is normal, and that any improvisation or technique which facilitates the expression of his sexuality is a step towards overcoming one of the handicaps of his disablement.

Where the disabled member of the family is a child, not only is the parent/child relationship likely to be affected, which most people can readily understand, but also the relationship between the spouses. It is significant that the Spastic Society leaflet 'The Handicapped Child Within the Family' intended for parents of cerebral-palsied children, carries a paragraph headed 'How is your marriage holding up?' It begins: 'Not such an impertinent question as it sounds – there are many problems in having a handicapped child which can be a great strain in marriage'.

The leaflet does not go on to spell out the strains in detail, but from other publications by the Society, and from studies of families with handicapped children (Hewett, 1970; Tizard and Grad, 1961), one fact soon becomes obvious – that caring for a handicapped child absorbs even more of the mother's time and energy than does the care of an able-bodied infant, and the dependence of the handicapped child lasts much longer. These studies also indicate that mothers with handicapped children went out with their husbands less often, on average, than did mothers of able-bodied children of the same age. One can assume, therefore, that the degree of active companionship a mother with a handicapped child can offer her husband is less than the couple would otherwise share. In the case of disabled wives, it appears that husbands do not find home-bound companionship an adequate substitute for the companionship of their wives in outside activities. It may well be that even if fathers of handicapped children shared a good deal of the care of the child, such home-bound companionship with their wives would not compensate for the loss of more active forms of companionship, and marital dissatisfaction and stress would result. Once again, if the American findings are correct (Fink *et al.*, 1968), there will be a tendency for such husbands, however loyal to their wives, to seek self-satisfaction in their careers, but this could mean they were less available to help at home, and would leave the burden of care for the handicapped child on the mother, leading to still greater stress.

Despite the strain of caring for a handicapped child, however, most families do give such care in their own homes. With a severely disabled child, the difficulties of caring increase with time. A tiny child can be lifted and carried about, protected and restricted, without too much physical effort on the part of the caring person. The older, heavier and stronger the disabled child, the more physically demanding becomes the caring role. Ultimately the ageing parent is unable to continue giving such care, and a residential placement for the disabled person becomes the only practical solution. It is the anticipation of this time that adds to the distress of parents with a handicapped child, and indeed to the distress of the disabled person himself. In Southampton it was found that while only 28 respondents out of over 1,000 disabled people who were surveyed had ever considered the possibility of residential care, six of these were parents of quite young handicapped children who said they dreaded the time when they could no longer cope and would have to let their disabled son or daughter go into a home.

The agony of mind of such parents is revealed by a letter which appeared in the *Birmingham Evening Mail* of 14 March 1974, written by the elderly parents of a severely mentally handicapped son who was then 34. They had been searching vainly for a home where they felt their son could be happy, now that they were too old to look after him much longer, and they concluded their despairing letter:

We would give every penny we possess if we could know that this kind of future [i.e. what he had been used to at home with them] is a possibility for him.

    If it isn't, then it may well be that the kindest thing we could do is to take him with us when we go, if we could summon the courage to take that step.

It is clear, from the ages of the majority of unmarried disabled people who enter residential care, that parents go on looking after their disabled sons and daughters long after the parents have reached an age when they themselves could do with a respite. This means that there are a number of extremely vulnerable households where elderly parents are caring for a disabled offspring, and where any moment there could be a complete breakdown of care, due to the illness or death of the parent. This was indeed the picture revealed in Southampton when emergency admissions of disabled people to hospital care were examined. (This information comes from a study, not yet published, by the Department of Rehabilitation at the University of Southampton Medical School.) The admissions were frequently necessitated not by illness of the persons admitted, but by a breakdown of their care system, and this breakdown was most frequently due to the collapse of an elderly parent.

RESIDENTIAL CARE

At present the only real choice for a disabled person is between family care, for the most part unsupported by outside help or services, and institutional care. Although in theory the personal social services can provide a good deal of assistance to disabled people living with their families in the community, in practice the help received is minimal. The Home Help Service, for example, is concentrated on the elderly, and less than seven per cent of calls made by this service are to families looking after a disabled member. Again, it is only a minority of disabled people living in the community who, through the social services, receive home adaptations, attend clubs or occupational centres, or are given holidays or offered transport to and from leisure activities (D.H.S.S., 1975).

    There is no indication that, despite greater public concern about disabled people, there is any increase in the supporting services received by them. For instance, whereas in 1969 83 per cent of all home-help cases were elderly people, in 1975 when the numbers of home helps had increased, 87 per cent of home-help cases were elderly people, and these 87 per cent of cases took up 93 per cent of the total number of calls made by home helps during 1975. These figures, of course, reflect the increasing numbers of people living into old age. A number of these will suffer disabilities associated with advanced age and increasing frailty, and the increase in the home-help service by 44 per cent since 1969 has understandably been absorbed by the increasing numbers of elderly people. It is also understandable, for the same reasons, that 83 per cent of households receiving aid from the social services in the form of adaptations to the home to facilitate mobility or increase safety were elderly-person households. Nonetheless, however understandable it may be that the bulk of social service support goes to the elderly, it remains that the disabled person under retirement age living in the community still has to depend on his family for care, and the family receives little relief or assistance in the task.

This undoubtedly means that the lives of disabled people and their families are often very restricted, owing to a combination of limited finance, restricted mobility in homes which are often unsuited to the accommodation of disabled individuals, and lack of energy, after the necessary tasks of care have been performed, to arrange leisure and social activities outside the home. One middle-aged disabled woman living with her elderly parents, for instance, was invited to attend a club for disabled people organized by a voluntary body and held one evening a month. It would have been a welcome outing, but the elderly father found driving at night very trying. Volunteers were found to collect the disabled woman and bring her home, but this meant she had to wait until the club premises had been tidied, the washing-up done, and the volunteer was free to drive her home. By that time it was after 11 p.m., and the elderly mother resented having to wait up when she was tired, in order to be available to help her disabled daughter undress and into bed. This was a case where the burden of unrelieved care of a very disabled daughter left the elderly parents with no reserves of energy at all, and therefore made even the limited opportunities for outings available to their daughter a further burden, rather than a relief.

Residential care, by contrast, offers the convenience of purpose-built, or at least extensively adapted, premises specially planned for the greatest mobility and independence of disabled occupants, with staff to give the necessary care and attention. Despite these advantages, it seems quite clear that few disabled people, however seriously handicapped, *choose* to enter residential care. They enter it, if at all, only when home care has completely broken down, or become an intolerable burden for caring relatives. This may be when a parent dies, or becomes too frail to cope, or it may be when the disabled person's marriage breaks up, or when the degree of handicap becomes so gross that the family can no longer give adequate care. Whatever the reason, institutional care is seen by most disabled people as a last resort and not as a preferable alternative to living at home, however unsuitable the dwelling may be which is called home, and however restricted to four walls may be the life of the disabled person.

This means that, except for a few residents, units for disabled people cannot rely on people entering residential care with enthusiasm for the opportunities which can be afforded. Nonetheless, if residential care is to be more than a waiting room for death, it must somehow involve the residents in living, and for them as for all of us, living means planning ahead and taking decisions, choosing between alternatives, deciding priorities and thus, implicitly, deciding what will be gone without. In other words, disabled residents of institutional care units need to be involved in the management of the places which they must regard as their home, since they can cope in no other.

In practice the philosophy which underlies the provision of care for disabled people has not often encouraged such resident participation. Residential care has been provided for those 'unable to care for themselves' and has been seen as meeting the needs of residents for physical care. This is, of course, essential, as it is for all of us. But for able-bodied people, meeting their physical needs for food and shelter, though essential, only serves as the preliminary to living, as distinct from existing. It is what *else* is in life, after food and shelter is assured, that most of us regard as giving meaning to our existence, and we consider it very much a matter for our own choice and effort as to what else we create or develop in our lives.

There is no reason to think that disabled people take any different view of life and its meaning. Their disablement may remove some areas of choice from them and to these constraints may be added the limitations of financial hardship and of social restriction due to lack of facilities. It is likely, therefore, that disabled people entering residential care may have become a little out of practice in taking decisions about their own life. Moreover, the fact that the step of entering residential care is seen not as a choice which has been made for positive reasons, but as an inevitable stage in the sad course of disablement, means that few will be equipped to exploit the opportunities for independence afforded by the better physical standards of their surroundings in a unit for disabled.

As a result most residential care units become places of apathy – warehouses of handicapped humanity, according to one study of residential units for the disabled (Miller and Gwynne, 1972), unless the ethos of the units is that of encouraging maximum independence and individuality. The kindly humanitarianism which promoted the development of residential units for the disabled – the desire to give necessary care – has in so many cases, however, become an urge to give *total* care.

The very concept of total care has been enthusiastically embraced by progressive thinkers in the field of health care, where, it is argued, the great need is to see the patient as a whole person, not simply as a case, and to plan for the total care of the person. This approach may be entirely justified in the case of someone who is sick, but disabled people are not simply permanently sick people. They are people who are adapting to life with a degree of handicap. They may, as may able-bodied people, become sick from time to time, and then be willing to surrender themselves totally to the doctor or the nurse in return for treatment and care to make them well. Disability, on the other hand, is intractable and is not 'cured'. Consequently the well but disabled person is unwilling to surrender more of himself than he absolutely must to survive. He is limited physically in what he can do, where he can go, the contacts he can make and the facilities he can command. He might expect in a residential unit to receive physical care as and when he needed it, and 'enabling' services – suggestions of facilities and provisions which he might find helpful, information about resources and possibilities that he might explore, and assistance in making contacts that he would welcome. He does not, however, seek total care from the institution, even if he is almost totally dependent physically on others for his bodily needs.

This means that residents in units for disabled want to retain as wide an area of choice in their lives as possible – the sort of choice which they had, or would have, in their own home. For example, there should be the choice of when to get up and when to go to bed. This choice should be unrestricted in the case of those able to get themselves into and out of bed unaided, and the better physical facilities of residential care as compared with those in the average private home ought to expand the numbers able to do this. Of course, if in the unit the staff prepare breakfast for a certain hour, the late riser may find the meal has been cleared away and he has to go without. He may choose to do so, nonetheless, just as many able-bodied people choose to get up too late to be able to eat breakfast before leaving for work. The disabled resident may choose to equip himself with an electric kettle, some instant coffee, powdered milk and biscuits to make good the lack of breakfast. He may be unsteady or clumsy and run the risk of scalding himself, but he may choose to do so, just as he would in his own home. He may choose to take a bath unsupervised in order to be able to take it when he feels like it, rather than when the staff find it convenient to help him. He may be at risk of falling, perhaps knocking himself unconscious and drowning himself in the bath, but he may choose to take this risk, just as he would in his own home.

Where a disabled person's activities, such as getting up, or taking a bath, demand the assistance of residential care staff (and the disabled person should be the judge of this), then the freedom of choice is bound to be limited by the availability of the staff. This will be conditioned not only by the actual numbers of people working in the unit, but also by the priority which is attached to their various duties – such as changing beds, preparing meals, taking residents to the lavatory, and so on. The priorities are the sort of thing each private household has to work out – is it more important that the family eats home-made jam, or that the mother spends time playing with her children? Is it more important to see a particular film showing that week, or to attend an evening class? In the same way, the priorities to be attached to the duties of staff in residential care units should be worked out with the participation of the residents. They may choose to forgo some aspects of care in order to make staff available for some other activity which they value more. It may be difficult to get some agreement on priorities to be established within the unit, but to ignore the views of residents in such matters simply because it takes time to reach agreement, and because no agreement will please everyone, is to remove a vital area of choice, decision, independence and living from the disabled residents.

The areas of choice so far discussed may seem trivial. They are trivial when we are sure we retain the right of choice, but they become very significant in the lives of people who have to make their home in a residential unit. Even so, such areas of practical choice do not exhaust the range of decisions which ought to be left with the individual, but which have often been absorbed into the paternalistic, total-care role of the staff in residential care units. A disabled person in residential care may have many physical limitations but he still has his emotional needs and strengths. He probably still needs and could enjoy close personal relationships, but the development of such relationships needs privacy – the courting couple monopolizing the privacy of the parlour is a generally recognized phenomenon – and residential care should afford and respect opportunities for privacy.

Unfortunately, even in the residential units which afford each resident a room of his or her own, there is often no assurance of privacy, since the staff can and do enter a resident's room at any time of the day or night. In some units, a Head of Home who is sensitive to the residents' need for privacy, will ask the staff to knock before entering a resident's room, but even where this request is complied with, the knock is often a perfunctory warning followed by immediate entry, and not a request for permission for entry to be awaited before opening the resident's door. In any case, some residents will suffer hearing loss, or find speech difficult, and in these cases staff may be forgiven if they regard a preparatory knock as of doubtful advantage to the resident.

What is needed is a simple lock on the inside of the resident's room so that he can secure his door against entry, and assure himself of privacy for whatever purpose. This, of course, opens the possibility of a disabled person locking himself in, and then finding he needs help which can only reach him by forcing the door. This is undoubtedly a risk, but the disabled person may choose to take it, in order to guarantee himself the privacy he values more. Some relationships formed between disabled people in residential care may be extra-marital, promiscuous or homosexual. That is true of some relationships outside residential care, too. The disabled person who enters residential care does not thereby expect to surrender moral choice, nor is there any reason for him to do so, whether in the matter of sexual morality, or in other spheres.

The disabled person who is supported by the local authority, either in one of its own units or by full or part payment of the cost of care in a unit provided by a voluntary organization, is encouraged to look on the unit as his home, and on himself as one of the 'family' in the unit. Quite apart from the fact that this analogy with the family suggests that a disabled resident's role is that of a child, while the staff take the role of the parents, which is hardly conducive to encouraging attitudes of independent self-determination, the images of home and family imply the security of a special permanent place in which one belongs and over which one exercises territorial rights, and in which one's possessions can be safely displayed and enjoyed. Yet the disabled resident who leaves the unit for a short stay with relatives, or to go to another residential unit, simply for a change of environment and companions, has no choice but to allow his room and his possessions in his 'home' to be taken over by a stranger. This is because, while he is away, another disabled person will be taken into his place. In all probability it will be a disabled person who is normally resident with his family in the community, and his admission to the residential unit will be a way of affording a short holiday to his family. This can be of enormous help and relief to families who are caring for a heavily disabled member, but it is a relief which is afforded them not by us, the able-bodied working members of society contributing a little extra to provide a holiday service, but by the severely disabled person in residential care. Some disabled residents may be glad to think that their room and their possessions in their 'home' are being used to bring relief to an unknown family, but some may resent the degree of generosity that this policy forces upon them. They may wish to choose, as you and I can choose, the extent to which, and the terms on which, their home will be available to benefit others while they are away. In other words, this moral choice should be one which each resident makes for himself rather than one which is forced upon him by the decree of others.

Although the concept of total care is widespread, and in the context of acute ill-health may be an excellent principle of medical care, there is in fact no legal obligation on the staff of residential units to assume responsibility for the total care of adult disabled who are not mentally defective. They will not be called to account for the actions of a disabled resident, since, as far as the law is concerned, the physically disabled person in residential care is as much in charge of his decisions as any other mentally competent adult. Many staff in residential units justify their prohibitive regulations, such as no baths to be taken without an attendant present, or no smoking in bedrooms, on the ground that they will be held responsible for any injury which residents sustain, but this is not true. If a disabled person in residential care is injured as a result of his own actions and behaviour, it is not the responsibility of the staff. But if staff deliberately assume responsibility of, say, bathing a disabled resident and in so doing the resident is injured, the staff could be held responsible if they were shown to have been neglectful or careless in the way they performed the task.

It is unlikely that merely stating the legal position in respect to responsibility will change the attitudes of staff in residential care units. The assumption of responsibility for the welfare of residents is part of the total care image which is prevalent. To relinquish such responsibility would create uncertainty about the proper limits of their caring role in the minds of many of the staff of residential units. So far the inappropriateness of the concept of total care in the field of residential care of disabled people has not been adequately stressed. This reflects the failure to distinguish clearly between the position in society of people who are ill, but who are expected to recover, and the position of those for whom a permanent degree of malfunction is the norm, and who cannot be expected to recover full competence. In other words, the failure to distinguish between the role of the sick and the role of the disabled has led to a confusion of the roles of those giving care to the respective groups. In the case of a person who is ill, society will excuse his failure to fulfil his obligations, such as going to work or keeping an appointment, provided the cause of his failure is recognized to be illness. This recognition will be given if the ill person behaves as if he wishes to get well. If he consults a doctor and follows medical advice, or if he retires to bed and follows accepted procedures for restoring health, he will be regarded as fulfilling the obligations of the sick role and will be temporarily excused normal obligations (Parsons, 1964).

Implicit in this formulation of the sick role is the willingness of the ill person to surrender himself to the treatment and care which *others* judge most likely to restore him to health and his normal duties. This is, as it were, the bargain which is struck between the person assuming the sick role and the rest of society. The man who, claiming to be unable to fulfil his obligations as a worker due to ill-health, rejects his doctor's advice to stay at home and rest and instead goes to a football match, may find that he is not accorded the sick role, but is regarded as in breach of duty. He is not, in other words, allowed to decide for himself what will make him well, but must surrender this decision to others, and they in turn must justify this surrender of his judgment by making him well as quickly as possible. It is clear that such an interpretation of the sick role makes it inappropriate for a person who is chronically ill or disabled. Their medical advisers cannot make them well, the limitation on their normal activities is not temporary but permanent, and there is no justification for requiring them to surrender their judgment as to what represents the best adjustment of their residual capacities to their particular circumstances. For these people the concept of the sick role is unhelpful, but no other clearly formulated social role has been defined for them. In the absence of this, staff involved in giving care to disabled people have tended to apply to them the same expectations and standards as are applied to sick people.

This tendency has been further encouraged because in the development of residential care provision for disabled people, the immediate past history was that of hospital provision – the geriatric hospital, or before that, the Poor Law Infirmary. The model for residential care tended to be the hospital model, and the senior staff recruited tended to be nurses with hospital backgrounds. It is not surprising, therefore, that the ethos of most residential care for disabled persons continues to be very much that of total care. As our society has become more affluent (despite recurring economic crises) the standard of total care offered has improved. Residential units have been increasingly established in purpose-built premises, with single rooms for residents, with workshop facilities, with special transport to enable residents to be taken out, and so on. The rising standard of total care, however, has not altered the fact that it is often a bad bargain for the residents. They still cannot expect a cure as a result of surrendering to total care, but they may very well find that, despite the better physical facilities of a residential unit, their independence, far from increasing, is decreased because so many areas of their life become controlled by decisions taken by others over whom they can exercise little or no influence.

It is odd that the value of total care has been accepted so uncritically, when the surely related phenomenon of total institutions (Goffman, 1961) has been widely regarded as anathema in what may broadly be described as social welfare circles. Goffman, who originated the term 'total institution' to describe places where individuals were collected together for the whole or virtually the whole of their activities, over a long period of time, was very critical of the effect such places had on individual personality. For him, the inevitable result was a destruction of the unique and independent personality, and the creation of a docile institutionalized inmate. Part of the process of institutionalization, according to Goffman, was the denial of the individual's right to exercise independent judgment over his activities, such as when to eat, or what to eat, when to get up, when to idle, with whom to make friends, or over what to quarrel.

The tremendous impact of Goffman's analysis of total institutions was due to the fact that he pointed out that, whether an individual was in a prison for punishment, or in hospital for care, the effect after any length of time in either environment was the same – institutionalization, or destruction of the individual personality.

Many of the features Goffman identified as contributing to the institutionalization process, such as uniformity of dress, lack of choice in food, and lack of contact with the community outside the institution, have now been considerably modified in long-stay care institutions. Few, if any, homes or hospitals for geriatric, mentally defective, or physically disabled people deliberately inflict institutionalized dress on the residents. Most offer as much choice in food as resources permit, and nearly all make quite strenuous efforts to bring members of the outside community into the unit, and to take residents of the unit to outside activities. To this extent, the total institution has been rejected, at least as a way of providing care, as distinct from custody. Nonetheless, the fundamental view that those who demonstrate a need for help in some spheres of life are 'dependent' in a generalized and global way, has not really been challenged, and has indeed been given a new and more attractive form in the idea of total care.

However progressive and laudable the aim of total care may be in the sphere of treatment of the acutely sick, it is unfortunate indeed that it has been adopted so uncritically as an appropriate aim in residential provision for handicapped individuals. The result has been to slow down considerably the de-institutionalization of such units, which was seen as an urgent necessity once the dangers of total institutions had been recognized. Now, although increasingly residential units recognize the need to involve residents in decisions about their lives, and some have attempted to organize residents' committees, the sad truth is that in many cases the residents have been so robbed of their independence by submitting to total care, that they are unable, even unwilling, to exercise the responsibilities of committee membership. As a couple of disabled people living in a residential unit perceptively comment, 'Management . . . says the typical resident doesn't want to be involved [in management] and seems apathetic. We say such apathy is caused by lack of real opportunity' (Bell and Cartwright, 1976).

It is not, as these residents have realized, real opportunity simply to create a residents' committee, or appoint one or two residents to the management committee of a residential unit, if in other ways the residents are denied the right to choose their way of life. The unit, for example, which invited its residents to elect two of their number to the management committee, and then heavily outvoted the residents' request to be allowed to use the well-equipped workshop whenever they wished during reasonable hours, without the necessity of seeking staff permission first, ought not to have been surprised when the residents became apathetic about serving on the management committee. The solicitous insistence on total care – residents might fall and injure themselves in, or going to and from, the workshop, and therefore staff must know when they were there and no-one could be there alone – had sapped the independence of the residents, kindly, but just as surely as any total institution regime.

What is needed in residential care for disabled people is not total care, but enabling care. This is a particular challenge, because most of those who enter residential care will not bring with them a positive expectation of improved opportunities for independence, but will regard the move as a failure – a failure of their ability to cope, or their family's ability to care, in the community. In this situation it is only too easy to envelop them in care. It takes much greater demands on the understanding and skill of the staff in such units for them instead to offer only that assistance with physical care that the individual disabled person must have to meet his basic require-ments, and then to leave him free, with encouragement and advice when needed (and it may often be at first), to run as much as possible of his own life. This approach requires the staff in residential units to work *with* the residents and not always to do things *for* them. It is not an approach which follows naturally from the training which a nurse receives, yet many of the tiny minority of staff in residential care work who have qualifications (two per cent) are nurse-trained. It is for this reason that a recent report (C.C.E.T.S.W., 1976) suggested that if qualified nurses were to be ap-pointed to run residential units for elderly or disabled people, they ought to be given some orientation course to equip them with the understanding and approach necessary for successful care of such groups. The report also recommends a rapid development of part-time courses, leading to a Certificate in Social Services, on a day-release basis for those staff in residential care who are at present untrained. In both cases the course would undoubtedly include some study of the effect of total institutions. It is to be hoped that the concept of total care will also be critically examined.

One final aspect of residential care ought also be considered. It is an aspect that one hopes will involve very few individuals at all: the matter of complaints about standards of care received in such units. A few years ago there were a series of shock reports about the conditions in which some elderly people were kept in institutions (Townsend, 1962; Robb, 1967), and there were some scandals about the hospital treatment of some men-tally handicapped individuals (H.M.S.O., 1969, 1971, 1972). There have been no such horrifying reports about the care given to physically dis-abled people who are in institutions. One hopes this means that standards of care are uniformly good, but one can only be confident of this if, with every opportunity to make dissatisfaction known, no disabled resident complains. Those who are in National Health Service hospitals or units for the younger chronic sick, will be covered by the complaints procedure being developed for the National Health Service, and will, if not satisfied with the way their grievance is dealt with, have recourse to the Commissioner for Health and Social Services. For those disabled people in local authority homes, complaints can be made to the relevant social services department of the county in which the home is located, and once again, if not satisfied with the outcome or with the manner in which the matter is investigated, there is the opportunity to refer the issue to the Commissioner. Although it may be difficult for a disabled person to operate the machinery of the complaints procedures, at least such machinery exists and steps are taken to see that residents know of it.

Just about half the physically disabled under retirement age, however, are in homes run by independent voluntary organizations. The majority of these people are sponsored by their local authority, which undertakes to pay the fee for their care to the voluntary organization concerned, when, as is usual, the means of the individual are inadequate to meet the cost. In this case the disabled individual presumably has the right to refer to his local authority any complaints he may have about the standard of care he is receiving. There is, however, no obligation on a local authority to investigate the matter. Their obligation with regard to homes for disabled people run by voluntary bodies is to register them, and make sure that the facilities (size of rooms, numbers of lavatories, number of staff, etc.) are adequate, but the standard of care is not otherwise assessed.

One Director of Social Services, asked about this matter said that the big voluntary organizations, which provide the majority of non-profit-making homes for disabled people, were assumed to give reasonable care. He was not aware that any complaint from a resident living in one of such homes and sponsored by his authority had ever been investigated nor did he think that any complaint had ever been received.

If this attitude is general on the part of local authority staff, it means that few disabled individuals, once in a home run by a voluntary organization, will be aware of any possible channel of complaint through their local authority. Yet if the local authority does not accept responsibility for investigating and pronouncing upon this type of grievance (and it is difficult to see how it could do this effectively in respect of a home run by an independent voluntary body), the disabled individual has recourse only to such complaints machinery, if any, that the voluntary body, or the particular management of the home, allows. Moreover, however dissatisfied such an individual might be with the outcome of his complaint, or the way it was dealt with, he would have no appeal to the Commissioner, who is concerned only with the statutory health and social services.

It may be that there is not and never will be, any cause for complaint by any disabled individual accommodated in homes run by voluntary bodies, or that all such homes have entirely adequate procedures, well-known and understood by all residents, for investigating any complaints which may arise. It is, however, absolutely at the discretion of the individual homes, or the various voluntary organizations, as to what complaints procedure to adopt, or whether to have any at all. At a time when the D.H.S.S. has seen fit to standardize the complaints procedure for the health service, and the government has bowed to the necessity of appointing a Commissioner to investigate unresolved complaints against the health and social services, it seems unfortunate that about 6,000 very vulnerable disabled individuals in residential care are left outside these protective provisions.

INTEGRATION OR SEGREGATION?

Many people would regard the provision of residential care for disabled persons as altogether the wrong approach, involving the segregation from the ordinary community of persons who suffer disablement. The right approach is seen to be that of integrating the disabled person into normal living as far as possible.

As has been pointed out already, the vast majority of disabled people *do* live in the community, and very few of those in residential care have chosen to live in that way in preference to living in a private household in the community. It may well be argued, therefore, that residential provision is both an unwanted and uneconomic form of care which imposes an unnecessary degree of segregation on the recipients. The comparative costs of residential and home care of disabled people have been examined (Economist Intelligence Unit, 1973) and the conclusion reached that home care, even of very severely disabled people, is cheaper than residential care.

It is tempting to decide that, simply by eliminating residential care, one could at a stroke meet the wishes of disabled people, facilitate their continued integration into the community, and also save money. This would be too facile a conclusion. The examination of the comparative costs of residential and home care for disabled individuals, mentioned above, made it quite clear that home care was cheaper because of the enormous amount of unpaid care given by the families of disabled individuals. The sort of social services domiciliary support which was costed as part of the home-care expenses, only supplemented family care, but even that, as the report makes plain, represents a degree of support which is seldom available to families at present. This immediately suggests that residential care will continue to be necessary in those cases where a severely disabled person has no family, or no family capable of giving the continuous care which is necessary. A less obvious implication is that where a very severely disabled person is cared for at home, with the very limited amount of social services support which is in practice available, the restrictions of disablement are shared by the whole family unit involved in giving care. These restrictions can be so numerous as to result in the disabled person and his family living in the community, but being unable to be *part of* it in any meaningful way.

It is not, in other words, enough to assume that integration of disabled people is automatically assured by their living in private households in the community. We need to be very clear what we mean by 'integration'. It is one of those words which needs the approach of a Humpty Dumpty, who, as anyone who knows their Alice in Wonderland will be aware, insisted that words meant what he, Humpty Dumpty, chose they should mean – no more and no less. As far as integration is concerned, it can, and probably has, meant a number of different things at different times to different people, and to discuss the 'integration' of disabled people, involves specifying what we mean by integration in any given context.

If, for example, we mean that by caring for a very disabled person in a private household, such a person will be more integrated into his family than if he were to be in residential care, that is likely to be accepted as true. If, however, we mean he will be more integrated into the community in the sense of participating in such community activities as local bingo clubs, or ratepayers' associations, or employment, it is quite possible that the better facilities of residential care could promote such activities rather more than the family is able to do whilst absorbed in and often exhausted by, giving the necessary basic care. There are, in short, several dimensions of integration, and for a disabled person to live in a private household rather than a good residential unit may promote one aspect of integration (with the family) but at the expense of others.

It may well be that most disabled people, and their families, are willing to sacrifice other forms of integration in order to retain the integration of the disabled individual in his family. But we should not, as a society, pretend that this is the same as integration into the community, or even that, with the level of social support currently available to the families caring for a disabled member, it is *compatible* with integration into the community. It is perhaps better to be seen as the willing acceptance by society of the natural inclination of disabled individuals and their families to put family unity before community involvement. If it leads to segregated families, rather than a segregated individual, society is able to ease its conscience by claiming that it is what disabled people want.

The danger of this self-deception on the part of society is that it encourages the complacent view that, as long as disabled people are living in private households and not in institutional care, a desirable state of 'integration' has been achieved. There is then little incentive to improve the facilities for families caring for a disabled member (except insofar as such support can remove the necessity for residential admission) or to recognize that the economies of home care as compared with residential care rest on the enormous unpaid labour of self-sacrificing relatives. Real social integration of the disabled person and his family in economic and leisure activities of life, would involve a much greater expenditure of resources in community care than is (usually) envisaged and would not be at all a cheap alternative to residential care.

Much the same line of argument applies to the issue of integrated or segregated education for disabled children. In 1954, it was stated (Ministry of Education, 1954): 'No handicapped child should be sent to a special school who can be satisfactorily educated in an ordinary school.' This view was unequivocally endorsed in the Plowden report in 1967, when it was said: 'The unnecessary segregation of the handicapped is neither good for them nor for those with whom they must associate. They should be in the ordinary school wherever possible' (H.M.S.O., 1967).

Although many people felt that a number of education authorities were tardy and unenthusiastic in their compliance with these injunctions, there were some voices warning that to place a severely disabled child in a normal school without making special help available to him, might be less satisfactory than a special school placement (Younghusband *et al.*, 1970; D. E. S., 1972). Once again, there is no clear understanding of what is meant by 'integrated' education, let alone of what the benefits may be. Merely to allow disabled children to attend schools planned primarily for able-bodied children is in effect to follow the practice adopted in the last century, when the schools that were being built to bring elementary education to the children of the working classes, accommodated any disabled child who could be contained within the classroom. It was regarded as a progressive development when the Elementary Education (Blind and Deaf Children) Act 1893 provided for special educational facilities for blind and deaf children, and pressure was mounted to extend this special consideration to mentally and physically handicapped children, as was made mandatory on educational authorities in the Education Act 1918. At that time, the arguments were that unless special educational provision was made for disabled children, they would be denied the benefits of education since their disabilities made ordinary schooling impossible or unsatisfactory.

There is now a tendency to revert to the idea that ordinary schooling is preferable for practically all physically disabled children, and for many mentally handicapped children. The Education Act passed by the government in 1976 seeks to change the emphasis of the Education Act 1944, which required local authorities to provide special schooling for handicapped children with special needs, to requiring local authorities to educate handicapped children in ordinary schools unless it is quite impracticable, against the best interests of the children, or would involve unreasonable cost. This move has been made without waiting for the report of a government committee, chaired by Mary Warnock, which was set up in 1974 to inquire into the education of handicapped children. Dr Mia Kellmer Pringle, director of the National Children's Bureau, has also been quoted (*The Times*, 11 November 1976) as saying that she believed that much more work needed to be done before anyone could be sure that integrating handicapped children with ordinary children was the best solution in every case, as few ordinary schools had enough equipment or enough specialist trained staff to deal with the special needs of handicapped children.

A child is only considered handicapped if he or she is restricted in the areas of activity which are basic to a child's development mentally or physically. If a disabled child is handicapped in only a small area of school life but can hold his own in others, he doubtless could benefit from education in an ordinary school, compensating for his disadvantage in one sphere by his proficiency in others. But severe disability which affects proficiency in many if not all spheres of school life, requires special facilities if the disadvantages of disablement are not to be compounded with lack of educational achievement, and possibly lack of self-confidence due to growing up in an environment where failure is inevitable, constant and widespread.

The cost of providing such special facilities, in the form of special equipment and specialist trained staff, in all or the majority of ordinary schools to cope with the, mercifully, small number of severely handicapped children in their catchment areas, would probably be far greater than the cost of equipping one or two specialist units to serve the whole educational area. The latter provision would undoubtedly segregate the severely handicapped children attending such units from the children at ordinary schools, but should, if such units are of high standard, encourage a level of educational achievement, and the development of self-confidence in what they could achieve, so that their ultimate integration in the adult community was promoted.

This is not to say that there may not be some children in special schools who could with benefit be educated in ordinary schools; the reverse may also be true. The selection of handicapped children for special or ordinary schooling does not seem to be carried out in a way to inspire confidence that the right decision is always, or almost always, made (Anderson, 1973). The point is that the integration of handicapped children is not necessarily advanced simply by increasing the numbers of them who are educated in ordinary schools as distinct from special units. Like many disabled adults living in private households, they may find themselves *in* the community (in this case, the ordinary school community) but unable to be *part of* it in any meaningful way.

One needs to be wary of the too glib emphasis on integration of disabled people, adults or children, into the community. Of course we need to look carefully at the special measures we introduce to ameliorate some of the difficulties of disablement, and do our best to ensure that the special measures themselves do not add to the segregation of the disabled. We also need to be very careful that we do not go to the other extreme and assume that the segregation that results from disability can be reduced by not providing special measures of help – in other words by leaving disabled adults in private households and sending disabled children to ordinary schools, to cope as best they can. We shall not reduce the tragedy of disablement by finding a new word for neglect and calling it integration.

CHAPTER 6

The Elderly

There is a rapidly growing range of literature now being produced about the elderly. Any consideration of this literature requires the disentangling of a number of basic features within the concept of 'old age'.

Writers have rarely been able to present ageing as a positive social experience. A few books have appeared urging the older reader to help himself and thrive by overcoming the ageing process. The disabilities of older people, it is suggested, are not so much due to the ageing process as to the individual's psychological reaction to it (Meares, 1975). 'What we make of our "old age" is largely up to us: it can be wretched, it can be verdant. But verdant old age does not happen of itself; we need to work at it' (Gore, 1973). Such attitudes perhaps serve only to emphasize the negative, darker side of ageing – growing old and being old are to be avoided at all costs – but this does imply an image of 'successful' ageing.

The concept of need in respect of older people has tended to be discussed in terms of social, physical and emotional problems. The fact that this has been so is closely linked to the emphasis on practical services for the elderly. Concentration in the field of social gerontology has frequently been on old age as a social problem and with the issues of policies aimed at the alleviation of problems. There have been relatively few contributions to the development of what might be termed a 'sociology of ageing' although a few attempts have been made (Shanas *et al.,* 1968; Rosow, 1967, 1974; Rose and Peterson, 1965; Blau, 1973). Perhaps the most extensive work in sociology in Britain has been done in relation to the family life of old people (Townsend, 1963) and the nature of institutional life in homes for the elderly (Townsend, 1962; Meacher, 1972).

It is both the strength and the weakness of gerontology as a body of research and thinking that it depends on a wide variety of disciplines for its

152

development. It is its strength insofar as the range of interests brings a depth of knowledge, but its weakness is that it is very difficult to systematize the different kinds of knowledge to produce coherent support for policy development. Two central points can, however, be highlighted. Research clearly suggests that ageing is not a simple, unified process that can be defined and described solely on a chronological basis: ageing is better viewed as a collection of processes affecting the individual and those around him. The second point is that there is a difference between ageing as a progression or collection of processes and old age as a social concept bound up with beliefs, perceptions and behaviour.

A sociology of ageing must take account of age-related behaviour within a social context: it will be concerned not only with old people and their behaviour, perceptions, interactions, needs, etc., but also with people who are growing older throughout their entire adult life. Several questions thus begin to emerge in relation to generalized preoccupations of particular age groups. Is the process of ageing the successful achievement of a series of tasks – procreation, creativity, caring, etc.? If there is such a series of tasks in any particular cultural context, then what are the mutual obligations and responsibilities implied? What do younger people expect of those who are older and what do older people expect of themselves and of those around them?

Biologically ageing is slow and symptomless (Anderson, 1967), not yet clearly understood and varying from one person to another. Anderson suggests that the outstanding thesis of modern geriatric medicine is that old people who are ill are unwell not because they are old but because there is some disease process present. Geriatric medicine has been defined as the branch of general medicine concerned with the clinical, remedial, preventive aspects of health and disease in the elderly (Royal College of Physicians, 1972), and having four central objectives: (1) to treat and study illness of all types in the elderly, (2) to help the elderly disabled to live independently by using rehabilitative methods, (3) to study the effects of social factors in the elderly and to take these into account, and (4) from the knowledge gained as a result of these studies to prevent illness and disability in the elderly (Hall, 1974). In summary the objectives of the physician in geriatric medicine are concerned with the control of disease and the maintenance of a life of optimum quality. Each of these objectives has obvious social consequence.

In 1976 Dr David Owen (Owen, 1976) stated that Departments of Geriatric Medicine contained about a quarter of all non-psychiatric hospital beds. In 1974 an average of 51,000 geriatric beds were occupied daily, although out-patient, and day-patient services have increased substantially over the last few years. Dr Owen estimated that the total running costs of Departments of Geriatric Medicine in 1975–6 were about £210 million, and capital expenditure of £30 million was spent on developing and improving the geriatric services. In addition people over 65 years of age are major users of all other beds (except maternity). In 1973 they were estimated to have occupied 49 per cent of general medical beds, 38 per cent of orthopaedic beds, and 47 per cent of psychiatric beds.

Clearly the provision of medical services to the elderly is extensive as well as expensive. It is essential to consider ways of ensuring that these vast sums of money are spent in a way that produces maximum individual and social benefit. It is important, also, to remember that preventive health and social services for the elderly are as extensive as hospital services.

It has already been suggested that those professionals who are concerned with providing care for older people in a social and health care context have tended to concentrate on the problem nature of old age. For a variety of reasons older people have been seen in stereotyped ways. It is perhaps hardly surprising that doctors, nurses, social workers, and others who are constantly in contact with those older people who are experiencing problems should view ageing in stereotyped, problem terms. However, the concept of old age, as distinct from ageing as a process or collection of processes, has very different meanings from individual to individual.

What, then, is old age? It is possible to identify a period of life, normally delineated by retirement in industrialized societies, as old age. Reaching the age of retirement and actually ceasing work have increasingly accompanied one another. Rates of participation in employment have fallen sharply among the population of retirement age: between 1951 and 1971 for instance the participation rate for men aged 70 and over in England and Wales fell by one-half. In Britain 50 years ago one in two men over 65 years of age was in employment: today the proportion is less than one in five. Retirement is, then, common, and leisure rather than work might be described as the social norm for people over 65. Is it, however, possible to describe those people within the age group homogeneously? Is there a recognizable role of 'old person' and, if so, what are the elements of role performance and how are they learned?

AGEING: A GENERAL VIEW

It has often been suggested that ageing is a process in which we are all involved to a more or less advanced degree. In the current state of knowledge chronological events during the process cannot be effectively related to normality but only to numerical frequency. Ageing involves the continuing interaction of a great many variables, physical, social, intellectual and emotional, and it is difficult to identify what is normal, healthy or natural during ageing because of this range of variables. It is perhaps easier to identify what is 'common' or usual but this can sometimes be misleading (Hall, 1972).

The concept of ageing as a process carries with it the implication that the ageing person will pass through a series of phases of life during the negotiation of the life cycle or in passing along what Bromley (1974) has called the life-path. To pass out of one stage of development of ageing is to pass into a new phase of life. One perception of this involves seeing ageing as a continual progression to something new, although there must be a degree of marking time and consolidation within each stage.

The value to the caring professions of the process view of ageing is that it points the way to the possibility of solutions. The problems experienced by old people are often the result of blocks – physical, social, emotional or material – to important life goals. If these blocks are removed then the normal process of ageing can proceed.

In one real sense there is a 'problem of old age'. The principal element in this is demographic – there are more older people around. At the beginning of the twentieth century there were less than $2\frac{1}{2}$ million people over retirement age in a population of over 38 million: 6.2 per cent of the population were old. In 1971, 16 per cent of the population of England and Wales were of retirement age: almost nine million people. Population trends suggest an expected increase from 1976 of about 36 per cent of people aged 75 and over until the year 1991, and 46 per cent for people aged 85 and over until the same year. This trend has obvious implications for service provision. Studies have shown a sharp increase in morbidity after the age of 75 years, and an increasing demand on geriatric services can be expected. Added to this will be a proportionately reduced workforce of an age to provide care, smaller family sizes, smaller houses, and more women – traditionally the care-givers – going out to work.

The condition and position of the elderly can be viewed, in general terms, from both the social and biological points of view. Each viewpoint is very much dependent on the other: the kind of life an old person leads is partly a function of his state of health and the converse is equally true. In attempting a discussion of theoretical standpoints the objective will be to highlight points of interdependence between physical and social experiences of old age.

ROLES AND AGEING

At least one writer (Pergeux, 1970) has discussed ageing from a functional-ist point of view, describing reciprocal obligations as the duty of society to educate the young who, in turn, must learn; to give work to the adult who must work; and to protect the aged who must participate. In this view a successful process of ageing involves the maintenance of an equilibrium between the needs of old and young in society.

The characteristics of the advanced industrial society include both an increase in the proportion of people living a long time and an increase in claims for independence from younger members of society. Together these two trends have led to an increase in the span of adulthood. This broaden-ing of the age band of adulthood has been associated with pressures to abandon, and certainly to move away from the gradation of powers and responsibilities on the basis of chronological age (as well as social seniori-ty). One effect has been to devalue age itself in assessing the value of the individual. Other factors have become important in considering expecta-tions, achievements and personal worth.

Some comments can be made on the perception of older people by younger age groups. Stereotyping seems common. Butler (1969) discussed some of the attitudes in the United States; he suggested that the repression of feelings about growing old leads to 'elder-rejection', that there is a feeling of powerlessness, uselessness and death, that the elderly are forced to withdraw from the mainstream of economic life and are often seen as impecunious and undeserving. One difficulty is immediately apparent: there is a chicken-and-egg phenomenon involved – old age is feared, therefore old people are rejected, therefore people fear to grow old, etc.

Blank (1971) reports a number of studies in the United States among professional social work students and medical students, who tend to reflect negative mental pictures of the aged. Similarly social workers in Britain tend to be reluctant to work with older people, although their clients make up the largest group in their caseloads (Neill *et al.*, 1973). During 1974–5 Age Concern England succeeded in generating the formation of around 800 local groups discussing various topics relating to older people, with a view to creating a manifesto for the elderly. Just over 80 of these groups discussed the emotional needs of the elderly. Although the underlying assumption seemed to be that people are people whatever their age, all the groups tended to project the stereotyped ideal. The groups felt the younger generation could learn courage, wisdom, loyalty, hard work, restraint and the importance of friendships and family life from the elderly (Gilhome, 1975). It is by no means surprising that groups so concerned for the elderly should produce positive stereotypes: there are of course plenty of negative stereotypes to go alongside these.

One characterization of the 'old person' is plainly based on stereotype and ideals and it is worth at least bearing in mind the effect of labelling and ideal-types on beliefs, self-perception and behaviour. Indeed the early pessimism of disengagement theory seemed to confirm the negative effects of these beliefs. Ageing was seen as a social process whereby society frequently imposed withdrawal on the older person but this did not necessarily mean that he was unable to experience a feeling of well-being (Cumming and Henry, 1961). Although it is not defended, even by its first proponents in this original form, disengagement theory has played a fundamental part in the development of gerontological theory in recent years. The stultifying effect on policies aimed at maintaining levels of stimulation, activity or involvement among older people is obvious. Accepted in its literal form, disengagement theory points to the wish of older people to sit quietly in the corner and watch the world go by.

More recent work, especially the cross-national study by Ethel Shanas, Peter Townsend, Henning Friis and others (1968) showed the inappropriateness of describing 'the old' as often ill, alienated or deprived. Older people, they argue, are fairly well integrated into their local communities by the services they provide for others and receive in exchange. The disengagement theorists, however, were not concerned primarily with the social integration of the old but were suggesting that decreasing role involvement and ego-energy are characteristic of ageing even under optimum conditions and that involvement with others is not a vital prerequisite for successful adjustment in old age.

A rather different argument has been put forward by Rose (1965) who suggests that there is a subculture of ageing. He argues that there is a positive affinity between older people, based to some extent on their physical limitations and consequent common interests in a physically easy and calm existence, and partly also on their having had common generational experiences in a rapidly changing society. Rejection of the elderly by younger age groups is based to some extent on the same factors but also on the low value given to inefficiency in our general culture. As a result of their common experiences, Rose suggests, older people tend to interact with each other and to share common values, attitudes and beliefs. The actual evidence that older people can be seen, or see themselves in such homogeneous terms is, however, very limited. Rose himself acknowledges that by no means all people past the age of 65 participate in the subculture: there are those who continue to identify with the cultural behaviour pattern of the middle aged.

Another American writer (Rosow, 1967, 1974) suggests that the social position of the elderly has several components: they are devalued, viewed in insidious stereotypes, excluded from social opportunities; and they lose roles, confront severe role ambiguity in late life, and struggle to preserve self-esteem through youthful self-images. These unpleasant elements are said to arise from a lack of effective socialization to old age. Rosow argues that older people's relative position in any society depends on a number of factors, including: their ownership of property and control of opportunities of the young; their command of strategic knowledge and skills; strong sacred and religious traditions; strong family bonds; a low or high productive economy; and mutual dependence. In industrialized and post-industrialized society the old have little power and are consequently devalued and devalue themselves.

Another view (Dowd, 1975) describes the problems of ageing as problems of decreasing power resources: older people are said to be increasingly unable to enter into 'balanced exchange relations' with other groups. In this view the disengagement process is the result of a series of exchange relations in which the power of the elderly in relation to those with whom they are in interaction increasingly deteriorates. The result is an imbalanced exchange relationship in which the elderly are forced to 'exchange compliance for continued sustenance'.

In general terms some elements are apparent. Stereotypes of old age are common but research has confirmed that the majority of older people are closely involved with others in their social environment. Many older people are, however, demonstrably less involved than they were when they were younger, and for a fairly substantial minority this creates problems. The authors of the cross-national study suggest that some, though by no means all, of their problems arise as a consequence of formal actions taken by society to confirm their separate retired status (social security legislation, pensioners' concessions, etc.). Other problems result from or are aggravated by, the quality of informal relationships, and the part played by primary relationships is central to the integration of older people. The assumption that the industrial society has no real structural place for the old is not upheld but nevertheless considerable difficulties exist for the individual in making an adjustment to the pressures of such a society.

THE INDIVIDUAL EXPERIENCE

Recent work (Gore, 1973) done on physical activity and ageing suggests that continuing exercise is a significant factor in the maintenance of activity levels in ageing individuals. Older people are able to maintain and even to improve their physical performance if given the chance of increased exercise and stimulation. Some work done in Californaia (Birren, 1972) suggests that the older nervous system, too, has a reserve capacity, and consequently the characteristic level of activity of an individual reflects a degree of chronic adaptation or adaptation to a chronic situation. It may be that this impaired adaptation is the result of relative sensory deprivation, which in turn results from diminishing environmental stimulation (Hall, 1973).

It is clear that the behaviour of many older people reflects an element of chronic adaptation in the sense that they have a reserve capacity on which they can draw if necessary, although this may be a reduced reserve. Older people are expected to do less and they become habitually less involved in social situations, and this tendency seems to be emphasized by the lack of opportunities to learn how to behave as an 'old person'. As a result of the stereotyping already discussed, some older people do not have a clear conception of the behaviour that is expected of them and will often accept the stereotyped role because of a lack of clear alternatives.

Blau (1973) has argued that serious consideration should be given to a proposition that illness fulfils a psychological function for older people. In a situation in which society has no clear guidelines on how old people should behave and no clear concept of the role of 'old person', sickness may serve as a socially acceptable way of legitimizing the rolelessness. Seen as a social role, sickness may provide the elderly patient with special rights and privileges that the old person who is well does not have access to.

The evidence on the extent of interaction in which the majority of older people take part suggests that they do tend to retain many family and community roles. It does seem, however, that on to this pattern of interaction is overlaid a degree of confusion and rolelessness which is characterized by under-performance. Two points are therefore suggested as central to this: firstly the physical activity levels of older people reflect an element of reserve capacity (albeit a reduced reserve); and the maintenance of physical activity is partly dependent on continuing exercise. Arising from this is a postulation that characteristic social behaviour of older people also reflects a level of chronic adaptation. Increased social activity may follow changed stimulation.

There is a large amount of data concerning individual processes of ageing which can be briefly summarized in the categories of physical, social and intellectual processes. Many of the physical effects are familiar; skeletal changes, changes in the skin and fatty tissues, muscle weakening, and hair changes mean that the older person is typically slightly stooped with comparatively long arms, some weight loss and redistribution of fat and with a general slowing of muscular response; the skin wrinkles and folds and the hair goes grey and is often lost. Other changes are less immediately visible. Changes in the central nervous system and deterioration of the senses are usual; older people have poorer sight and hearing as well as experiencing loss of brain cells and changes in the sense of smell and touch.

The nature of some of the social processes has already been discussed. The pattern that seems to emerge is one of gradually lessening involvement for most – though by no means all – older people, who tend to play fewer active roles but who seem to gain a more intensive satisfaction from the fewer roles that remain. Undoubtedly older people as a group do remain integrated into society and continue to achieve satisfactions from participation in relationships. For a minority of older people rather more roles may be lost for a number of reasons: some may choose to withdraw and actually favour disengagement, some may experience a crisis of illness, bereavement, etc., and be unable to overcome the immediate difficulties with the available social supports; others may lack the environmental opportunities necessary to successful or satisfying adjustment. It is these groups of older people compulsorily disengaged from active roles and relationships who are most likely to experience ageing in problem terms.

Intellectually the older person seems to have a tendency to be slower, less adaptable, but with a store of experience and learning with which to compensate for his losses. His memory, especially for recent events, is less efficient, but he is able to learn, given time and opportunity. Unfortunately the available evidence does not provide an adequate basis for anything more than very broad generalizations. One fact that may be of particular importance is the suggestion that older people may require more cues than younger ones before they have an adequate basis for their judgment and will, therefore, have to process more information before reaching a conclusion (Chown, 1972). The consequence of this is that decision-making tends to take rather longer, and older people are also more cautious, especially in giving advice.

The attitudes of the ageing individual to these changes depend on numerous factors. Older people tend not to identify themselves as 'old' although awareness of age is very closely related to the way other people react towards the person (Blau, 1973). The available studies of attitudes to retirement – perhaps the single most important age-related change for most people – before the event, have tended to examine attitudes to the choice between work and retirement. Clearly people are very much influenced by prevailing expectations and values in the specific social and occupational groupings involved. Some important points can be drawn from the evidence: when approaching retirement, workers commonly give 'ill-health' or 'work too tiring' as a reason for retiring; compulsory retirement is also a common reason (Shanas *et al.*, 1968). Work by Jacobson (1972) suggests that attitudes to retirement are associated with negative rather than positive factors and that a majority of older workers would have liked a flexible system of part-time work rather than complete retirement. Jacobson's study also found that workers in 'heavier' occupations were much more likely to give ill-health as a reason for retirement. A study by Crawford (1972) suggests that attitudes in the pre-retirement period are also influenced by the extent of activity and engagement outside the immediate work situation. This tends to involve social class differences. Bearing in mind class, occupational and value differences, there is some evidence that a proportion of workers would wish to remain in employment, given the opportunity. Jacobson suggested that 63 per cent would have continued on a part-time basis and 20 per cent would have worked even if there was no financial necessity. The cross-national study of Shanas and others suggested a figure of 32 per cent giving 'forced to retire' as their reason for retirement.

There is, of course, a difference between looking forward to retirement with apprehension and wanting to continue in full-time or part-time employment. Crawford's study suggests that men in manual occupations, for example, are more likely to fear retirement, yet these are also the workers who are in 'heavier' or less remunerative jobs and who consequently tend to say that they must retire because of ill-health or the tiring nature of the work.

It is possible that the unwillingness to retire which many express is evidence not of a wish to remain at work but of uncertainty about how to use retirement. The cross-national study found that a substantial proportion of people in Britain (39 per cent) who had been retired for less than three years said that they wished to work – although again class differences were evident. The same study showed that one other factor which seems to affect the retired person's wish to work is the length of time he has been retired. There appears to be a cut-off period after about three years in retirement: the man who wants to work is the recently retired person who feels physically capable of doing so. It may be that this period represents an adjustment period and that after the three-year cut-off the retired person has accepted the role – or has become resigned to it.

Adjustment to ageing and to old age is very difficult to measure: it seems to be entirely an individual matter. A study by Age Concern of 2,700 people of pensionable age living in private households was concerned with the attitudes of the elderly and retired to the situation in which they found themselves (Age Concern, 1975). Almost two-thirds felt that they do help other people in some way, and a majority felt that 'someone relies on you nowadays to do things for them' but eight per cent of the sample were unable to think of anything that they 'look forward to nowadays'. Seventy-nine per cent did not agree at all that they 'enjoyed being retired at first but after a while got fed up with it': only nine per cent agreed strongly with the statement. Therefore, it may be that the majority make a good and satisfying adjustment to retirement but up to one in ten find the retirement period unsatisfying.

In summary, it has been suggested that many older people do remain closely involved in relationships and social activities. Some old people, however, experience problems which are not necessarily caused by ageing but which are age-related. Most people are able to cope with the barriers to a satisfying process of life with the help of family and friends, but a minority require help from health and social services. It is difficult to generalize on such an individual concept as adjustment but good physical and mental health, adequate income and material environment (the nature of adequacy being very subjective) and physical and social activity seem essential prerequisites to successful adjustment.

THE HEALTH OF THE ELDERLY

Total health refers not just to the absence of active disease but to the sense of well-being that comes from a subjective feeling of emotional, physical and social security. Physical health is essential for the elderly person to be able to avoid illness or disease. Old age cannot and should not be regarded as a state of ill-health but as a time when certain physical changes can be expected to take place. During the course of ageing the rate of physical change will vary from one person to the next, and with one individual may accelerate or slow down noticeably. As a result of these physical changes the ageing person may become vulnerable to ill-health and all the restrictions associated with this.

In studying the health of older people most work has been directed towards answering the question, 'How ill are old people?' rather than the question, 'How well are old people?' Some work has, however, been done on the health of all elderly people. Townsend has developed an index of incapacity (Townsend, 1962) based on a two-part score designed to find out whether an old person can carry out without aid a number of activities. The first part relates to personal incapacity, assessing activities believed to be representative of those essential to personal care; the second part is an assessment of capacity to manage a household unaided. This index has been applied in several studies which all show how incapacity commonly increases with age. However, at all ages both among those living in institutions as well as private households there are wide differences in incapacity. Even at advanced ages around half of all old people at home and one-tenth of those in institutions have little or no incapacity as measured by this index. Townsend (1973) suggests that altogether 83 per cent of older men and 74 per cent of older women living in private households have little or no incapacity, compared with 24 and 14 per cent in institutions.

The cross-national study conducted in Britain, the United States and Denmark (Shanas *et al.*, 1968) suggests that about one in ten of the elderly in the three countries studied are in hospitals and other institutions, or are bedfast or incapacitated at home. The majority of the elderly, the researchers suggest, maintain good health and are physically active. They are physically able to continue to participate in social relationships.

A lack of incapacity does not necessarily imply that individuals will experience their health as good. Good health may be perceived in a number of ways. One old person labouring under appalling conditions may deny the need for help whilst another, in much less stressful circumstances, may give up the struggle and become dependent. Health may be defined by the independent observer, or by a busy physician as well as by the old person himself. Defining and redefining of personal health status continues throughout life.

Most old people say that they are in good health for their age. Several studies of groups of old people have found up to 75 per cent with at least one unknown, moderate or severe disability. Williamson (1964, 1967) has used the term 'unreported illness' to refer to the fact that old people tend not to bring the fact that they feel unwell or in pain or discomfort to the notice of their doctor. The tendency seems to be to relate their experiences to an assumption that growing old inevitably involves physical discomfort. Older people tend not to complain of illness unless there is a real physical basis causing, particularly, difficulties in mobility. Williamson showed that when the older person himself realizes that he has some disease process he usually calls in the doctor, this type of illness being something recognized as a departure from the normal, such as breathlessness, ankle swelling or loss of power in an arm or leg. Symptoms such as painful feet, difficulty in micturition, mental confusion and dizziness tend to be less commonly reported and are attributed to ageing.

A study by Age Concern (1975) amongst elderly people found that self-assessment of health for age varies little across age groups but that with increasing age the difference in self-assessment between men and women becomes more marked. Men who survive into old age are more likely to consider their health good for their age. Self-assessment was also found to vary with social class, more 'middle-class' people considering themselves in good health than 'working-class'. Seventy-eight per cent of the elderly were found to be happy with the amount of interest their doctor takes in them, although only a quarter were in regular contact with their doctor.

Bearing in mind the large proportion of unreported disease and illness among the elderly, some general trends can be noted. The increase that has come about in the average expectation of life is the result of the conquest of major epidemic diseases, of improvements in obstetric methods and neonatal care; of improved nutritional, living and occupational standards;

and of the therapeutic mastery of major infectious disease (Agate, 1970). Before these developments it was possible to regard the elderly as survivors: to last to old age in the face of all the threats to health implied a great deal of physical resilience. This is no longer the case and in later life it is common for people to suffer from several diseases at once: multiple disease is the rule rather than the exception (Agate, 1972). Sensory loss is common and, in particular, changes in sight and hearing. About one-third of elderly people have hearing difficulties, about six per cent to a severe extent. Severe visual disorders affect about eight per cent of the elderly and 22 per cent experience some degree of impairment of sight (Townsend and Wedderburn, 1965). Heart disease, arterial disease and hypertension as well as arthritis and rheumatism cause problems for many. Cancer also presents a serious problem. Acute illness does occur in the elderly but this is not necessarily associated with the ageing process although it may be aggravated by physical changes. The problem for the geriatrician is the one in which disease, illness and disability are connected with factors in the ageing process – psychiatric, emotional and social as well as physical.

The social and emotional implications of physical and health changes among the elderly are many and varied. The physical changes which are commonly associated with the ageing process, as well as the accumulation of disease and disability, combine to bring about changes in self-image. Each person has a view of himself which includes a conception of what he can and cannot do; of who he is and who he would like to be. For some people physical factors of strength and appearance are very important aspects of this self-concept. The changes brought about by ageing involve self-reappraisal, which may be a painful and difficult process. Additionally, physical changes have accompanying practical consequences. Older people cannot walk as far, are less physically strong and are slower. They may be unable to get to the shops, to climb stairs, or to use the bath alone. It is inevitable in these circumstances that some older people become increasingly dependent on others. Sometimes this is the result of a gradual process of change but it may also follow from a crisis illness. In the latter event adjustment may be particularly difficult.

Linked to this change in self-concept and, perhaps, in self-esteem is the increase in frustration at being unable to do all the things that were previously possible. In growing through adolescence it is necessary to come to terms with becoming a separate, whole individual whilst still recognizing the need for a degree of interdependence with others. Growing into old age involves a reverse process of learning once again to be dependent on others for basic necessities; for some older people this will be to a much greater extent than for others. The objectives of caring services should be to enable those older people who are physically dependent, still to retain self-respect and dignity, to be whole individuals.

The social impact of health changes in old age will depend largely on the availability of substitute supports to the older person. Hobman (1972), in discussing some of the problems which relate to the changing roles and relationships involved in the process of ageing, suggests that the solution for many people lies in the attitudes and behaviour of those who surround them. He feels that it is up to the community as a whole to display greater understanding of the needs of those who are less able to help themselves. Problems arise principally because of the fact that some old people either have no family at all or live too far from relatives to receive regular help.

Adjustment to retirement changes has already been discussed in relation to standards of health. People approaching retirement, especially those in heavier, physically demanding work frequently give ill-health as a reason for wishing for retirement, yet studies have shown that those with poor health are less likely to enjoy the retirement period – or even to survive long after retirement. The ability to cope with change is closely related to good health.

Ability to cope with other social changes is also dependent on the standard of health. Living alone is a problem of the elderly as a group and is in fact on the increase in Britain. Older people are more likely than others to live alone, and living alone has been found to predispose to isolation, which in turn may predispose to loneliness (Tunstall, 1966). Being alone is not in itself a problem, but being alone in association with poor health and few social contacts will inevitably lead to isolation, loneliness and unhappiness.

The majority of elderly people live either alone or with only their spouse, but of those who have children well over three-quarters see at least one child regularly and frequently. In reality families often tend to cling to their elderly relatives when they are ill, and they usually wish to provide care, often only allowing the old person to go into hospital when they have reached full stretch – or beyond. It is not unusual, therefore, for elderly people to enter hospital in a situation of family crisis. This usually arises, not because families do not care but because they care too much, and hang on too long.

Another common experience of the elderly is that of bereavement. Growing old involves having to face the reality of personal death and making some form of adjustment to this. Younger people may be able to avoid facing death in a personal sense, but in middle age this becomes less easy as physical changes highlight the approach of death. This will be emphasized by the death of loved ones, which is increasingly likely as ageing progresses. Erikson (1964) has proposed that the person who can look back on life and see a clear and logical pattern in which good and bad events have a 'rightness' and inevitability is a mature and satisfied person. This will not necessarily be an easy task for many people who may not have the intellectual and emotional equipment to look back at the totality of life. In reality old age is a time of loss – of physical capacities, of friends, of good health, of family, of material and financial security – and for many people there may be insufficient compensations for these losses. For some people old age is a very unhappy time. Usually this is the result of what Saul (1974) has called the 'cluster of circumstances'. The convergence of many demands within a relatively short space of time, resulting from an accumulation of minor difficulties when there is a reduced resistance to stress leads to a need for help from outside the usual individual problem-solving areas.

Elsewhere (Brearley, 1975a) I have argued that adjustment will be encouraged if internal and external stresses are reduced and if support is available. The majority of old people seem to reach a rather more than less satisfying level of adjustment. Adequate adjustment does not necessarily seem to be directly related to good health – there are many chronically sick or disabled older people who have reached a level of personal integration and acceptance that has little to do with their physical being. Nevertheless, good or bad health plays a vital part in predisposing ageing individuals to adapt and compensate for social changes.

So far the discussion has been concerned with physical health rather than mental health. The elderly mentally infirm in the community are particularly vulnerable. Elderly people make up about 45 per cent of the total population of psychiatric hospitals, and this represents only the tip of the iceberg as most elderly patients are cared for at home (Blessed, 1974). The term 'psycho-geriatric' is, of course, a very loose term describing any form of mental illness experienced by an elderly person. Four main categories of psycho-geriatric illness have been suggested as a basis for service planning (Holford, 1972): firstly, those long-stay patients who have entered hospital earlier in life and have grown old; secondly, those patients in whom an episode of functional mental disorder presents in old age; thirdly, patients with what is often called the organic brain syndrome;

and finally, patients with acute confusional states, often associated with acute mental illness.

Hall (1973) stresses a number of points in relation to mental illness and the elderly. The incidence of mental illness increases markedly with age: probably one-third of people over 80 years of age have measurable mental impairment or an appreciable psychotic illness. Hall also argues that it is important to distinguish between chronic organic brain damage and memory changes resulting from 'normal' senescent changes. A special organization for the early diagnosis and management of affected patients is necessary, particularly as mental illness is often found with coexisting physical illness.

The social consequences of mental illness among the elderly are obvious: a large number of elderly, mentally ill old people are cared for in the community, usually by relatives who are often experiencing severe strain. The increasing incidence of morbidity with increasing age can only add to the burden on health and social services as more people live to be very old. It is the very old, or 'old old' who make the highest demands on services. If mental illness has social consequences for the elderly, the corollary has not yet been demonstrated. No clear causal effects of social deprivation have been found but the possibility that social deprivation does contribute to the mental illnesses of old age cannot be ruled out (De Alarcon, 1971).

PREVENTION

At a primary level, ill-health and the consequent breakdown of the elderly person in the sense of his becoming unable to function within the community might be prevented by wider changes in attitudes to the elderly. A fuller understanding of the nature of ageing and old age will lead to changes of approach from the general level of community relationships to more specific policy levels. If, for instance, the elderly are encouraged and enabled to remain active in either employment or in voluntary work they will remain involved and feel useful for longer. Equally an understanding of the effects of institutional care on older people may lead to a differential use of old peoples' homes in providing a short-term, more therapeutically orientated service than at present.

On another level the earlier identification of old people who are in known risk groups will facilitate the allocation of limited resources to prevent those older people who are at risk from deteriorating. Meacher

(1970) suggests that the main risk groups might be classified as the severely incapacitated, the mentally infirm, the socially isolated and the very old.

Research has indicated a number of important areas for the development of a register of elderly people at risk. Advancing age is a very important factor: the critical level seems to be at 70 years of age (Andrews, Cowan and Anderson, 1971). There is a need to visit people of 70 and over (Stanton and Exton-Smith, 1970), and Anderson (1973) suggests that with a properly constructed questionnaire the health visitor can select elderly patients who need to be seen by their own general practitioner for further screening.

Those who are subject to extreme social isolation are also at risk: without contact with others there is little stimulation and little need to observe the basic requirements of self-care. Those who are alone may tend to neglect themselves and enter a vicious circle in which the more they neglect themselves, the less likely other people are to bother with them – so the more they become withdrawn and rejected. A spiral of deterioration occurs, culminating in ill-health, hospital admission, and even death.

The recently bereaved are also a vulnerable group, and other important life changes may have the effect of increasing vulnerability of older people. Physical relocation – rehousing, admission to hospital or residential care – may have this effect. Studies suggest that opportunity for social interaction by the elderly with their environment is essential for life-adjustment. If substitute relationships are available at a time of bereavement, adjustment tends to be better (Blau, 1973). Adjustment to rehousing is more likely to be satisfactory if the old person can feel he has freely made the choice to move. The element of 'felt rejection' has a direct influence on such adjustment. There is a direct relationship between happiness and social activity (Graney, 1975). Bereavement or environmental change, then, will predispose to risk, particularly if the old person has few social supports in the way of family or friends.

Skelton (1973), in discussing geriatric care in general medical practice, suggests that general practitioners must be able to meet patient initiated demands as fully as possible and to practise prevention by medical examination and the social and economic assessment of as many old people as possible. Particularly vulnerable groups such as the recently bereaved, the isolated, the over-75s and the recently hospital-discharged should receive special attention. The primary health care team should be able to disseminate advice and health education and encourage the elderly to use it as a source of information. This concept of preparing and maintaining a register of those groups who are at risk is an attractive one, but the organization, administration and manpower as well as the financial commitment needed will be substantial.

Once a register has been compiled the main problem seems to be that of maintenance. Cochrane (1973) points out that the boundary within screening procedures in terms of cost-benefit has never been defined, although it certainly exists. He suggests that the preoccupation in discussions of screening has been with what might be considered abnormal within certain distributions, and proposes that a more rational approach might be to determine the points at which treatment starts to do more good than harm. Cochrane also suggests that it would be possible to produce a simple classification related to type of housing required (independent, sheltered housing, and hospital), to be carried out by a social worker or health visitor, as a more useful classification of need.

The primary responsibility for the identification and prevention of illness in the elderly rests with the general practice team. Common conditions may present in the elderly in unusual ways, and multiple pathologies are the rule. Patients can be described as falling into four categories. Firstly, there is a group of old people who are healthy and require only review every one or two years. Secondly, there are some who need the continuing support of the general practitioner team for minor or moderate ill-health. A group with more serious illness can be helped with out-patient, day-hospital or day-centre support, and a final group require admission to hospital or residential care (Skelton, 1974). The primary health care team is particularly concerned with the second and third of these. In order to provide a complete service to these groups of ill or at-risk elderly, it is essential that services are conceived and organized on the basis of a multidisciplinary approach.

ASSESSMENT

The concept of a multidisciplinary approach to the care of the elderly implies a concept of a geriatric team. This raises the question of who comprises the team. From one view the team might be a medical one including the general practitioner in the community and the hospital physicians, or it might be the primary health care team of doctor, community nurse, health visitor and social worker. Alternatively the team might be the hospital group of physicians, nurses, social workers, physiotherapists and occupational therapists. Ideally the team should involve all those people, although in reality various groupings do exist based on organizational barriers, administrative necessity, or simply personalities.

Only if clear communication between professionals is possible can a full assessment be made, and only if such an assessment is made can the most appropriate help be given to the patient. This raises another question which is perhaps the most important of all: is the elderly patient to be included in the team as an equal partner in the decision-making process? Not only does the patient have a right to be involved in what is being done for and to him, or her, but he also may have a need to be actively involved. It has been suggested earlier that ageing involves coming to terms with loss. One of the principal losses is that of decision-making. The range of options open to the older person tends to decrease partly as an inevitable result of physical change but also because of social pressures and deprivations. Older people often have the capacity to make decisions, but their ability to do so atrophies through disuse. If they can be re-educated in decision-making as part of the therapeutic exercise they will be better able to direct their own affairs after recovering from illness. In many cases this point of view is, of course, over-optimistic: sick and dependent old persons need care and concern as the first priority. Only when they begin to recover is it possible to bring them fully into the team.

Assessment of the ill old person almost always takes place in the community. The assessment will involve the collection and ordering of information in a way that will facilitate action. Information will be relevant insofar as it contributes to the understanding and solution of the presenting problem. At such a time the old person is particularly vulnerable and it is important not to violate his privacy with unnecessary questions. The assessment in the community will require the collection of information about the patient's physical and psychiatric state and also about his social situation. A decision on hospitalization will often depend not only on the nature of the illness or disease but also on the patient's wishes and whether he has someone at home to provide care.

Insofar as they provide new and different relationships for the patient, all the members of the geriatric team contribute to changing his life. Insofar, also, as they live within the same community, or function within the same hospital system, they play an important part in the ways in which the social systems interact. The process of assessment cannot be seen as a clinical and detached exercise since it involves social interaction between patient and doctor, and patient and other caring people. It is vitally important that each member of the geriatric team is made aware, and remains aware, of the impact of his own interaction on the patient's social functioning.

HOSPITAL CARE

Illness of the elderly person in the community is usually well covered by the general practitioner team, but admission to hospital can often be a time of frustration and anxiety for both the patient and the professional team. The admission procedures of hospitals differ, and procedures even within hospitals may differ from one unit to the next. Clear and manageable administrative procedures are an essential part of geriatric care. The minor irritations of delays, repeated telephone calls, etc., can create stresses within the team that prevent an optimum service being given to the patient.

The general practitioner should be quite sure that admission is absolutely necessary: if there is any doubt he should arrange a domiciliary consultation (Brocklehurst, 1966). It is also important that he should be aware of the risks inherent in admission to institutional care. The studies of the reactions of older people admitted to hospital or other forms of institutional care fall into two general groups: those which consider the physical effects and those examining the psychological and pyscho-social effects.

Complications unrelated to the illness that precipitates admission seem to be as frequent as those associated with the original diagnosis. Infections form the largest group of incidental complications (Rosin and Boyd, 1966). Reichel (1965) found a comparable rate of complications arising from hospital-caused factors and from intercurrent disease processes (also related to hospital factors such as excessive bed-rest, inactivity, medication or dehydration). In the psychiatric hospital setting three factors have been proposed as prognostic of early death following admission: serious physical illness, acute organic confusional state, and age over 80 years (Kay, Norris and Post, 1956).

Studies concentrating on psychological reactions to admission identify some of the reasons for stress (Kent, 1963). The patient expects the hospital to meet his needs in an almost magical way, as an all-giving parent might, and when their expectations are not met difficulties may arise. Disturbances that have occurred before admission may aggravate problems because of a feeling of rejection or being let down by family and friends. Kent argues that response to stress may take a number of forms from complete adjustment in a mature way on intellectual and emotional levels, through poor adjustment, to regression, rejection, paranoia and depression. Litin (1956) makes an explicit link between the behaviour of children and old people after admission to hospital. He describes the reactions of the child who may be terrified, and certainly becomes apprehensive and confused, with anxiety allowing full rein to the child's fantasies and imagination, especially at night. Many of these reactions are observed in the older patient, in whom aggression, panic, delirium and agitation may be seen – again particularly at night time.

The process of admission is an event, then, that exposes the already weakened and vulnerable old person to additional physical and emotional stress. When he leaves his home and family he is also leaving behind a large number of social roles. Sometimes this is only a temporary loss of roles, but for many elderly patients hospital admission may be a final move and they will have to readjust to changed status in having fewer roles.

Not all the elderly sick are cared for by the specialist in geriatric medicine. However, many elderly patients, when treated for their presenting illness, are not cured and may only be enabled to continue at home for a little while before being readmitted. It is the patients who present with a number of disease processes, in combination with frailty or disability, and lack of appropriate social supports, who will need the care of a specialist team with knowledge of the multiplicity of geriatric need. The increasing demand for such specialist knowledge has led to the growth in geriatric medicine in the United Kingdom as a branch of general medicine.

Geriatric medicine is concerned perhaps as much with the continuing management of illness and the future care of elderly patients as with the treatment of presenting illness. This concern inevitably extends to the social and emotional needs of the individual patient, who can only remain independent in terms of his total internal and external environment. The concept of maintaining independence is a central one in much of the literature on caring for the elderly. It is a concept that has diverse and very subjective meanings. There is very little that can be recognized as objectively independent in the life of an old person living alone on a limited pension on the ground floor of a house with stairs too steep for him to climb any more. Nevertheless it may be that he has a feeling of self-direction or control over his own life which is not available to the resident of an old people's home, who can potter around in his own room, get out to the shops occasionally and has all his meals prepared for him but who has no control over his pension book, or over what time he gets up or goes to bed. It is therefore important in using the concept of independence to remember that not all people need to be in their own home at all costs: flexibility in maintaining human dignity and self-respect is the central concept in providing a geriatric service.

Geriatric medicine is dealing not only with acute illness, recoverable diseases and rehabilitation – with helping people to get better – but also with the task of dealing with what might be described as medical failures. Some elderly patients are unlikely to recover because of the nature or the extent of their illness or disability. As a group such patients are very expensive since they require a period of extended hospital care – if their families (if they have families) are unable to provide care. The majority of such patients are very old, usually over 75 and often much older. They represent a pressing problem as continuing care wards of the hospital service are blocked by an ever-increasing number.

The main problem of providing continuing hospital care for the very frail elderly is associated with maintaining a satisfying quality of life for them. It is possible to encourage these elderly patients to take part in developing life opportunities for themselves (Brearley, 1975b). The experience of life in an institution is rarely a pleasant one, and elderly long-stay patients tend to perform at a minimum level, becoming apathetic and conforming to a stereotypical pattern of withdrawn behaviours (Barton, 1959). With encouragement, support and re-education they are capable of self-determination and participation in hospital life. Given a range of choices and extension of options, the elderly patient will be able to find new ways of occupying and extending himself and particularly of expressing his individuality; in order to achieve this extension of choice a total strategy will be necessary in order to bring all the social groupings in the hospital along a similar line of development. Such a strategy will involve direct work with patients individually and in groups, educational and training work with all staff groups, the development of community links (especially the bringing in of patients' relatives), and also looking at possibilities for changes in the ways in which the hospital's organizational structure impinges on individuals living and working within it.

The organization of a geriatric service of prevention, assessment and acute and long-term hospital care takes place within a community context in response to community needs. Hospital care is just as much a community service as is the primary health care service. In the same way a psycho-geriatric service, if it is to be efficient in operation, is a community service. Most mentally ill and infirm people are cared for by their families and neighbours within the community, and the organization of care is developing in ways that will make this easier and more possible.

The need for hospital beds varies in relation to the efficiency of community support services. Within the medical service day hospitals, out-patient clinics and intermittent hospital admissions are increasingly used as contributory elements in maintaining the elderly patient in the community.

Brocklehurst (1970) has defined the day hospital as a building to which patients come, or are brought in the morning, to spend a few hours in therapeutic activity before being returned home on the same day. Day hospitals differ from day centres in that the latter provide social facilities but none of the remedial services found in the day hospital. The primary function of the day hospital is not to provide the relief of social stress, although this may be a secondary, subsidiary result of day hospital care. During 1974 there were 187,000 out-patient attendances (including 32,000 new out-patients) and over 950,000 day hospital attendances (including 28,000 new day-patients) (Owen, 1976).

There seem to be no grounds for assuming that community care is cheaper than either residential or hospital care for the elderly. In certain circumstances, especially in those cases in the upper dependency levels the amount of service input needed to keep the individual at home may cost the same as, or even more than, institutional care. The right balance between cash and care is difficult to achieve (Owen, 1976).

Other forms of domiciliary care are important in determining demand on hospital services. Home nurses spend more than half their time in caring for old people, and the chiropody service is almost entirely devoted to the care of old people. Mobility is essential to physical independence, and regular chiropody treatment can do at least as much to maintain this as any other service.

Social services provision is equally important. Old people are poor people and this has direct consequences for their ability to acquire the basic necessities of life: food, warmth and housing. Poor nutrition and hypothermia are regrettably common, and lack of adequate accommodation is the commonest cause of application for admission to residential care. There is an inevitable interdependence between domiciliary, residential and hospital care.

Unfortunately the administrative barriers between social services departments and the health service often lead to difficulties in allocating help in the best way. A common example is the overlap of people in residential care, people on waiting lists for care, and people in hospital. There is no doubt that some people at home would be much better in residential care. Equally people in old people's homes should be in hospital and vice-versa. These overlaps represent a wastage of resources.

The home help service, meals and luncheon club provisions, and services for the physically handicapped (the majority of whom fall into the older age groups) are provided by local authority social services departments. Such services vary widely from region to region but many old people rely heavily on them. Once again it is clear that the administrative divisions in the forms of state provision (which in turn are separate from important areas of voluntary service for the elderly) point to a need for clear and close communication with the community geriatric team to overcome the potential blocks to optimum service.

CARE OF THE DYING

It is impossible to consider the social and medical needs of the elderly without taking account of death and dying. Most people who die do so when they are old, although men tend to die at an earlier age than women. Slightly more than half of both men and women die in National Health Service hospitals and just over one-third die at home.

It is not possible to lay down rules for the care of the dying: just as the care of the sick elderly requires flexibility and an individual approach, so the care of the dying must be based on individual need. It seems that the fear that is associated with death is linked not to the end of life as such, so much as with the pain that might go with the ending of life (Hinton, 1967). Lamerton (1973) has spoken of the joyful process of dying which can be achieved in the specialist hospice for dying patients. Whether or not death, or the process of dying, can be a joyful experience, it is possible to relieve pain in terminal illness. With modern tranquillizers and with the pain-relieving drugs there seems no reason at all why anyone should die in pain (Anderson, 1967).

The experience of dying and death is not an individual experience: it usually takes place within a family context and although the physical pains may be relieved emotional pain will still exist – if not for the patient, for his family. Dying people need others and the fear of death should not prevent others from giving the support they need. It is important, too, that relatives are given the opportunity to share in the business of death if they want to do so. If an old person is taken away to hospital to die – perhaps alone – relatives may feel guilty at abandoning him, however medically justified the hospital care may be. Once again the need seems to be for a service with sufficient flexibility to allow individual needs and wishes to be met.

CONCLUDING: SOCIAL CHANGE AND THE GERIATRIC TEAM

This chapter has set out to compress a large and rapidly growing range of knowledge and thinking into a very limited space. Inevitably much has been dealt with rather briefly, but the central fact remains: in providing a caring service for elderly people, social, biological and medical factors are interdependent. Not only are they interdependent but they are inextricably linked. It is impossible to describe the social conditions of the elderly without considering the implications these have for the health of the old. The implications for service delivery are clear: unilateral action to help an elderly person has little chance of success. Only with a multidisciplinary approach can the elderly person with problems be helped to lead a happy and healthy life. There is no point, for instance, treating a patient for hypothermia if he is to return home to a cold house. Similarly there is no point providing a gas fire and electric blanket without showing him how to use it and finding the money to pay for fuel.

Ageing can be represented as a collection of processes in which we are all involved. Most people experience ageing and old age in fairly satisfying terms but some face problems, for a variety of reasons, which they cannot overcome alone. These are seen as problems by the individual if they stop him achieving important personal goals: preventing the progress of ageing. The solution to problems lies in the restoration of the ageing process, and intervention aims are consequently limited. The elderly person, especially when he is suffering ill-health, is vulnerable, and the ways in which services are offered or imposed will have an important effect on the ways in which he can live his life. The caring professional has considerable power to alter the old person's life.

The usual tasks of the social worker have been seen as bringing about change in the elderly person's material environment by direct forms of social intervention, and helping the individual to make attitudinal adjustments to his changing physical and environmental circumstances. This concept of the social worker's role as the main agent of social change has to be closely reviewed in relation to the concept of the geriatric team. In many cases it will be the doctor, nurse, health visitor or chiropodist who will bring about personal or social change. If the feet are treated, for example, an older person previously dependent on neighbours or home helps may be able to get to the shops alone and consequently live a quite radically altered life. Social interventions should take account of the process of ageing and must aim to provide care that will take account of the developing needs of the old person. The social worker cannot hold a monopoly as agent of social change. The social work contribution, within the geriatric team, will be an interpretation of the ageing person's previous social and emotional development, of the way he views his current predicament and of the way his attitude to his illness, his family, the ageing process, etc., will influence his future functioning in society.

CHAPTER 7

Common Concerns in Health Care

The chapters of this book, written by different people, some with social work and some with academic sociology backgrounds, about a variety of aspects of health care, are nonetheless bound together by common interests. Four important themes emerge. One is the emphasis on the social significance of states of health. Another is the recognition that the decision as to whether an individual is in need of health care treatment, and whether or not that treatment is appropriate, is not purely or even mainly a professional decision: individual choice and self-determination play a very considerable part in such matters. Some of the chapters suggest this part should be greater still. A third theme is the changing emphasis on community rather than institutional care and the differences between these two forms of provision. Fourthly, an issue which appears in practically every chapter, is that of the 'medicalization' of society, which means that more and more facets of life are seen as being within the medical sphere and amenable to medical treatment (Illich, 1975).

Not every chapter deals explicitly with all the above four themes, but each section examines some aspect, or contributes a fresh perspective, on one or more of the four central issues. The emergence in the book of these areas of common concern is not, of course, simply fortuitous. Anyone familiar with the literature in the health care field will recognize all four themes as having been, separately or in combination, the focus of many works (Titmuss, 1963; Forsyth, 1966; Robinson, 1971; Illich, 1975). In one form or another, these issues have for some time been of great concern to the student of the health care sphere.

THE SOCIAL SIGNIFICANCE OF STATES OF HEALTH

Perhaps the most obvious way to demonstrate the social significance of health is to document the ever-increasing acceptance by society of responsibility for health care. Henry VIII legislated to license physicians in order to distinguish the doctor from the quack. Since that time there have been many Acts to regulate the training and qualifications of those claiming professional expertise in treating the sick, thus protecting the public from abuse by charlatans. Apart from this form of public regulation of health care, every advanced industrial nation has followed the same paths of assuming responsibility for controlling infectious diseases and the mentally disordered, and then for treatment of other types of sickness either for all, or for certain groups, such as those too poor to buy treatment for themselves, or those who are insured.

This pattern of the development of health care provision demonstrates clearly the awareness of governments of the social consequences of ill-health, and also in some cases of the social causes of some ill-health. For instance, Edwin Chadwick had, as early as 1842, identified insanitary environments as responsible for much sickness and consequent poverty (Chadwick, 1842). During the nineteenth century, public fever hospitals and mental asylums were established in all the industrializing countries of the West. These institutions could offer little therapy to the individual patient at that stage in medical knowledge, and served principally to isolate the fevered and the mentally disordered from their fellows in order that society should not be disrupted. The very location of these hospitals, some of which are still in use, ensured the geographical isolation of the patients from centres of population. The expression 'put away', popularly used when someone was admitted to a mental hospital, indicates that the public realized and tacitly accepted that the main function of such institutions was to tidy away disruptive elements.

Elsewhere in this book (chapters 2 and 3) some links are traced between social change and the development of collective responsibility for the provision of health care, and this is not the place to augment or summarize those accounts. The reader who is interested in this field should study for himself the debates which have preceded and accompanied health care legislation, and Brian Watkins' annotated extracts from health and social services' documents provides a useful starting point for such a study (Watkins, 1975).

Although, as has been suggested above, the most obvious illustration of the social significance of health is the ever-increasing collective involvement in health care provision, there are other aspects of the significance to society of the health of individuals. One such aspect has been emphasized by Talcott Parsons (1964) in his work on the concept of the sick role. While the usefulness of this concept is probably limited because of its doubtful relevance to the chronic sick and disabled (see chapters 5 and 6), the extent to which it has gained credence is due to the insights provided by the emphasis on the social, not simply the individual, significance of ill-health.

According to Parsons, every society has a generally accepted view of what is normal acceptable functioning for its members. The particular features which constitute normal functioning may vary from one society to another, but within any one society, variations from the norm are tolerated only within certain fairly narrow limits. Any greater deviation causes concern to society and results in efforts to secure conformity by means of punishment, such as penal sanctions; or in assistance, encouragement and re-education in conformity by social service agencies; or in formally acknowledging certain conditions as legitimate reasons for non-performance of normal functions. One such formally acknowledged reason is immaturity, or childhood. Another is sickness. According to Parsons, the sick role is the way in which society formally recognizes that an individual is excused the fulfilment of his normal obligations as a worker, parent, neighbour, church member, etc. The deviance of the sick person is thus socially condoned, provided he seeks the appropriate help and undertakes the prescribed measures to cure his malady and enable him to conform again to the normal patterns of functioning.

In chapter 6 it is suggested that the elderly are a group in our population without a clear role in society because, for the majority of adults, their role is defined mainly by their occupational and family responsibilities. The elderly, however, are retired from gainful employment and their family responsibilities are ended – many of them are living entirely alone. In past centuries there were not only far fewer elderly people than there are today, so that it was easier to ignore their marginal position in society, but they also had, as the few survivors of their generation, a greater measure of prestige. Moreover, their wisdom born of experience was still valued, as circumstances had changed only little and slowly during their lifetime. Today, with rapid technological development, the elderly person's past experiences are seldom relevant to the current problems, and the much larger group of elderly in our society cannot go unnoticed. There is no clearly defined 'older citizen role' which institutionalizes lack of conformity to the general patterns of gainful employment and family responsibilities in old age in the way that the child's role institutionalizes the lack of conformity at the other end of the age scale. The elderly therefore tend to have the sick role thrust upon them to explain and excuse their non-conformity, although this is often both inappropriate and unhelpful, as chapter 6 makes plain.

This discussion of the sick role has touched upon the concept of normality in health, or normal functioning. What may be taken as normal functioning is, as demonstrated in one way or another by every chapter in the book, usually socially determined. Only in a few situations, where biological survival is immediately threatened by some physiological state, do social norms play no part in the recognition of a state of abnormal or ill-health. In the vast majority of cases, the recognition of illness, physical or mental, and of disability, amounts to a recognition that there is a departure from some standard, usually implicit and ill-defined, of normality.

In this sense, the amount of ill-health or disability in a society is not only socially significant, but socially determined, because it is defined in relation to widely held social standards of normality, rather than in terms of departure from physiological perfection.

THE INDIVIDUAL AND HEALTH CARE

The socialization process which begins at birth and which transmits to new members of society the generally held values and standards, affects the individual's perception of his needs, including his health needs. Within a society there can be subgroups, based for example on social class, ethnic origins or religious affiliation, and the distinctive values and standards of the group or groups to which an individual belongs will also colour his perception of health need (Mechanic, 1968; Robinson, 1971; Kosa and Zola, 1975). In addition, however, the individual will bring unique considerations to bear on whether or not he considers himself ill, and whether or not he seeks, and then cooperates with, treatment.

It is not, however, only in the perception of when he is ill that an individual's attitude is significant in the sphere of health care. There is mounting evidence that much pathology is the result of styles of life which are physiologically harmful, and which are the consequence of individual choice. Cigarette smoking consistently over a long period, frequent alcohol consumption, food intake in excess of that required for replacement of energy expended, insufficient exercise, and exposure to man-made hazards such as road traffic accidents, are together responsible for a great and increasing amount of morbidity and mortality. Individual decisions about the value attached to health as compared with the value attached to the pleasures of physical comfort, smoking, drinking, eating and personal transport, are recognized to be of great significance to the amount of physiological pathology in the community. Considerable efforts are being made, with some success, to change people's scales of value, so that health, or more particularly future health, is more highly regarded by more people than are the pleasures of physiologically injurious habits.

Any increase in individual commitment to health will not only result in a changing hierarchy of values, as suggested above, but will probably also increase the readiness of such health-conscious individuals to see their state of health as abnormal and requiring treatment. As it is, in less than twenty years which elapsed between the first National Morbidity Survey in 1955–6 and the second in 1970–1, the readiness of people to see themselves as sick (though not necessarily as in need of professional advice but perhaps only of self-medication) had increased by 180 per cent (Crombie, 1974). Health education, if it is successful in encouraging a still higher commitment to health in preference to other previously valued habits, will surely accelerate this trend.

Apart from an individual's role in creating the circumstances in which he becomes unhealthy, and in the decision as to when professional advice is necessary, he is also seen as having an increasing share in the management of his illness and treatment. This is particularly true in the case of the types of illness which now predominate – chronic and degenerative illnesses.

In the case of episodes of acute illness, the effects of intervention by a health care professional are more dramatic, typically resulting in complete cure of the acute symptoms or failure to preserve life. The authority of the professional adviser is correspondingly greater and more readily accepted by the patient than in the case of chronic illness. Here the most that the professional can achieve is palliation, and in many cases his intervention may increase, at least temporarily, the patient's discomfort without the promise of any dramatic improvement. His role is thus seen as less crucial and his authority is less willingly tolerated. Instead, the patient's view of his needs, and the patient's expectations from treatment assume proportionately greater significance. Moreover, unless there is patient cooperation in long-term treatment regimes, they are doomed to failure.

In the training of health care professionals today, therefore, there is increasing emphasis on the patient as an individual – the one who bears in most cases the main burden of deciding when he is ill, how much he will sacrifice to avoid ill-health, and how far and in what ways and for what purpose he will accept and follow professional advice.

INSTITUTION AND COMMUNITY

Implicit in recent legislation and reports has been the view that institutions and community are two distinct and separate entities which, while it would be helpful to construct bridges between them, will remain clearly apart. The National Health Service reorganization in 1974 had, as one of its aims, the facilitation of cooperation between health services in hospitals and services in the community. The Mental Health Act 1959 aimed at restoring to the community as many as possible of the people who were currently in mental institutions, and at cutting down future admissions. The Chronically Sick and Disabled Persons Act 1970 required local authorities to provide supporting services which would enable the handicapped to live in the community rather than enter institutions. The government's policy for the health and social services (D.H.S.S., 1976) stressed an intention to build up community rather than institutional services.

Further support for the view that institutional life is essentially different from life in the community comes from the literature on institutionalization (e.g. Goffman, 1961). Undesirable consequences have been attributed to institutional living *per se*, whereas living in the community has been accepted as being without such disadvantages.

At various points throughout this book, the notion of this dichotomy between institutions and community has been challenged. Explicitly, hospitals and residential units have been claimed as part of the community. This must mean that the value systems of such institutions cannot be totally at odds with those of the wider society within which they operate but must be assumed to change in line with those of the general population – although perhaps not often in advance of ideas becoming prevalent in the community.

This surely implies that one cannot isolate the institutional approach from the community approach: one cannot, then, regard institutional life as inherently and inescapably 'institutionalizing' while life in the community is not. If one studies Goffman's account of the effect on the individual of being resident in what he calls a 'total institution', i.e. one that encompasses the whole of each inmate's waking and sleeping, working and leisure life, it becomes apparent that the institutional processes which he described as depersonalizing the individual inmates are those processes which deny the individual the opportunity to exercise individual choice. If life in an institution is depersonalizing because it removes choice from residents, community living will also be depersonalizing to the extent that opportunities for choice are limited. In the case of the elderly and the disabled, opportunities to choose between alternative courses of action, even while living in their own homes, are often severely restricted by the constraints of poverty, by over-protective relatives, and by lack of practical assistance to overcome the limitations of their functional incapacities. For those affected by such restrictions, their lives will be constrained and their capacity for exercising judgment in choosing between different possible courses of action will atrophy or fail to develop. Dependence and apathy are the likely outcome, whether the setting in which they live is that of the community or a residential unit.

It may be that an institutional setting is likely to limit opportunities for choice more often than a community setting, but this may not always be so. For some individuals, the better physical facilities of a modern institution could promote greater freedom of activity than their family environment permitted. One behaviour modification theorist, comparing the effects of institutional and community living on behaviour, argued that unhelpful and unconstructive responses to handicapped people are as likely and as harmful whether the individual is in a hospital or cared for at home (Goldiamond, 1976).

The refusal to see institutions as apart from, and different in kind from, community life does not mean that we can comfortably forget Goffman's disturbing insights into the consequences of the care given in long-stay hospitals and in Homes. On the contrary, it means we must now apply these insights in order to amend the objectives of long-stay institutions from that of giving total care in all cases, with the inevitable result of the destruction of individual choice and independence, to that of *offering* the help necessary to supplement the residual capacities of each individual while leaving him free to decide what assistance he will accept in pursuit of a life-style of his own choice. It means, also, that we must examine critically the actual as distinct from the assumed advantages of care in the community.

We can then concentrate on developing ways in which varying levels of support and care may be given according to individual need and choice. Financial support, purpose-built housing, domiciliary services, sheltered accommodation, grouped homes around day-centre facilities, hostels, residential units, and hospitals, then become part of a wide range of provision all made by the community for use, in sequence or in combination, by members of the community as their wish for care makes appropriate.

MEDICALIZATION OF SOCIETY

The increasing readiness of people to perceive themselves as ill has been referred to above, and the likely effect on this trend of greater emphasis on health education has been noted. These are aspects of the medicalization of society. Illich (1975, p. 44) has argued that many normal processes have come within the orbit of medical care. He points out that it is now taken for granted '. . . that people require routine medical ministrations for the simple fact that they are unborn, newborn, infants, in their climacteric, or old . . . life turns from a succession of different stages of health into a series of periods each requiring different therapies.'

It is, of course, arguable that where medicalization of a normal process has led to less discomfort and better survival, the process has been justified. Illich, however, stresses the unnecessary treatments imposed on people experiencing normal processes, which can sometimes cause or increase discomfort, or even jeopardize health – as, for example, in the tragic cases of thalidomide prescribed to deal with normal discomforts or normal pregnancies and resulting in the birth of seriously deformed infants.

Not everyone is likely to regard as undesirable the medicalization of conditions such as those listed by Illich in the passage quoted, despite doubts about the balance between good and bad outcomes in some cases. Rather more people would be concerned about the medicalization of conditions which are normal for the individual concerned and which are not amenable to medical intervention: in other words, the medicalization of intractable disability. And even more would question the medicalization, as mental illness, of various forms of anti-social behaviour (Flew, 1973; Norton, 1973).

To some extent, the readiness to reject the medical model in respect of disability, or frail old age, springs from the conviction that professional control over such persons' conditions of living – their daily timetable, diet and activities – is an unjustifiable restriction on individual choice, because the returns in improvements in health are negligible or non-existent. De-medicalizing disability and old age is thus seen as increasing the independence and freedom of choice of these groups, which most of us would agree is entirely desirable. It must be recognized, however, that the severely disabled and the very frail elderly do need help, and freeing them from inappropriate medical care will only leave them prisoners of their functional limitations unless an alternative pattern of help is provided.

Whether this help is given by health care professionals, relatives, or others is not really relevant to whether or not such help is appropriate to the needs of the recipient – although it may be very relevant to the cost of such care. The important point is that, whoever gives assistance should assess, in conjunction with the recipient, the need for help, the objectives of such help and the way in which it may best be given. In this way the individual retains responsibility for the direction and balance of his life, and his freedom of choice, but still receives the help necessary to make good his functional loss.

When it comes to the medicalization of anti-social behaviour, the issues are rather different. A number of people are reluctant to see excessive drinking, for instance, as mental illness rather than lack of standards or of self-control. The same is true of callously aggressive behaviour, sometimes labelled as psychopathy and treated as mental illness. The reluntance to equate such forms of anti-social behaviour with mental illness may, as in the case of non-remediable disability, arise from a desire to restore to the individual the responsibility for his own life, but it is a responsibility for his *past* life and actions which is emphasized, not so much his future. De-medicalizing anti-social behaviour means that the individual is denied access to the sick role, and the appropriate response to his failure to conform to accepted patterns of behaviour is no longer treatment, but punishment or re-education. This implication may dismay some of the advocates of de-medicalization who may have thought of the process of de-medicalizing behaviour of which society disapproves mainly in terms of freeing political dissidents in other countries from incarceration in mental hospitals. The realization that there are other implications may be less unacceptable when it is appreciated that treatment of anti-social behaviour in many cases restricts the perpetrator's liberty for a longer period than any court would award as punishment, and without having been shown to be any more effective in securing future conformity.

De-medicalization, therefore, while it has become a popular aim – one referred to in several chapters of this book – has a number of different implications according to the condition which is suggested for de-medicalization. The issue, like many health care issues, is complex and has far-reaching consequences – for other social services and for policy decisions (which in turn have financial implications) and for social values and attitudes. This is an example of the interaction between the health care sphere and other aspects of society: an interaction which makes it impossible to develop a full understanding of health care policies and practices, problems and proposals, without considering them in their social context.

References

Chapter 1   The Social Context of Health

Alderson, M. R. (1970) 'Social Class and the Health Service' *The Medical Officer* vol. 124.
Anderson, O. (1963) 'The Utilisation of Health Services' in H. Freeman *et al.* (eds.) *Handbook of Medical Sociology* Englewood Cliffs, N. J., Prentice-Hall.
Apple, D. (1960) 'How Laymen Define Illness' *Journal of Health and Human Behaviour* 1.
Backett, E. M. (1961) 'Social Aspects of the New Patterns of Disease: the Role of the Family Doctor' *Advancement of Science* p. 541.
Balint, M. (1964) *The Doctor, His Patient and the Illness* Pitman.
Baumann, B. (1961) 'Diversities in Conceptions of Health and Physical Fitness' *Journal of Health and Human Behaviour* 2.
Blum, R. and E. (1965) *Health and Healing in Rural Greece* Stanford University Press.
Cartwright, A. (1967) *Patients and Their Doctors* Routledge.
Cartwright, A. (1970) *Parents and Family Planning Services* Routledge.
Cartwright, A. (1976) 'What Goes on in the General Practitioner's Surgery?' in Acheson, R. and Aird, L. (eds.) *Seminars in Community Medicine Vol. 1.*
College of General Practitioners Research Committee (1963) *Journal of the College of General Practitioners* 15.
Dubos, R. (1959) *Mirage of Health* New York, Harper.
Dubos, R. (1965) *Man Adapting* Yale University Press.
Dunnell, K. and Cartwright, A. (1972) *Medicine Takers, Prescribers and Hoarders* Routledge.
Epson, J. E. (1969) 'The Mobile Health Clinic' interim mimeographed report, London Borough of Southwark Health Department.
Feldman, J. (1966) *The Dissemination of Health Information* Chicago, Aldine.
Freidson, E. (1973) *Profession of Medicine* New York, Dodd Mead.
Gordon, G. (1966) *Role Theory and Illness* New Haven College and University Press.
Herzlich, C. (1973) *Health and Illness* Academic Press.
Hinkle, J. *et al.* (1960) 'An Examination of the Relation between Symptoms, Disability and Serious Illness in Two Homogeneous Groups of Men and Women' *American Journal of Public Health* 50.
Illich, I. (1975) *Medical Nemesis* Calder and Boyars.
Jefferys, M. (1965) *An Anatomy of Social Welfare Services* Michael Joseph.
Jefferys, M., Brotherston, J. and Cartwright, A. (1960) 'Consumption of Medicine on a Working Class Housing Estate *British Journal of Social and Preventive Medicine* 14.
Kasl, S. V. and Cobb, S. (1966) 'Health Behaviour, Illness Behaviour and Sick-role Behaviour *Archives of Environmental Health* 12.
Koos, E. (1954) *The Health of Regionville* Columbia University Press.
Last, J. N. (1963) 'The Iceberg' *Lancet* 2, 28.
Mechanic, D. (1964) 'The Influence of Mothers on their Children's Health Attitudes and Behaviour' *Pediatrics* 33.

Mechanic, D. (1965) 'Perception of Parental Responses to Illness' *Journal of Health and Human Behaviour* 6.

Miles, A. forthcoming

Milio, N. (1975) 'Values, Social Class and Community Health Services' in Cox, C. and Mead, A. (eds.) *A Sociology of Medical Practice* Collier-Macmillan.

Morris, J. N. (1967) *Uses of Epidemiology* Livingstone.

Noyce, J. *et al.* (1974) 'Regional Variations in the Allocation of Financial Resources to the Community Health Services' *Lancet* 1.

Office of Health Economics (1968) *Without Prescription.*

Office of Health Economics (1971) *Off Sick.*

Office of Health Economics (1974) *The Work of Primary Medical Care.*

Office of Health Economics (1975) *The Health Care Dilemma.*

Parsons, T. (1951) 'Social Structure and Dynamic Process: the Case of Modern Medical Practice' in his *The Social System* Routledge.

Parsons, T. (1964) 'Definitions of Health and Illness in the Light of American Values and Social Structure' in his *Social Structure and Personality* New York, Free Press.

Pearse, I. and Crocker, L. (1944) *The Peckham Experiment* Allen and Unwin.

Robinson, D. (1971) *The Process of Becoming Ill* Routledge.

Robinson, D. (1976) *From Drinking to Alcoholism: a Sociological Commentary* Wiley.

Rosenblatt, D. and Suchmann, E. (1964) 'Blue-collar Attitudes and Information towards Health and Illness' in Shostak, A. and Gomberg, W. (eds.) *Blue Collar World* Englewood Cliffs, N. J., Prentice-Hall.

Royal College of General Practitioners (1970) *Present State and Future Needs of General Practice.*

Samora, J. *et al.* (1962) 'Knowledge about Specific Diseases in Four Selected Samples' *Journal of Health and Human Behaviour* 2.

Scheff, T. J. (1972) 'Decision Rules, Types of Error, and their Consequences in Medical Diagnosis' in Freidson, E. and Lorber, J. (eds.) *Medical Men and their Work* Chicago, Aldine and Atherton.

Schenthal, J. E. (1960) 'Multiphasic Screening of the Well Patient' *Journal of the American Medical Association* 172.

Sedgwick, P. (1973) 'Illness – Mental and Otherwise' *Hastings Center Studies* vol. 1, no. 3.

Straus, M. A. (1962) 'Deferred Gratification, Social Class and the Achievement Syndrome' *American Sociological Review* 27.

Suchmann, E. A. and Rosenblatt, D. (1964) 'Under-utilisation of Medical Care Services by Blue-collarites' in Shostak and Gomberg *op. cit.* under Rosenblatt and Suchmann (1964) above.

Thomas, K. B. (1974) 'Temporarily Dependent Patients in General Practice' *British Medical Journal* 1, p. 625.

Titmuss, R. (1968) *Commitment to Welfare* Allen and Unwin.

Tudor Hart, J. (1975) 'The Inverse Care Law' in Cox and Mead *op. cit.* under Milio (1975) above.

Wadsworth, M., Butterfield, W. J. H. and Blaney, R. (1971) *Health and Sickness: the Choice of Treatment* Tavistock.

Weeks, A. *et al.* (1958) 'Apathy of Families towards Medical Care' in Gartley Jaco (ed.) *Patients, Physicians and Illness* Glencoe, Ill., Free Press.

Zborowski, M. (1958) 'Cultural Components in Response to Pain' *ibid.*

Zola, I. K. (1964) 'Illness Behaviour of the Working Class' in Shostak and Gomberg *op. cit.* under Rosenblatt and Suchmann (1964) above.

Zola, I. K. (1966) 'Culture and Symptoms: an Analysis of Patients' Presenting Complaints' *American Sociological Review* 31.

Zola, I. K. (1972) 'Medicine as an Institution of Social Control' *Sociological Review* 20, 4, p. 487.

Chapter 2   Health Care Policies

Abel-Smith, B. (1964) *The Hospitals* Heinemann.
Bevan, A. (1952) *In Place of Fear* Heinemann.
Beveridge, W. (1942) *Report on Social Insurance and Allied Services* Cmd. 6404, H.M.S.O.
B.M.A. (1929) *Proposals for a General Medical Service for the Nation* B.M.A.
B.M.A. (1938) *A General Medical Service for the Nation* B.M.A.
B.M.A. (1977) *Evidence Submitted by the British Medical Association to the Royal Commission on the National Health Service* B.M.A.
Bradshaw, J. (1972) 'A Taxonomy of Social Need' in G. McLachlan (ed.) *Problems and Progress in Medical Care* 7th ed. Oxford University Press.
Briggs (1972) *Report of the Committee on Nursing* (the Briggs Report) Cmnd. 5115, H.M.S.O.
Chadwick, E. (1842) *Report of an Inquiry into the Sanitary Conditions of the Labouring Population of Great Britain.*
Dawson (1920) *Future Provision of Medical and Allied Services* Cmd. 693, H.M.S.O.
D.H.S.S. (1968) *The Administrative Structure of the Medical and Related Services in England and Wales* (Green Paper 1) H.M.S.O.
D.H.S.S. (1970) *The Future Structure of the National Health Service* (Green Paper 2) H.M.S.O.
D.H.S.S. (1971) *National Health Service Reorganization: Consultative Document* H.M.S.O.
D.H.S.S. (1972a) *National Health Service Reorganization: England* Cmnd. 5055, H.M.S.O.
D.H.S.S. (1972b) *Management Arrangements in the Reorganized National Health Service* (the Grey Book) H.M.S.O.
D.H. S.S. (1974) *Democracy and the National Health Service* H.M.S.O.
D.H.S.S. (1976a) *Priorities for Health and the Personal Social Services* H.M.S.O.
D.H.S.S. (1976b) *Sharing Resources for Health in England: Report of the Resource Allocation Working Party,* H.M.S.O.
Forsyth, G. (1966) *Doctors and State Medicine* Pitman.
Goldberg, E. (1970) *Helping the Aged* Allen and Unwin.
Goodenough (1944) *Report of the Inter-departmental Committee on Medical Schools* (the Goodenough Report) Ministry of Health and Department of Health, Scotland, H.M.S.O.
Harvard-Davis, R. (1971) *Report of a Sub-Committee of the Standing Medical Advisory Committee of the Central Health Services Council,* H.M.S.O.
Hicks, D. (1976) *Primary Health Care* H.M.S.O.
Hyde, G. (1974) *The Soviet Health Service* Lawrence and Wishart.
Klein, R. and Lewis, J. (1976) *The Politics of Consumer Representation* Centre for Studies in Social Policy.
McKeown, T. (1965) *Medicine in Modern Society* Allen and Unwin.
Manson, T. and Taylor, J. (1976) 'Demand, Need and Efficiency', unpublished paper delivered at a seminar at the University of Nottingham.
Maynard, A. (1975) *Health in the European Community* Croom Helm.
Pilkington (1960a) *Report of the Royal Commission on Doctors' and Dentists' Remuneration* (the Pilkington Report) Minutes of Evidence 3–4, Question 1023, H.M.S.O.
Pilkington (1960b) *Report of the Royal Commission on Doctors' and Dentists' Remuneration* Cmnd. 939, H.M.S.O.
Porritt, A. (1962) *Medical Services Review Committee: A Review of the Medical Services in Great Britain* (the Porritt Report) Social Assay.
Poynter, F. N. L. and Keele, K. D. (1961) *A Short History of Medicine* Mills and Boon.

192   *References*

Royal Commission (1976) Royal Commission on the National Health Service *The Task of the Commission* H.M.S.O.

R.C.N. (1977) *Evidence Submitted by the Royal College of Nursing to the Royal Commission on the National Health Service* R.C.N.

Rutter, M. L., Tizard, J. and Whitmore, K. (1970) *Education, Health and Behaviour* Longman.

Stevens, R. (1966) *Medical Practice in Modern England* Yale University Press.

Todd (1968) *Report of the Royal Commission on Medical Education* (the Todd Report) H.M.S.O.

Topliss, E. (1975) 'The Role of Community Health Councils' *Royal Society of Health Journal* (Dec.).

Topliss, E. (1970) 'Selection Procedure for Hospital and Domiciliary Confinement' in G. McLachlan and R. Shegog (eds.) *In the Beginning* Oxford University Press.

Willcocks, A. J. (1967) *The Creation of the National Health Service* Routledge.

Woodward, J. (1974) *To Do the Sick No Harm* Routledge.

Chapter 3   Primary Health Care

Abel, A. (1969) *Nursing Attachments of General Practice* D.H.S.S. Social Science Research Unit, H.M.S.O.

B.M.A. (1965) *A Charter for the Family Doctor Service* B.M.A.

B.M.A. (1970) *Report of the Working Party on Primary Medical Care* Planning Unit Report no. 4.

B.M.A. (1974) *Primary Health Care Teams* Board of Science and Education.

Brooks, M. B. (1973) 'Management of the Team in General Practice' *Journal of the Royal College of General Practitioners* 23, pp. 239–52.

Byrne, P. (1973) 'University Departments of General Practice and the Teaching of General Practice in the United Kingdom' *Journal of the Royal College of General Practitioners* 23, suppl. no. 1.

Cartwright, A. (1967) *Patients and Their Doctors* Routledge.

Central Health Services Council (1963) Standing Medical Advisory Committee *The Field of Work of the Family Doctor* (the Gillie Report) H.M.S.O.

Clark, J. (1973) *A Family Visitor, a Descriptive Analysis of Health Visiting in Berkshire* Royal College of Nursing.

Cooper, B. (1971) 'Social Casework in General Practice: The Derby Scheme' *Lancet*, 1, pp. 539–42.

D.H.S.S. (1970) *Report of the Joint Party on Group Attachment of Nursing Services to General Practice* H.M.S.O.

D.H.S.S. (1973) *Report of the Committee on Nursing* (the Briggs Report) Cmnd. 5115 H.M.S.O.

D.H.S.S. (1974) *Community Hospitals: Their Role and Development in the N.H.S.* H.M.S.O.

D.H.S.S. (1976a) *Priorities for Health and Personal Social Services in England* Consultative Document H.M.S.O.

D.H.S.S. (1976b) *Annual Report, 1975* Cmnd. 6565. H.M.S.O.

D.H.S.S. (1976c) *Report of the Committee on Child Health Services* Cmnd. 6684, H.M.S.O.

Dubos, R. (1968) *Man, Medicine and Environment* Pall Mall Press.

Ferguson, T. and McPhail, A. N. (1954) *Hospital and Community* Oxford University Press.

Forman, J. A. S. and Fairbairn, E. M. (1968) *Social Casework in General Practice* Oxford University Press.

Fry, J. and Farndale, W. A. J. (1972) *International Medical Care* Oxford Medical and Technical Publishing Co.

Goldberg, E. M. and Neill, J. (1972) *Social Work in General Practice* Allen and Unwin.

Harwin, B. G., Cooper, B., Eastwood, M. R. and Goldberg, D. P. (1970) 'Prospects for Social Work in General Practice' *Lancet*, 2, pp. 559–61.

Hockey, Lisbeth (1966) *Feeling the Pulse. A Study of District Nursing in Six Areas* Queen's Institute of District Nursing.

Jefferys, M. (1965) *An Anatomy of Social Welfare Services* Michael Joseph.

Kuenssberg, E. V. (1970) 'The Nurse – a Luxury or a Necessity in General Practice' *Journal of the Royal College of General Practitioners* 19, suppl. no. 3.

Lamberts, H. and Riphagen, F. E. (1975) 'Working Together in a Team for Primary Health Care – a Guide to Dangerous Country' *Journal of the Royal College of General Practitioners* 25, pp. 745–52.

Last, J. (1963) 'The Iceberg' *Lancet* 2, pp. 28–31.

Marsh, G. and Kaim-Caudle, P. (1976) *Team Care in General Practice* Croom-Helm.

McKeown, T. (1965) *Medicine in Modern Society* Allen and Unwin.

Mead, A. (1975) *The Actual and Potential Role of the Social Worker in the Primary Health Care Team* D.H.S.S.

Ministry of Health (1920) Consultative Council on Medical and Allied Services *Interim Report of the Consultative Council on Future Provision of Medical and Allied Services* (the Dawson Report) Cmd. 693 H.M.S.O.

Office of Health Economics (1975) *The Health Dilemma or Am I a Kranken Doctor?* no. 55.

Payne, L. (1976) 'Interdisciplinary Experiment: an Account of the Southampton Study Group' *Social Work Today* (5 Feb. 1976) 6, no. 22.

Ratoff, L., Cooper, B. and Rockett, D. (1973) 'Seebohm and the N.H.S. A Survey of Medicosocial Liaison' *British Medical Journal* suppl. no. 2.

Robinson, W. (1974) 'Britain's First Community Hospital' *Nursing Times*, 70, no. 13.

Seebohm, E. (1968) (Chairman) *Report of the Committee on Local Authority and Allied Personal Social Services* Cmnd. 3707, H.M.S.O.

Theophilus, A. (1973) 'General Practitioners and Social Workers – Collaboration or Conflict? *Clearing House for Local Authority Social Services Research* no. 10.

Todd (1968) *Royal Commission on Medical Education: Report* (the Todd Report) Cmnd. 3569, H.M.S.O.

Weston Smith, J. and Mottram, E. M. (1967) 'Extended Use of Nursing Services in General Practice *British Medical Journal* 4, pp. 672–4.

Chapter 4   The Mentally Ill

Bateson, G., Jackson, D. D., Haley, J. and Weakland, J. H. (1956) 'Toward a Theory of Schizophrenia' *Behavioural Science* 1, pp. 251–64.

Bornstein, P. E., Clayton, P. J., Halikas, J. A., Maurice, W. L. and Robins, E. (1973) 'The Depression of Widowhood After Thirteen Months' *British Journal of Psychiatry* 110, pp. 198–204.

Brown, G. W., Brolchain, M. N. and Harris, T. (1975) 'Social Class and Psychiatric Disturbance among Women in an Urban Population' *Sociology* 9, pp. 225–54.

Brown, G. W. (1976) 'Social Causes of Disease' in D. Tuckett, *An Introduction to Medical Sociology* Tavistock.

Bunch, J. (1972) 'Recent Bereavement in Relation to Suicide' *Journal of Psychosomatic Research* 16, pp. 361–6.

194   References

Butler (1975) *Report of the Committee on Mentally Abnormal Offenders* (the Butler Report) Cmnd. 6244, H.M.S.O.

Clare, A. (1976) *Psychiatry in Dissent* Tavistock.

Cumming, E. and J. (1957) *Closed Ranks: An Experiment in Mental Health Education* Harvard University Press.

D.H.S.S. (1971) *The Nottingham Psychiatric Case Register* Statistical Report Series no. 13, H.M.S.O.

D.H.S.S. (1975) *Better Services for the Mentally Ill* H.M.S.O.

D.H.S.S. (1976a) *Psychiatric Hospitals and Units in England,* Statistical and Research Report Series no. 12, H.M.S.O.

D.H.S.S. (1976b) *Priorities for Health and Personal Social Services in England* H.M.S.O.

D.H.S.S. (1976c) *Review of the Mental Health Act 1959* H.M.S.O.

Faris, R. E. L. and Dunham, H. W. (1939) *Mental Disorder in Urban Areas* Chicago University Press.

Freud, S. (1950) *Mourning and Melancholia: Collected Papers* vol. IV, Hogarth Press.

Freud, S. (1961) *Letters 1873–1939* Hogarth Press.

Goffman, E. (1961) *Asylums: Essays in the Social Situation of Mental Patients and Other Inmates* New York, Doubleday.

Goldberg, E. M. and Morrison, S. L. (1963) 'Schizophrenia and Social Class' *British Journal of Psychiatry* 109, pp. 785–802.

Goldhamer, H. and Marshall, A. W. (1949) *Psychosis and Civilisation: Two Studies in the Frequency of Mental Disease* Glencoe, Ill., Free Press.

Gostin, L. O. (1977) 'The Mental Health Act from 1959 to 1975. Observations, Analysis and Proposals for Reform' *MIND* Special Report, N.A.M.H.

Grad, J. and Sainsbury, P. (1968) 'The Effects that Patients Have on Their Families in a Community Care and a Control Psychiatric Service – a Two Year Follow Up' *British Journal of Psychiatry* 114, pp. 265–78.

Greer, C. (1975) 'Living with Schizophrenia' *Social Work Today* 6, no. 1, pp. 2–7.

Hawks, D. (1975) 'Community Care: an Analysis of Assumptions' *British Journal of Psychiatry* 127, pp. 276–85.

Hirsch, S. R. and Leff, J. P. (1975) *Abnormalities in Parents of Schizophrenics* Oxford University Press.

Hollingshead, A. B. and Redlich, F. C. (1958) *Social Class and Mental Illness* New York, Wiley.

Holmes, T. H. and Rahe, R. H. (1967) 'The Social Readjustment Rating Scale' *Journal of Psychosomatic Research* 11, p. 213.

Jones, K. (1972) *A History of the Mental Health Services* Routledge.

King, R. D., Raynes, N. V. and Tizard, J. (1971) *Patterns of Residential Care: Sociological Studies in Institutions for Handicapped Children* Routledge.

Kohn, M. (1972) 'Class, Family and Schizophrenia: a Reformulation' *Social Forces* 50, pp. 295–303.

Laing, R. D. and Esterson, A. (1971) *Sanity, Madness and the Family* Penguin Books.

Langner, T. S. and Michael, S. T. (1963) *Life Stress and Mental Health* Glencoe, Ill., Free Press, p. 27.

Leighton, A. H. (1959) *My Name is Legion* New York, Basic Books.

Lewis, A. (1953) 'Health as a Social Concept' *British Journal of Sociology* 4, pp. 109–24.

Morgan, H. G. (1975) 'Urban Distribution of Non-fatal Deliberate Self-harm' *British Journal of Psychiatry* 126, pp. 319–28.

National Association for Mental Health (1974) 'Patients' Rights: The Mentally Disordered in Hospital' *MIND Report* no. 10.

Neill, J. E., Warburton, R. W. and McGuiness, B. (1976) 'Post Seebohm Social Services' *Social Work Today* 8, no. 5.

Parkes, C. M. (1964) 'Recent Bereavement as a Cause of Mental Illness' *British Journal of Psychiatry* 110, pp. 198–204.
Parkes, C. M., Benjamin, B. and Fitzgerald, R. G. (1969) 'Broken Heart: a Statistical Survey of Increased Mortality among Widowers' *British Medical Journal* 1, pp. 740–3.
Plunkett, R. J. and Gordon, J. E. (1960) *Epidemiology and Mental Illness* New York, Basic Books.
Sainsbury, P. (1955) *Suicide in London* Chapman and Hall.
Seebohm, E. (1968) (Chairman) *Report of the Committee on Local Authority and Allied Personal Social Services* Cmnd. 3707, H.M.S.O.
Shaw, C. R. and McKay, H. D. (1939) *Juvenile Delinquency and Urban Areas* University of Chicago Press.
Shepherd, M. *et al.* (1966) *Psychiatric Illness in General Practice* Oxford University Press.
Spitzer, S. P. and Denzin, N. K. (1968) (eds.) *The Mental Patient: Studies in the Sociology of Deviance* New York, McGraw-Hill.
Srole, L., Langner, T. S., Michael, S. P., Opler, M. K. and Rennie, T. A. C. (1962) *Mental Health in the Metropolis: the Midtown Manhattan Study* New York, McGraw-Hill.
Szasz, T. S. (1972) *The Myth of Mental Illness*, Paladin.
Szasz, T. S. (1974) *Law, Liberty and Psychiatry* Routledge.
Vaughn, C. E. and Leff, J. P. (1976) 'The Influence of Family and Social Factors on the Course of Psychiatric Illness' *British Journal of Psychiatry* 129, pp. 125–37.
Whately, C. D. (1968) 'Social Attitudes Towards Discharged Mental Patients' in Spitzer, S. P. and Denzin, N. K. (eds.) *The Mental Patient* New York, McGraw-Hill.
Wing, J. K. and Bransby, E. R. (eds.) (1970) *Psychiatric Case Registers* D.H.S.S. Statistical Report Series no. 8, H.M.S.O.
Wing, J. K. and Brown, G. W. (1970) *Institutionalism and Schizophrenia* Cambridge University Press.
Wing, J. K. and Hailey, A. M. (eds.) (1972) *Evaluating a Community Psychiatric Service* Oxford University Press.
World Health Organization (1973) *International Pilot Study of Schizophrenia* Geneva.

Chapter 5   The Disabled

Anderson, E. (1973) *The Disabled Schoolchild* Methuen.
Bell, G. and Cartwright, D. (1976) 'Management '76 – A New Look' *Cheshire Smile, Journal of the Leonard Cheshire Foundation* (autumn).
Blaxter, M. (1976) *The Meaning of Disability* Heinemann.
Buckle, J. (1971) *Work and Housing of Impaired Persons in Great Britain* H.M.S.O.
Carpenter, J. O. (1974) 'Changing Roles and Disagreement in Families With Disabled Husbands' *Archives of Physical Medicine and Rehabilitation* (vol. 55, June).
Central Council for Education and Training in Social Work (1976) *Manpower and Training for the Social Services* C.C.E.T.S.W.
D.E.S. (1972) *The Health of the School Child* H.M.S.O.
D.H.S.S. (1974) *Social Work Support for the Health Services* H.M.S.O.
D.H.S.S. (1975) *Personal Social Services and Local Authority Statistics* H.M.S.O.
D.H.S.S. (1976a) *Prevention and Health: Everybody's Business* H.M.S.O.
D.H.S.S. (1976b) *Priorities for Health and Personal Social Services* H.M.S.O.
Dubos, R. (1965) *Man Adapting* Yale University Press.
Economist Intelligence Unit (1973) *Care with Dignity* National Fund for Research Crippling Diseases, Horsham.

Fink, S. L., Skipper, J. K. and Hallinbeck, P. (1968) 'Physical Disability and Problems in Marriage' *Journal of Marriage and the Family* (Feb.).

Garrad, J. (1974) 'Impairment and Disability, their Measurement, Prevalence, and Psychological Cost' in Lees, D. and Shaw, S. (eds.) *Impairment, Disability, and Handicap* Heinemann.

Goffman, E. (1961) *Asylums* New York, Doubleday.

Goffman, E. (1963) *Stigma: The Management of a Spoiled Identity* Englewood Cliffs, N. J., Prentice-Hall.

Harris, A. I. (1971) *Handicapped and Impaired in Great Britain* H.M.S.O.

Hewett, S. (1970) *The Family and the Handicapped Child* Allen and Unwin.

H.M.S.O. (1967) *Children and Their Primary Schools* (the Plowden Report).

H.M.S.O. (1969) *Report of the Committee of Inquiry into Allegations of Ill-Treatment of Patients and Other Irregularities at Ely Hospital, Cardiff* Cmnd. 3975.

H.M.S.O. (1971) *Report of the Farleigh Hospital Committee of Inquiry* Cmnd. 4557.

H.M.S.O. (1972) *Report of the Committee of Inquiry into Whittingham Hospital* Cmnd. 4861.

Home Office (1971) *Habitual Drunken Offenders* H.M.S.O.

Hunt, P. (1966) *Stigma* Chapman.

Lancaster-Gaye, D. (1972) *Personal Relationships, the Handicapped and the Community* Routledge.

Miller, E. J. and Gwynne, G. V. (1972) *A Life Apart* Tavistock.

Ministry of Education (1954) Circular no. 276 (25 June 1954).

Parsons, T. (1964) *Social Structure and Personality* New York, Free Press.

Parsons, T. and Bales R. (1955) *Family, Socialization and Interaction* New York, Free Press.

Robb, B. (1967) *Sans Everything* Nelson.

Sainsbury, S. (1970) 'Registered as Disabled' *Occasional Papers in Social Administration* no. 35, Bell.

Sainsbury, S. (1973) 'Measuring Disability', *Occasional Papers in Social Administration* no. 54, Bell.

Sanford, J. R. A. (1975) 'Tolerance of Debility in Elderly Dependents by Supporters at Home: its Significance for Hospital Practice' *British Medical Journal* (23 Aug.).

Schontz, F. C. (1962) 'Severe Chronic Illness' in Garrett, J. F. and Levine, E. (eds.) *Psychological Practices with the Physically Disabled* Columbia University Press.

Stewart, W. F. R. (1976) *Sex and the Physically Handicapped* National Fund for Research into Crippling Diseases, Horsham.

Tizard, J. and Grad, J. C. (1961) *The Mentally Handicapped and Their Families* Oxford University Press.

Topliss, E. (1975) *Provision for the Disabled*, Basil Blackwell and Martin Robertson.

Townsend, P. (1962) *The Last Refuge* Routledge.

Younghusband, E., Birchall, D. and Kellmer-Pringle, M. (1970) *Living With Handicap* National Bureau for Cooperation in Child Care.

Chapter 6   *The Elderly*

Agate, J. (1970) *The Practice of Geriatrics* 2nd. ed. Heinemann.

Agate, J. (1972) *Geriatrics for Nurses and Social Workers* Heinemann.

Age Concern, England (1975) *The Attitudes of the Retired and the Elderly* Age Concern.

Anderson, W. F. (1967) *Practical Management of the Elderly* Blackwell.

Anderson, W. F. (1973) 'Health Needs of the Elderly' in Canvin, R. W. and Pearson, N. G. (eds.) *Needs of the Elderly for Health and Welfare Services* University of Exeter. Institute of Biometry and Community Medicine.

Andrews, G. R., Cowan, N. R. and Anderson, W. F. (1971) 'The Practice of Geriatric Medicine in the Community: An Evaluation of the Place of Health Centres' in McLachlan, G. (ed.) *Problems and Progress in Medical Care* Nuffield Provincial Hospitals Trust, Oxford University Press.

Barton, R. (1959) *Institutional Neurosis* Wright.

Birren, J. E. (1972) 'The Organisation of Behaviour, Adaptation and Control of Aging' *Proceedings of the Ninth International Congress on Gerontology,* Kiev.

Blank, M. L. (1971) 'Recent Research Findings in Practice with the Aging' *Social Casework* pp. 382–8 (June).

Blau, Z. S. (1973) *Old Age in a Changing Society* Watts.

Blessed, G. (1974) 'Psychiatric Illness in Old Age' *Medicine* 25 (1972–4) pp. 1457–516.

Brearley, C. P. (1975a) *Social Work, Ageing and Society* Routledge.

Brearley, C. P. (1975b) *Self Help, Participation and the Elderly* University of Southampton.

Brocklehurst, J. C. (1966) 'Coordination in Care of the Elderly' *Lancet* p. 1363 (June).

Brocklehurst, J. C. (1970) *The Geriatric Day Hospital* King's Fund.

Bromley, D. B. (1974) *The Psychology of Human Ageing* Penguin.

Butler, R. N. (1969) 'Agism, Another Form of Bigotry' *The Gerontologist* 9, pp. 243–6.

Chown, S. M. (1972) *Human Ageing* Penguin.

Cochrane, A. L. (1973) 'Screening for the Elderly' in Canvin, R. W. and Pearson, N. G. (eds.) *op. cit.* under Anderson (1973) above.

Crawford, M. (1972) 'Retirement and Role Playing' *Sociology* vol. 5, no. 1.

Cumming, E. and Henry, W. E. (1961) *Growing Old – The Process of Disengagement* New York, Basic Books.

De Alarcon, J. G. (1971) 'Social Causes and Social Consequences of Mental Illness in Old Age' in Kay, D. W. K. and Walk, A. (eds.) *Recent Developments in Psychogeriatrics* Royal Medico-Psychological Association.

Dowd, J. J. (1975) 'Aging as Exchange: A Preface to Theory' *Journal of Gerontology* vol. 30, no. 5., pp. 584–94.

Erikson, E. H. (1964) *Childhood and Society* rev. ed. New York, Norton.

Gilhome, K. (1975) *The Place of the Retired and the Elderly in Modern Society* Age Concern, England.

Gore, I. Y. (1973) *Age and Vitality* Allen and Unwin.

Graney, M. J. (1975) 'Happiness and Social Participation in Aging' *Journal of Gerontology* vol. 30, no. 6, pp. 701–6.

Hall, M. R. P. (1972) 'Physical Health' in *Easing the Restrictions of Ageing* Age Concern, England.

Hall, M. R. P. (1973) *A Green and Smiling Age* Southampton University.

Hall, M. R. P. (1974) 'Aspects of Geriatric Medicine' *Medicine* 25 (1972–4) p. 1465.

Hinton, J. (1967) *Dying* Pelican.

Hobman, D. (1972) 'Changing Roles and Relationships' in *Easing the Restrictions of Ageing* Age Concern, England.

Holford, J. M. (1972) 'Old Age and Mental Illness' in *The Elderly Mind* British Hospital Journal/Hospital International.

Jacobson, D. (1972) 'Fatigue-producing Factors in Industrial Work and Pre-retirement Attitudes' *Occupational Psychology* 46, p. 193.

Kay, D. W. K., Norris, V. and Post, F. (1956) 'Prognosis in Psychiatric Disorders of the Elderly' *Journal of Chronic Diseases* 19, pp. 307–13.

Kent, E. A. (1963) 'Role of Admission Stress in Adaptation of Older Persons in Institutions' *Geriatrics* pp. 133-8 (Feb.).

Lamerton, R. (1973) *Care of the Dying* Priory Press.

Litin, E. M. (1956) 'Mental Reaction to Trauma and Hospitalisation in the Aged' *Journal of the American Medical Association* vol. 162, no. 17, pp. 1522-4.

Meacher, M. (1970) 'The Old: the Future of Community Care' in *The Fifth Social Service* Fabian Society.

Meacher, M. (1972) *Taken for a Ride: Special Residential Homes for Confused Old People* Longmans.

Meares, A. (1975) *Why Be Old?* Fontana.

Neill, J. *et al.* (1973) 'Reactions to Integration' *Social Work Today* vol. 4, no. 15.

Owen, D. (1976) 'The Costs of Ageing' in *Old Age - Today and Tomorrow* British Association for the Advancement of Science.

Pergeux, Y. (1970) 'The Aged and Society' *First International Course in Social Gerontology*, Lisbon.

Reichel, W. (1965) 'Complications in the Care of 500 Hospitalised Patients' *Journal of the American Geriatrics Society* vol. 13, no. 11, pp. 973-81.

Rose, A. M. and Peterson, W. A. (eds.) (1965) *Older People and Their Social World* Davis.

Rosin, A. J. and Boyd, R. V. (1966) 'Complications of Illness in Geriatric Patients in Hospital' *Journal of Chronic Diseases* vol. 19, pp. 307-13.

Rosow, I. (1967) *Social Integration of the Aged* New York, Free Press.

Rosow, I. (1974) *Socialization to Old Age* University of California Press.

Royal College of Physicians, London (1972) Committee on Geriatric Medicine *Report of the College Committee*.

Saul, S. (1974) *Aging: An Album of People Growing Old* New York, Wiley.

Shanas, E. *et al.* (1968) *Old People in Three Industrial Societies* Routledge.

Skelton, D. (1973) 'Comprehensive Geriatric Care in General Practice' in *Care of the Elderly* Wessex Regional Hospital Board.

Skelton, D. (1974) 'The Elderly at Home' *Medicine* 25 (1972-4) p. 1513.

Stanton, B. R. and Exton-Smith, A. N. (1970) *A Longitudinal Study of the Dietary Intake of Elderly Women* King's Fund.

Townsend, P. (1962) *The Last Refuge* Routledge.

Townsend, P. (1963) *The Family Life of Old People* Penguin.

Townsend, P. (1973) 'The Needs of the Elderly and the Planning of Hospitals' in Canvin, R. N. and Pearson, N. G. *op. cit.* under Anderson (1973) above.

Townsend, P. and Wedderburn, D. (1965) *The Aged in the Welfare State* Bell.

Tunstall, J. (1966) *Old and Alone* Routledge.

Williamson, J. *et al.* (1964) 'Old People at Home: Their Unreported Needs' *Lancet* 1, p. 1117.

Williamson, J. (1967) 'Ageing in Modern Society' paper presented to Royal Society of Health, Edinburgh, quoted in Anderson (1967).

Chapter 7   Common Concerns in Health Care

Chadwick, E. (1842) *Report of an Inquiry into the Sanitary Conditions of the Labouring Population of Great Britain*.

Crombie, D. (1974) 'Changes in Patterns of Recorded Morbidity' in Taylor, D. (ed.) *Benefits and Risks in Medical Care: A Symposium Held by the O.H.E.* Office of Health Economics.

D.H.S.S. (1976) *Priorities for Health and Personal Social Services* H.M.S.O.

Flew, A. (1973) *Crime or Disease* Macmillan.

Forsyth, G. (1966) *Doctors and State Medicine* Pitman.

Goffman, E. (1961) *Asylums* New York, Doubleday.

Goldiamond, I. (1976) 'Coping and Adaptive Behaviours of the Disabled' in Albrecht, G. L. (ed.) *Socialisation in the Disability Process* University of Pittsburgh.

Illich, I. (1975) *Medical Nemesis* Calder and Boyars.

Kosa, J. and Zola, I. K. (1975) *Poverty and Health: a Sociological Analysis* 2nd ed. Harvard University Press.

Mechanic, D. (1968) *Medical Sociology* New York, Free Press.

Norton, A. (1973) *Drugs, Science and Society* 2nd ed. Fontana.

Parsons, T. (1964) *Social Structure and Personality* New York, Free Press.

Robinson, D. (1971) *The Process of Becoming Ill* Routledge.

Titmuss, R. (1963) *Essays on the Welfare State* 2nd ed. Allen and Unwin.

Watkins, B. (1975) *Documents of Health and Social Services 1834 to the Present Day* Methuen.

Index

ageing: and activity, 159, 162, 163; adaptation to, 159–63; and loss, 167; and mental illness, 98, 167–8; physical effects of, 160; and roles, 156–9, 160; sociology of, 152–3
Apothecaries Act (1815), 73
Area Health Authorities, 53, 54, 59, 74, 79, 81, 83
Attendance Allowance, 127, 128

bereavement, 106–7; and the elderly, 166, 169
British Medical Association, 42, 73

Central Board of Health, 38, 39
Certificate in Social Service, 145
Chronically Sick and Disabled Persons Act (1970), 122, 184
chiropodist, 175, 178
Commissioner for Health and Social Services, 145–6
community care: and the elderly, 175–6; and institutions, 184–5; and the medically ill, 71–2; and the mentally ill, 113, 117–21
Community Health Councils, 54

day care: and the elderley, 175; and the mentally ill, 119
demographic changes, 55, 70, 155
depression, 94, 105, 107
disabled, 122–151; children, 133–5, 149–51; married women, 127, 128, 129–31
disablement: definition of, 122–3; and employment, 124, 126–7; and family relationships, 129–35; and household income, 124–8; and marital roles, 129–31; and residential care, 135–47; and sexual problems, 131–3; and the sick role, 142; social services in the community, 135–6

200

disease: new patterns of, 26, 55–6, 69–70; prevention of, 28–9, 70–1; undiagnosed, 27, 70–1
disengagement, 157, 158, 160
District Management Team, 53, 74
doctors, 22, 27, 29, 35, 36, 39, 40, 42, 46, 61, 86, 87, 154, 170, 171, 178
double-bind, 112
drugs: consumption of, 19, 30–1, 34
dying, care of, 176–7

ecology, 102
elderly, 152–78, 181–2; and assessment, 170–5; and exchange, 158; and family, 155, 160, 162, 166, 168; growing numbers of, 55, 155; and hospital care, 172–5; and independence, 173, 174; and residential care, 163, 172–5, 176; stereotypes of, 156–7, 158; and subculture, 158
Elementary Education (Blind and Deaf Children) Act (1893), 149
Emergency Medical Service, 43–4, 45
ethnicity, and attitudes to health, 16

family doctor, see general practitioners
Family Practitioner Committee, 74

General Medical Council, 73
general practitioners: divided from specialists, 45–6; and the elderly, 169, 170, 172; and family planning, 30; and health insurance, 42; reasons for consulting, 32–4, 69; role under N.H.S., 46–8, 67, 73–4; and social services, 83–5; specialization, 88
geriatric medicine, 153–4, 173, 174
group homes, 120

health: behaviour, 18–25; definitions of, 7–8, 37, 71; of the elderly, 163–8; knowledge, 17; lay conceptions of,